*Reappraising Repub*

# Studies on Contemporary China

The Contemporary China Institute at the School of Oriental and African Studies (University of London) has, since its establishment in 1968, been an international centre for research and publications on twentieth-century China. *Studies on Contemporary China*, which is edited at the Institute, seeks to maintain and extend that tradition by making available the best work of scholars and China specialists throughout the world. It embraces a wide variety of subjects relating to Nationalist and Communist China, including social, political, and economic change, intellectual and cultural developments, foreign relations, and national security.

## Series Editor

Dr Frank Dikötter, Director of the Contemporary China Institute

## Editorial Advisory Board

Professor Robert F. Ash
Professor Hugh D. R. Baker
Professor Elisabeth J. Croll
Dr Richard Louis Edmonds
Mr Brian G. Hook
Professor Christopher B. Howe
Professor Bonnie S. McDougall
Professor David Shambaugh
Dr Julia C. Strauss
Dr Jonathan Unger
Professor Lynn T. White III

# *Reappraising Republican China*

*Edited by*

FREDERIC WAKEMAN, JR

and

RICHARD LOUIS EDMONDS

UNIVERSITY PRESS

*This book has been printed digitally and produced in a standard specification in order to ensure its continuing availability*

OXFORD
UNIVERSITY PRESS

Great Clarendon Street, Oxford OX2 6DP

Oxford University Press is a department of the University of Oxford.
It furthers the University's objective of excellence in research, scholarship, and education by publishing worldwide in

Oxford New York

Auckland Cape Town Dar es Salaam Hong Kong Karachi
Kuala Lumpur Madrid Melbourne Mexico City Nairobi
New Delhi Shanghai Taipei Toronto
With offices in
Argentina Austria Brazil Chile Czech Republic France Greece
Guatemala Hungary Italy Japan South Korea Poland Portugal
Singapore Switzerland Thailand Turkey Ukraine Vietnam

Oxford is a registered trade mark of Oxford University Press
in the UK and in certain other countries

Published in the United States
by Oxford University Press Inc., New York

Oxford is a registered trade mark of Oxford University Press
in the UK and in certain other countries

Published in the United States
by Oxford University Press Inc., New York

© The China Quarterly 2000

The moral rights of the author have been asserted

Database right Oxford University Press (maker)

Reprinted 2005

All rights reserved. No part of this publication may be reproduced, stored in a retrieval system, or transmitted, in any form or by any means, without the prior permission in writing of Oxford University Press, or as expressly permitted by law, or under terms agreed with the appropriate reprographics rights organization. Enquiries concerning reproduction outside the scope of the above should be sent to the Rights Department, Oxford University Press, at the address above

You must not circulate this book in any other binding or cover
And you must impose this same condition on any acquirer

ISBN 0-19-829617-7

# *Contents*

# *Notes on Contributors*

MARIE-CLAIRE BERGÈRE is Professor of Chinese Civilization at the Institut National des Langues et Civilisations Orientales (Paris). She is the author of *The Golden Age of the Chinese Bourgeoisie*, *La République populaire de Chine de 1949 à nos jours*, and *Sun Yat-Sen*, and has co-authored and co-edited *La Chine au Xxe siècle*.

LOREN BRANDT is Associate Professor in the Department of Economics at the University of Toronto. His research focuses on both contemporary and historical issues relating to the Chinese economy. For the last few years, he has been involved in extensive survey work in China, including a household-level survey that extended to many of the villages surveyed by Japanese researchers in the 1930s, and a survey of Shanghai firms examining technology transfer and FDI. He is currently working on projects analysing the evolution of property rights in China's rural economy and, and the dynamics of growth and inflation in China's economy under reform.

RICHARD LOUIS EDMONDS is Senior Lecturer in Geography with reference to China at the School of Oriental and African Studies (SOAS), University of London. Previously Director of the Contemporary China Institute at SOAS, he is also Editor of *The China Quarterly*.

WILLIAM C. KIRBY is Professor in the Department of History and Chair of the Council of East Asian Studies at Harvard University. He is a historian of modern China and his work examines China's economic and political development in an international context. His current projects include a study of the international development of China in the 20th century; the history of modern Chinese capitalism; and the international socialist economy of the 1950s and China's role in it.

MARY BACKUS RANKIN is the author of *Early Chinese Revolutionaries: Radical Intellectuals in Shanghaa and Chekiang, 1902–1907* and *Elite Activism and Political Transformation in China: Chekiang Province, 1865–1911*.

JULIA C. STRAUSS is a lecturer with reference to China in the Department of Political Studies at SOAS, University of London.

HANS VAN DE VEN is a lecturer in modern Chinese history at Cambridge University. His publications include *From Friend to Comrade: The Founding of the Chinese Communist Party* and *New Perspectives on the Chinese Communist Revolution* (co-edited with Tony Saich). He is currently working on a study of the economic, political, and social impact of the military in 20th-century China.

FREDERIC WAKEMAN, JR is the Haas Professor of Asian Studies and Director of the Institute of East Asian Studies at the University of California, Berkeley. His most recent book is *The Shanghai Badlands: Wartime Terrorism and Urban Crime 1937–1941*.

WEN-HSIN YEH is Professor of History and Chair of the Center for Chinese Studies, University of California at Berkeley. She is the author of *The Alienated Academy: Culture and Politics in Republican China* and *Provincial Passages: Culture, Spaces, and the Origins of Chinese Communism*. Her current research concerns the urban culture of modern Shanghai.

# The State of Studies on Republican China

Richard Louis Edmonds

The opening of China to economic reforms from 1978 and subsequent political and social developments both in mainland China and in Taiwan have facilitated substantial reassessment of China's Republican era. The Republican years are seen by researchers increasingly as part of a continuous transition during which China modified its traditional society and adapted to new roles in world affairs – sometimes with considerable success. This special issue brings together recent studies of China's Republican era, the legacy of which can still be observed in current Chinese affairs.

The contributions to this special issue were first presented as papers at the conference entitled "Reappraising Republican China" convened by *The China Quarterly* and held at the School of Oriental and African Studies in December 1996. The conference was jointly organized by the former Editor of *The China Quarterly*, David Shambaugh, and the Guest Editor of this issue, Frederic Wakeman. Its aim was to reassess the state of scholarship in Republican studies as at 1978 and to introduce new research directions undertaken since publication of the last major survey of the field, volumes 12 and 13 of the *Cambridge History of China*, more than a decade ago. Thanks are due to the Guest Editor, the former Editor of *The China Quarterly* and to the authors who made such a comprehensive assessment possible. The papers also benefited from the comments of all those who participated in the conference as discussants and guests: Robert Bickers (who also served as rapporteur), Lisa Croll, Frank Dikötter, Christopher Howe and Gary Tiedemann. This special issue is the result of these combined efforts and will testify to the accomplishments of Republican studies during the 1980s and early 1990s.

Mary Rankin opens the volume with her interpretation of the transition from the late Qing dynasty to the Republic in order to explain political and social development of the early Republican period. In contrast to conventional wisdom which has seen the 1911 Revolution as a less radical break than the New Culture movement or the May Fourth movement of 1918, Rankin points out that although the 1911 Revolution may not have brought about a new order, the "heritage of 1911 was an obstacle to centralized state-building." The militarized oppression of Yuan Shikai spurred various segments of society to react by supporting self-government and local autonomy. The motivation of these various groups differed: warlords wanted to increase their power base, gentry were dissatisfied with the central government, and local people wanted to protect their home areas. Rankin also notes the recent shift in focus away from early Republican national governments and national revolutionary movements towards local social organizations and cultural history. There is much work yet to be done, such as looking at the efforts of the central government to assert control, local attempts to foster autonomy, and

© The China Quarterly, 1997

studies of the relations between local civil and military power. To Rankin the death of Yuan Shikai marks as significant a change in the pattern of government as any event in the early Republican era.

The economic historian, Loren Brandt, concentrates on agricultural development from the mid-1890s to 1937. Scholarship of the 1970s viewed economic development in the early Republican period as fairly dismal. Agricultural production was considered to have lagged behind population growth, rural marketing and industry were limited, and income gaps supposedly widened, both within rural areas and between urban and rural areas. Recent studies conducted in the People's Republic and the Republic of China on Taiwan, and scholarly work on the Qing economy since 1980 have taken a less pessimistic view. Brandt finds that the record of Republican era agricultural production was quite respectable when compared with industrializing 18th and 19th-century England and pre-Second World War Japan and Taiwan, though he concedes that the Chinese economy of that time was subject to world economic patterns so that "success" is hard to measure. Data problems also loom large but Brandt estimates that agricultural production grew faster than population over the 40 years of his study and concludes that agricultural growth in China was largely limited by the supply of technology and education to rural areas. Japanese government investment in agricultural development during this period contrasts sharply with weak efforts by the various Chinese governments.

In her review of the developments in the study of Republican urban history, Marie-Claire Bergère makes the point that no single year provides a turning point in the evolution of Republican society. Limiting her reassessment to Chinese urban history written by Western historians, Bergère notes that after several decades of focusing on the political aspects of 20th-century Chinese urban history, many recent studies have shifted attention to the lower classes and non-empowered groups, symbolism in cities, and case studies of individual cities. Bergère elucidates the difficulties of employing terms developed in a European context, such as "civil society" or "post-modernist" deconstruction, to describe Chinese urban social history. She also points out that the field of Republican urban history still requires foundation work such as a basic chronology of events and surveys of individual personalities and political organization before a thorough cultural reassessment of the period can be effectively undertaken.

In her article, the political scientist Julia Strauss looks at the problems of capacity building for Republican era governments. Although Strauss dwells less on dating the specific period for her study than many of the authors, she makes the point that the existing Qing bureaucracy left its imprint on Republican governments and that the political issues faced by the Republic have reappeared both in the People's Republic and on Taiwan. For example, although the late Qing saw the formal end of the Confucian bureaucratic system, its replacement with a proper functioning civil service was not successful. Strauss feels that overall, Republican governments vacillated between promoting a Weberian technocracy and attempting to implement a Soviet-style, or perhaps more appropriately put, a Whampoa-style "controlled mobilization" which fostered patriotism and party loyalty through "training sessions." Strauss sees the failure to merge effectively these two forms of institution-building during the years of the war against Japan (1937–45) as one of the factors leading to the demise of the Kuomintang on the mainland. The task of balancing government priorities between these two models of governance remained a problem in the post-1949 era, most notably with the "Red and Expert" issue of the 1950s. Strauss also notes that although researchers have a good picture of the pattern of institution-building at the national level, much work remains to be done at the provincial and local level.

The most prominent manifestation of "controlled mobilization" during the Republican era probably was the omnipresent military. Hans van de Ven points out that developments in late Qing China were to have a profound impact upon the Republic's military matters. The defeat of China in the Sino-Nipponese War of 1895 and the rise of social Darwinism strengthened the hand of the military in late Qing society and made military efficiency a matter of prominent importance during the Republic. However, the Republican central governments had very little money – in fact they often had less money than the provincial governments. This situation led to decentralization of power and set the stage for the warlord period. While the warlord period was considered bad by most people, van de Ven agrees with Arthur Waldron that the need for arms for the warlord armies was probably an important stimulus for the industrialization of China. He also thinks that militarization improved social discipline within the government. By the 1930s both the Communists and the Nationalists regarded the soldier, more than the intellectual or the worker, as the paragon of the nation and soldiers were rewarded as such. For instance, the radical land policies of the Communists were put in place in part to ensure that their soldiers were prime recipients of redistributed land. Emphasis on the military was important for political control: Yuan Shikai, Chiang Kai-shek and Mao Zedong were all backed up by their armies, and the military and military ways have continued to influence politics in mainland China and Taiwan. This can be seen most notably in party organization and the existance of party armies.

Shanghai in the Republican period was the main centre of Sino-foreign commercial contact. Wen-hsin Yeh looks specifically at Shanghai's modernization process during this era. Contemporary research on Sino-foreign contact has been divided into humanistic and socio-economic spheres with few studies crossing the line. Yeh's work suggests that it is far too simplistic to describe certain cultural phenomena and goods as either traditional/Chinese or modern/Western. To the Chinese living in Republican Shanghai, commercial goods and life-styles existed either as "Chinese" or "foreign." The view of what was foreign and what was Chinese changed over time as marketing of new goods necessitated their adaptation to Chinese culture and hence in many cases, led to their being considered Chinese. An example is Yeh's analysis of the "national goods" (*guohuo*) campaigns of the 1920s and the 1930s, where one can find producers of Chinese goods who held foreign passports, and where ambiguity of identity, such as whether a foreign product meant that it was produced outside China or whether it was an object that was not considered as part of Chinese culture, arises. In her conclusion. Yeh notes that the opinion of some social scientists that place associations and parochialism were dominant in Shanghai society was probably overstating the case as: "the forces of commerce and cultural history ... altered the basic structure of urban life."

Frederic Wakeman's article focuses specifically on the politics of the Kuomintang during the Nanjing decade and sheds new light on the question of just how fascist was Chiang Kai-shek's rule. As fascism refers to the Italian Fascists and development of the German Nazi Party, any comparable Chinese phenomenon inevitably will stray from this norm. Wakeman labels the Nationalist organization of authoritarian political groups with personal loyalty to Chiang Kai-shek as "Confucian Fascism." A labyrinth of groups is described: the top secret Lixingshe or Society for Vigorous Practice and its front organizations, the short-lived Revolutionary Army Comrades Association (Geming junren tongzhi hui), the Revolutionary Youth Comrades Association (Geming qingnian tongzhi hui), and the Renaissance Society (Fuxingshe); the notorious Blue Shirts Society (Lanyishe); and even the reorganized Chinese Boy Scouts. The identity of most of these groups became confused in the public eye because some of them had clandestine activities (the elite Lixingshe, for instance, remained unknown to the public for 40 years), and membership in one group often overlapped with another. Wakeman points out that Chiang muddled fastidious neatness and orderliness with fascism as well as with Neo-Confucianism. Chiang never used the word fascism to refer to his regime's ideology but faithfully referred to Sun Yat-sen's *Sanminzhuyi* as the philosophy of his reign. In sum, Wakeman stresses that Chiang's regime was a military dictatorship and more purely authoritarian than fascist. Chiang never wanted to create a mass movement and for Wakeman that was the key difference between his rule and European fascism. Even the Blue Shirts were never analogous to the Black or Brown shirts of Italy and Germany as they were a far more heterogeneous group. The hetereogeneity and ambiguousness of Chiang's regime also led to its demise. In terms of continuity with the People's Republic, Wakeman ends by noting that, as Lloyd Eastman once wrote, the Red Guards and the Blue Shirts were not that far apart.

William Kirby agrees with Wakeman that Republican China lacked a fascist social movement; only fascist trappings were present – rhetoric, pageant and propaganda. For Kirby, however, even these trappings show that China was more internationalized during the Republican era than at any previous time in its history. He goes so far as to say that during the Republican era everything important had an international dimension and that the international aspects grew with each successive regime. Kirby further posits the idea that Republican diplomacy was actually quite successful. For a start, the Republic was able to maintain sovereignty over the entire Qing empire with the exception of Outer Mongolia. In

Tibet, Xinjiang and the North-east this diplomacy required a considerable amount of tenacity. Furthermore, sovereignty over Taiwan was acquired even though no Republican government ruled the island prior to 1945. The Republic was also successful at getting extraterritoriality and other foreign privileges repealed. Kirby recognizes that the end of foreign privileges was the result as much of changes in relations amongst the foreign powers as of Chinese diplomacy *per se* but none the less, this was a major diplomatic accomplishment for the Chinese. The Republic was also the first government to deal with foreign powers on a bilateral basis as an equal. Alliances were forged first with Germany, then the USSR, and finally the United States. Kirby considers the greatest role the West played in Republican China was in the advancement of militarization. At the end of the Second World War, the Republic found itself recognized as a world power with its ascent on to the United Nations Security Council. Kirby concludes that the area most in need of research on the internationalization of Republican China relates to the interaction between Western sojourners in China and the Chinese.

Much work remains to be done, particularly at the local scale and on rural areas. As *The China Quarterly* has received rather few submissions on the Republican period in the past, it is hoped that this special issue will send a signal to scholars to use the journal as an outlet for publication and enter into the lively debates found in the pages that follow.

# State and Society in Early Republican Politics, 1912–18

Mary Backus Rankin

The 1911 Revolution profoundly disrupted the mixture of bureaucratic power, cultural and religious symbolism, and force upon which the authority of the Qing imperial state had rested. Tacit agreements, shared assumptions and mutual interests defining balances between state and society could no longer determine political relationships. Thus the republican revolution opened the way for a long series of redefinitions, and changed the political contexts in which actions would take place. As knowledge of the early years of the Republic grows, so does appreciation of how actions were contingent upon unpredictable new circumstances.

Historical interpretations of the early Republic have often focused on two themes. One is political failure, both of the revolution and the state. In this view, the revolution was betrayed by Yuan Shikai, who crushed opponents and destroyed incipient democratic institutions. Revolutionaries and their militarist allies overthrew Yuan in 1916. However, Sun Yat-sen could not organize his party into an effective force. The state centre disintegrated. Power became militarized and devolved upon warlords. In the absence of effective and equitable government, rural societies were dominated by conservative gentry and local bullies who manipulated institutions to their own advantage.[1]

The second theme emphasizes intellectual change and cultural iconoclasm, the political disillusionment of urban intellectuals, and their dissatisfaction with familial authoritarianism. During the second half of the 1910s, such factors produced intense attacks on Confucianism, coupled with searches for individual freedom and cultural solutions for China's problems. A common interpretation suggests that these attitudes reflected liberal democratic ideas. The ensuing New Culture and May Fourth movements are often seen as more revolutionary breaks with the past than was the 1911 Revolution – the real beginnings, leading to the more varied cultural experimentation and more radical socio-political movements of the 1920s.[2]

These characterizations point to important aspects of the 1910s, but some specific interpretations have been questioned by historians. The politics of Yuan Shikai's presidency have been persuasively interpreted as competition between centralized bureaucratic state-building and

1. John K. Fairbank, Edwin O. Reischauer and Albert M. Craig, *East Asia: The Modern Transformation* (Boston: Houghton Mifflin Co., 1965), pp. 642–46; Chuzo Ichiko, "The role of the gentry: an hypothesis," in Mary Clabaugh Wright (ed.), *China in Revolution: The First Phase, 1900–1913* (New Haven: Yale University Press, 1968), pp. 306–308.

2. Chow Tse-tsung, *The May Fourth Movement* (Cambridge, MA: Harvard University Press, 1960), pp. 1–6.

© The China Quarterly, 1997

socially based political initiative. Other historians have argued that radical students were inspired by anarchism rather than liberal individualism or that an economic boom ushered in a "golden age of the Chinese bourgeoisie."[3] Such revisions underline the need to define political issues of the early Republic broadly. Although the 1911 Revolution did not realize goals of national strengthening or limited elite democracy, it gave old frameworks and integrative systems a sharp jolt from which they did not recover. Along with the disorder and uncertainty came ferment from various sources and locations. State authorities were only one of a long list of political actors that included central officials, provincial leaders, local officials, members of elite civic and voluntary organizations, publishers and journalists, warlords and their armies, revolutionaries and their forces, and the loosely organized students in urban centres.[4] Instead of clear dichotomies between state power and social action, there were shifting intersections between different processes of bureaucratic centralization, militarization, elite civic participation or nationalistic protestation. Societal action continued to be locally rooted even when connected to national or inter-regional issues, and events at different urban levels constantly intersected.

Recent research in social and cultural history suggests interpretations less focused on the national centre and revolutionary parties. Studies of social institutions and local history have broadened conceptions of arenas of change and increased appreciation of how local, regional and national activities and orientations might intertwine. Renewed emphasis on agency has encouraged a view of culture and relationships emerging through practice. From this perspective, both cultural change and modernization can appear as continuous reworking and recombining of practices and attitudes in new contexts. At a time when previous certainties had been disrupted, so many relationships were in flux and so many initiatives were being undertaken, it is difficult to fit them into one or two trajectories. As events unfolded during the 1910s, those involved had perhaps even less than the usual murky understanding of what the outcome of actions would be.[5]

A related issue is the interaction between continuity and change during these years. Although there was no decisive event, national politics after 1911 were characterized by a series of closely spaced disjunctures: Yuan Shikai's imposition of dictatorship in 1913–14, his abortive attempt to

3. Ernest P. Young, "Politics in the aftermath of revolution: the era of Yuan Shih-k'ai, 1912–1916," in John K. Fairbank (ed.), *The Cambridge History of China*, Vol. 12, *Republican China, 1912–1949, Part I* (Cambridge: Cambridge University Press, 1983), p. 208; Arif Dirlik, *Anarchism in the Chinese Revolution* (Berkeley: University of California Press, 1983), ch. 5; Marie-Claire Bergère (trans. Janet Lloyd), *The Golden Age of the Chinese Bourgeoisie* (Cambridge: Cambridge University Press, 1989), p. 8.

4. This list leaves out workers and rural lower classes. They had sporadic local impact in some places. But workers were only beginning to take part in general political movements in the later 1910s, and peasant involvement really began in the 1920s.

5. The concept of unfolding comes from Edward A. McCord, *The Power of the Gun: The Emergence of Modern Chinese Warlordism* (Berkeley: University of California Press, 1993), p. 11.

restore the monarchy, the "Third Revolution" in 1915–16, renewed civil political activity and the entry of warlords into the Beijing government. Political crises became the norm, the context of politics changed constantly and the level of violence increased. Nevertheless, one finds many continuities between the last Qing decade and the early Republic and between the early Republic and the May Fourth period. Some arose from surviving traditional institutions, practices and attitudes. Modern-minded women and young men repeatedly sought solutions to problems arising from Confucian familial relationships. In such cases, continuing traditional conservatism stimulated increasingly radical attempts to change it.

Much of the ongoing change within society, on the other hand, was not produced by deliberate reform agendas and is better conceived as transmutation or reformulation of existing institutions, values and practices in changing contexts. Native place associations, for instance, persisted in large cities like Shanghai. However, new forms appeared along with new functions and agendas, and new vocabularies rearticulated connections between native place and nation. In more rural areas, degree-holding gentry were gradually replaced by modern school graduates or military men, thereby changing the character of local leaders and the institutions through which they acted – even when the same lineages and families remained powerful.[6]

Paralleling such unplanned social reformulations were continuities in the modernizing reforms instituted by both officials and local elites during the last Qing decade. Within the government, the efficient operation of some new central ministries like education, justice and communication contributed to maintaining a bureaucratic state centre while warlords controlled the top layer of government.[7] Within localities, modern schools, chambers of commerce and other New Policies institutions increased further during the early Republic. Ramifications of such changes permeate the political processes of the 1910s.

The early Republic is defined here as the period from the establishment of the revolutionary provisional government in January 1912 to the May Fourth Movement in 1919. This was a phase in a long revolutionary process that had roots in the late Qing and continued through the 20th century. The 1911 Revolution did not either usher in a strong modern state or remake society, but it did introduce a powerful radical current into Chinese politics. The early Republic inherited the "revolutionary party," whose members were willing to fight against "tyrannical" governments that strayed too far from their ideals of nationalism, republicanism and democracy. A mystique of revolution

6. Bryna Goodman, "New culture, old habits: native place organization and the May Fourth Movement," in Frederic Wakeman, Jr. and Wen-hsin Yeh (eds.) *Shanghai Sojourners* (Berkeley: Institute of East Asian Studies, University of California, 1992), p. 77 and *passim*; R. Keith Schoppa, "Contours of change in a Chinese country, 1900–1950," *Journal of Asian Studies*, Vol. 51, No. 4 (1992), p. 778.

7. Andrew Nathan, "A constitutional republic: the Peking government, 1916–1928," in Fairbank, *Cambridge History, Early Republic*, p. 267.

with Sun Yat-sen as its leader was kept alive and redefined first against Yuan Shikai and then against warlords, imperialists and the inequities of Chinese culture and society. More fundamental redefinitions would occur during the 1920s, but the political transmission between 1911 and the Nanjing regime (1927–37) followed a revolutionary thread.

1911 was a complex revolution, and its different aspects carried strongly over into the early Republic. Revolutionaries were the ones who injected violence as an oppositional political tactic into the new politics developing at the beginning of the 20th century. Officers and soldiers of the Qing new army were brought into politics by revolutionary and nationalist ideas, and post-revolutionary militarism was fostered by armies supporting revolution as well as by Yuan Shikai's troops and those of warlords. Late Qing urban elite movements for constitutionalism, self-government and reform, which contributed so much to the 1911 Revolution, fostered an emergent urban elite civic culture in the early republican environment. Nationalism, arising in anti-foreign demonstrations before 1911, stimulated politics of protest of the late 1910s culminating in the May Fourth Movement. Even though revolutionaries did not control politics, the themes associated with 1911 had a continuing place in the emerging civic culture and the heritage of 1911 was an obstacle to centralized state-building.

*Crisis in Central State Authority*

The Chinese state had for many centuries been defined by combinations of imperial and bureaucratic power. The Qing New Policies had modified the administrative structure, establishing new ministries and abolishing the old examination system. The 1911 Revolution left much of the bureaucracy intact, and Yuan Shikai carried on Qing centralizing and modernizing policies within a republican format. Yuan's conviction that a strong centre was required for modernization, national strengthening and maintaining order was shared by other political leaders, including Sun Yat-sen who believed that too much democracy would impede the "rapid, peaceful and orderly" mobilization of resources.[8]

The authority crisis, arising from the collapse of the centralized bureaucratic monarchy, had several aspects. Because the locus of political authority had become uncertain, Beijing governments had to solidify control by recentralizing power and continuing state-strengthening modernization to survive. Legitimacy, on the other hand, now not only derived from the way governments exercised power but also depended on satisfying expectations and aspirations of diverse groups within changing urban society. Militarization increasingly affected the exercise of central power, the ability of the centre to control the provinces and the support forthcoming from society.

8. Edward Friedman, *Backwards toward Revolution: The Chinese Revolutionary Party* (Berkeley: University of California Press, 1974), pp. 169, 178.

By the end of the 1910s, the formal state structure sometimes seemed almost irrelevant amidst the fighting, fragmentation, governmental corruption and urban demonstrations, but it did provide a fairly consistent framework in which central power was exercised or contested. It combined the restructured bureaucracy inherited from the Qing New Policies with the republican constitutional order first set out in the 1912 provisional constitution. The New Policies' inheritance was relatively stable. Such new central ministries as interior, finance, industry and commerce, education, and foreign affairs and technical programmes to collect statistics, promote trade and standardize education carried through the political turmoil despite name changes, modifications and mixed local success. Professionalized government bureaus were gradually established in provincial capitals as well. The Nanjing government thereby inherited at the end of the 1920s a substantial modern professional administrative capacity even though central political leadership had collapsed after 1916.

The constitutional structure was politicized, contested, volatile and often modified by coercion. Nevertheless, the general outline continued to reflect the provisional document of 1912. There was a president and vice-president. A premier, responsible to the president, headed the cabinet composed of ministry heads. The initial provisional council of provincial representatives (*canyiyuan*) became an upper legislative body. The parliament (*guohui*), first elected in the autumn of 1912, would be twice dissolved, once recalled and once re-elected during the decade.[9] Coercion and corruption increasingly shaped the functioning of constitutional governmental organs, and initial hopeful beginnings of representative participation in the Qing provincial assemblies were undercut.

The general structure persisted despite two attempts to restore the monarchy, suggesting an urban public commitment to republicanism buttressed by new symbols like constitutions and flags, supported by participatory aspirations, and nourished in assemblies and local organizations. Central power-holders might maintain their positions for a while by military force, coercion and bribery, but they violated the entire constitutional structure at their peril. The dictatorial use of executive authority and contentious disarray of parliamentary politics reflected more than personal ambitions, factional feuds and corruption. There were serious disagreements over how authority should be constructed and apportioned. How, too, could a new republican legitimacy resting on national strength, modernization, cultural and social reform, and political participation be defined and achieved? How could unity and local self government be combined?

It does not seem an exaggeration to say that Yuan's four years in power ensured that the modernizing programmes at the end of the Qing

9. Li Chien-nung (trans. Su-yu Teng and Jeremy Ingalls), *The Political History of China, 1840–1928* (New York: D. Van Norstrand Co., 1956), pp. 272–310, 352–394. For a summary on assemblies see Chang Peng-yuan, "Provincial assemblies: the emergence of political participation, 1909–1914," *Zhongyang yanjiuyuan jindai shi yanjiusuo jikan* (*Bulletin of the Institute of Modern History, Academica Sinica*) No. 22 (1983), pp. 273–299.

would continue, but his chances for success were doomed by unwillingness to accommodate the politicized segment of the elite populace. This political failure continued and amplified the late-Qing conflict between centralized state-building and demands for political participation.[10] Yuan sought to continue Qing plans to centralize administrative control and extend bureaucracy downwards into society. His scheme for local government in Shandong, for instance, was an extension of his programmes under the Qing to bring local men into the new county and sub-county agencies under the direction of the magistrate. Had he had the power and the time he would have further strengthened the state centre by eliminating the provinces and their politically powerful governors, thereby making county magistrates directly responsible to ministries in Beijing. These and other ambitious plans were immediately undercut by lack of funds. Fiscal weaknesses inherited from the Qing were compounded by military expenses to maintain control and the difficulties of collecting taxes in many areas.

Post-revolutionary politics were also more complex. Yuan had to contend with political parties seeking power in a national assembly, revolutionaries contesting his authority, provincial and local elites establishing their own self-government organs, provincial administrations with autonomous ambitions, and all those groups who in one way or another were angered by new national taxes or additional foreign loans. As a high Qing official, Yuan had already shown little tolerance for independent initiatives by social elites. His response to the mounting participatory drive in 1912–13 was to arrange the assassination of Kuomintang parliamentary leader Song Jiaoren, crush the "Second Revolution" in 1913 and dissolve all assemblies in 1914.

Gentry, businessmen and much of the urban professional elite initially favoured Yuan as an experienced and effective leader who could preserve unity and order, but support was eroded when revolutionary opposition pushed him into maintaining power through repression and terror. His military appointees arrested, tortured and executed alleged revolutionaries on sometimes slight evidence after the Second Revolution. Newspapers and organizations suspected of opposition were closed. Nanjing was pillaged for two weeks after Zhang Xun's troops retook the city, and the repression in Hunan and Hubei began with the startling execution of 16 prominent gentry members of the former Hunanese government. Yuan declared martial law in the summer of 1913 and the following year promulgated press and police laws formalizing censorship and banning public meetings. These laws were often ignored, but the political atmosphere made even people accustomed to privileges arising from social status and wealth feel insecure. The repression was widespread enough to suggest that the power of Yuan and his appointees was significant, and

10. Young, "Politics" p. 208; Mary Backus Rankin, *Elite Activism and Political Transformation in China: Zhejiang Province, 1865–1911* (Stanford: Stanford University Press, 1986), ch. 7.

after the Second Revolution he temporarily made considerable progress in consolidating his control.[11]

There certainly were gentry and merchants who favoured Yuan's strong measures, but generally speaking the repression, coupled with his attempt to become emperor, persuaded those who placed a high premium on stability that it would be prudent not to support him when Sun Yat-sen's allies launched the "Third Revolution" in 1916. The ambivalence of support for Yuan was illustrated in Shanghai. Gentry and merchants in that city had vigorously established local self-government and supported constitutionalism. They had loaned large sums to supply revolutionary armies in 1911, held civil positions in the city's revolutionary government and ensured a secure base by maintaining order with merchant corps. However, after the Tongmenghui's Shanghai military government had raised money by extortions, numerous taxes and kidnappings, the alienated merchants and gentry were very willing to support Yuan Shikai. During 1912 they expanded their self-government activities, and co-operated with chambers of commerce elsewhere to promote ideas of economic modernization, peace, unity and limited constitutional democracy.

Although a few city leaders joined the Shanghai branch of the Kuomintang, most held aloof from "party matters," including the assassination of Song Jiaoren. Most did not support the Second Revolution, but neither did they unreservedly back Yuan Shikai. Instead they tried to persuade both Yuan and Sun Yat-sen to negotiate and then sought to protect the city when war broke out. As fighting over the Jiangnan Arsenal became imminent, the Shanghai General Chamber of Commerce boldly protested to the commanders of both armies: "Shanghai is a marketplace of China, not a battlefield. The arsenal is a public factory of the Republic, not a prize in the struggle between north and south armies. Whichever side initiates hostilities will be in opposition to the people, and the people will consider them rebels." After the end of the fighting, Yuan's military commander in Shanghai interpreted such neutrality in defence of city and trade as treason. Among those who fled to avoid arrest was the highly respected self-government leader, Li Pingshu. The Shanghai Municipal Government Office was soon turned into an official bureau when Yuan abolished all local self-government councils in February 1914.[12]

Although the Second Revolution failed to advance the radical cause it clarified political relationships, first by revealing differences between revolutionaries and progressive social elites that had been obscured by

11. McCord, *Power of the Gun*, pp. 195–200; Zhang Yufa, "Erci geming: Guomindang yu Yuan Shikai de junshi duikang (1912–1914)" ("The Second Revolution: military confrontation of the Kuomintang and Yuan Shikai"), *Zhongyang yanjiuyuan jindai shi yanjiusuo jikan*, No. 15 (1986), pp. 286–291; Ernest Young, *The Presidency of Yuan Shih-k'ai: Liberalism and Dictatorship in Early Republican China* (Ann Arbor: University of Michigan Press, 1972), pp. 143–46.

12. Li Tajia, "Cong 'geming' dao 'fan geming:' Shanghai shangren de zhengzhi guanhuai he juezhe" ("From revolution to anti-revolution: Shanghai merchants' political concerns and priorities"), *Zhongyuan yanjiuyuan jindai shi yanjiusuo jikan*, No. 23, Part 1 (1994), pp. 239–282. Quotation from *Shenbao* is on p. 278.

mutual opposition to the Qing, and subsequently by driving a wedge between these self-government elites and Yuan Shikai. In 1914 Yuan made a fateful turn away from his heritage of Qing authoritarian bureaucratic reform toward unsuccessful dictatorship. His immediate political legacy was to strain further the already uneasy relations between state authority and politicized social elites. He used state power in ways that impeded co-operation with social groups, perhaps forestalling a developmental partnership, however undemocratic, between officials and progressive social leaders.[13]

Although the relationship between the state and urban elites was very different from that between officials and villagers, one can suggest an analogy to the breakdown of the symbolic and normative cultural nexus that one historian suggests had infused countless interactions and negotiations between officials and village leaders, fostering unity between rural society and government during the Qing.[14] The resulting bonds were eroded during the Republic as governments became more impersonal, extractive and regulatory, and officials attacked the religious beliefs in which symbolic bonds between centre and village were embedded. During the Qing a process of interchange, interaction and dialogue between local elite leaders and officials in effect combined tacit state approval of local public activity with elite recognition of state legitimacy and authority. In this arena, too, governmental power had strong symbolic underpinnings, and local officials did not normally press authority beyond the cultural bounds defined through continual interactions with local notables. Redefinition and reformation of these relationships had already increased conflict between the state and social leaders at the end of the Qing. After 1911, symbolic representations sustaining the imperial political structure became obsolete, as had old mechanisms giving elites a stake in the national polity through formal examinations and informal connections.

The Yuan Shikai government (like the Qing before it) missed an opportunity to redefine ties of state and elite society in terms of preserving order, modernizing and strengthening China, and broadening opportunities for participation in government. Although gradual fragmentation of elites would have made it difficult to redefine the old bonds into a more participatory relationship, governmental repression made it impossible. Tensions between governmental authority and societal activism would not be resolved during the Republic. Yuan, in effect, failed to create a new republican nationalist legitimacy and squandered the goodwill of progressive urban elites. Most immediately, his failure to mobilize societal support for orderly reform and modernization under central bureau-

13. On state failure to support bourgeoisie and modernization, see Bergère, *Golden Age*, pp. 7–10.

14. Prasenjit Duara, *Culture, Power, and the State: Rural North China, 1900–1942* (Stanford: Stanford University Press, 1988), pp. 5, 39, 217–18. Helen Chauncey, *Schoolhouse Politicians: Locality and the State during the Chinese Republic* (Honolulu: University of Hawaii Press, 1992), pp. 210–12, appears to draw on a generalized concept of cultural nexus in discussing relations of officials and town elites.

cratic direction encouraged the rise of military power as a political determinant.

*Military Components of Political Power*

Whether they trace warlordism back to the Qing 19th-century regional armies, see it beginning under Yuan Shikai or believe it arose after Yuan's death, historians have related militarism to weakening state authority, devolution of power and disintegration of national structures.[15] The central state certainly weakened, but concepts of devolution and disintegration tend to assume that power was static and the property of either the state or warlords. However, the exercise of power was constantly changing in the early 20th century, and new forms were being created. As observed for the late Qing, politics was not a zero-sum game.[16] Interaction of militarization with other political processes perhaps raises more fundamental issues than national disintegration.

Warlordism has been described as unfolding unevenly as civilian politicians sought help in resolving political conflicts by force, thereby empowering and politicizing military men. In a province such as Hunan, military governors co-operated with civilian elites and progress was made in instituting a kind of authoritarian self-rule.[17] Opportunities for military intervention increased, however, during the Yuan Shikai years. By the end of 1916, warlordism was penetrating the tops of governmental structures, diverting revenues and fragmenting power.

Nevertheless, military power *per se* was not necessarily disintegrative even though central government was eventually undermined. It buttressed the civil authority of the Qing and Yuan Shikai. In Zhejiang, it was more associated with commanders appointed from Beijing than with autonomy. In the north after 1916, powerful warlords fought to control the national government rather than for independence. Even in the remote south-west, military governors remained involved in national politics, and Lu Rongting in Guangdong maintained uneasy ties with Beijing to buttress himself against local rivals. Many warlords appear to have demanded partial autonomy, but saw advantages in retaining ties with Beijing. Fluctuating relations rested on time-honoured methods of negotiation and accommodation as well as military force, allowing the concept of a political centre to survive the weakness of specific governments.[18]

15. Franz Michael, "Introduction: regionalism in nineteenth-century China," in Stanley Spector, *Li Hung-chang and the Huai Army: A Study in Nineteenth-Century Chinese Regionalism* (Seattle: University of Washington Press, 1964), pp. xxxix-xliii; James E. Sheridan, *China in Disintegration: The Republican Era in Chinese History, 1912–1949* (New York: The Free Press, 1975), pp. 18–21.

16. Stephen R. McKinnon, *Power and Politics in Late Imperial China: Yuan Shihkai in Beijing and Tianjin, 1900–1908* (Berkeley: University of California Press, 1980), p. 10.

17. McCord, *Power of the Gun*, pp. 10–11, 82, 160–63, 205–207, 245–46, 267.

18. Allen Fung, "Center and province after Yuan Shikai: a study of Guangdong, 1916–1919," *Papers on Chinese History*, Vol. 4 (Cambridge, MA: Fairbank Center, Harvard University, 1995), pp. 24–26.

The two revolutionary uprisings also contributed to militarization, and especially the Third Revolution encouraged formation of more local forces amidst widespread fighting. The Kuomintang itself came close to becoming an unsuccessful military coalition. However, Sun Yat-sen managed to keep commitment to revolution alive when he withdrew to Guangzhou with some parliamentary members and much of the Chinese navy in 1917 after the national parliament was dissolved and Zhang Xun briefly restored the Qing monarchy. His government there failed to establish an effective army, could not rely on the provincial militarists with whom it competed for resources, and did not win over the Guangdong civil elites who balked at paying for Sun's national ambitions. On the other hand, by establishing his government in the name of protecting the constitution and steadily affirming his defence of the Republic, Sun distinguished his movement morally and politically from warlords controlling Beijing. His tenacious insistence that he was a national figure with whom the Beijing government had to reach agreement maintained the revolutionary thread even if he did not determine national events.

The continual fighting was hardest on rural societies. Fear and uncertainty pervaded villages and towns in areas like the north China plain where armies, bandits and local defence forces competed and intermixed. Strongmen needed to protect communities were too often unscrupulous, but without such protection inhabitants were worn down by the uncertainties of daily life and the exactions of passing armies. Existing infrastructure declined and there was little money or incentive to make repairs or undertake new investments.[19] In Beijing and other cities, administrative structures were more secure, but shallowly rooted, repressive and greedy governments plagued the urban populace and did little to foster economic development. Nevertheless, militarism left more room for elite civic and associational activities restricted by Yuan Shikai. These rebounded at the same time as warlordism became established, and the interactions of these two processes did much to shape politics in the late 1910s.

### *Ambiguities of Self-Government and Participation*

Central power-holders, militarists and local civil elites all appealed to the idea of self-government, but gave it different meanings during the debates and power struggles of the early Republic. Sorting out the claims and the realities requires, first of all, a distinction between local self-government (*zizhi*) as a supplement to bureaucratic administration and as a vehicle for societal initiative. Secondly, it needs to be recognized that elite participatory ambitions often put a higher premium on taking part in government than on safeguarding autonomy and defining rights against the state.

Contradictory implications of local self-government had been evident ever since the Qing included this concept in its constitutionalist pro-

19. Diana Lary, "Violence, fear, and insecurity: the mood of Republican China," *Republican China*, Vol. 10, No. 2 (1985), pp. 55–63.

gramme. The court planned to formalize the long-established societal-elite role in local affairs through establishing local councils and professional organizations at the base of a unitary bureaucratic framework. This policy unintentionally gave societal elites public forums from which to argue with local officials and discuss national issues impinging on local affairs. Proliferation of county and town councils during 1912–13 attests to the interest of local elites in this form of local participation. Yuan's order dissolving all provincial and local deliberative bodies in early 1914 reflected not only his suspicions of revolutionaries among assemblymen but also his conviction that participatory aspirations *per se* threatened central control. His subsequent self-government regulations carried on the Qing policy of bringing local men into the bottom of rationalized governmental structures under the control of magistrates.[20]

On the provincial level, the 1911 expedient of dividing authority between revolutionary military governors and civil governors drawn from prominent gentry supporters or co-opted Qing officials survived. Military governors became a permanent fixture, acting sometimes as independent warlords and sometimes as representatives of Beijing. Provincial self-government became a convenient slogan for the militarists, but was also used by civilian reformers opposed to Yuan's control. Debates among politicians and in the press over such issues as the division of power between civil and military governors and whether to abolish the provincial administrative unit were really about Yuan's centralizing policies. Proponents of provincial self-government advocated a *de facto* federalism that had not yet been conceptualized as a "movement" as in the 1920s. In practice, there was a considerable military component with room for civilian participation in provinces like Hunan. Perhaps even more clearly in the Lower Changjiang provinces, self-government encompassed strong sentiments of provincial pride and native place loyalties that combined with the late-Qing idea that the nation could be rebuilt from below.[21]

The extension of native place loyalties into newly constructed national identity was encouraged by the political expansiveness of the 1900s and the first year of the Republic. This process continued in the cities during the 1910s, but might exhibit more defensive overtones. In a speech at a January 1917 rally in Hangzhou opposing Beijing's appointment of outsiders as military and civil governors of Zhejiang, the radical provincial assembly member, Shen Dingyi, asserted: "Zhejiang is the Zhejiang of the people of Zhejiang. If Zhejiangese can not protect Zhejiang, then the people of the nation can not protect the nation.... The whole country's affairs are the responsibility of the people of Zhejiang. Likewise, the whole of China should bear some responsibility to the people of Zhejiang.

20. Lu Jianhong, "Yuan Shikai difang zizhi pouxi" ("An analysis of Yuan Shikai's local self-government") *Shixue yuekan*, No. 4 (1991), pp. 59–61.

21. Hu Chunhui, *Minchu de difang zhuyi yu liansheng zizhi* (*Localism and Federalism in the Early Republic*) (Taibei: Zhongyang shuju, 1983), pp. 24–31; Rankin, *Elite Activism*, pp. 249–250; R. Keith Schoppa, "Province and Nation: the Zhejiang Provincial Autonomy Movement, 1917–1927," *Journal of Asian Studies*, Vol. 36, No. 4 (1977), pp. 673–74.

If the Zhejiangese are not self-governing, then one by one they [in Beijing] will appoint outsiders...."[22]

After Yuan's death, self-government stood for three agendas. It justified provincial warlord governments, encompassed reformist aspirations of intellectuals and progressive gentry disillusioned with the centre, and embodied desires of local men to protect their home areas from predatory outsiders. Reformist self-government sponsored in Nantong by the nationally prominent native son, Zhang Jian, was an alternative to degenerate central regimes. Such progressiveness strengthened local self-consciousness, but did not imply desire for autonomy as much as conviction that reform fared better in non-official contexts.[23]

Participation involved the related but different question of who could take part in government at all levels. The principle found institutional expression in both elective assemblies and associations – either the state-authorized, elite-run professional organizations or voluntary private societies. Legislative assemblies, first elected in 1909, had the shallowest historical roots and proved to be fragile vehicles for political participation. Yuan Shikai's dissolution of assemblies in 1913–14, with attendant political repression, has been called a blow from which "elite-based political liberalism" did not recover, and later constitutions have been characterized as tools in factional struggles.[24] These observations seem particularly true for the Beijing government. In some southern provinces, at least, provincial assemblies continued to cause headaches for military governors. Assertive assemblymen did not alter balances of power, but throughout the 1910s and into the 1920s they remained a factor that could not be simply ignored.[25]

Local elite organizations and associations were more substantial, safer vehicles for participation in local governance. Insofar as societal elites had an institutionalized role in public affairs (*gongshi*) during the Qing, it was performed through local institutions providing local services and by native place associations (*huiguan*) that became involved in the affairs of the city where their members resided. Gentry and merchant leaders interacted constantly with state officials who authorized their organizations, and were often able to pursue their own agendas by negotiating, appealing to their connections and using their local prestige. Their institutions had an ambivalent relationship with official yamen. They were not autonomous, but nevertheless enjoyed sometimes considerable latitude within culturally and politically constructed boundaries and derived part of their power from local societies or groups. This earlier

22. Translated in R. Keith Schoppa, *Blood Road: The Mystery of Shen Dingyi in Revolutionary China* (Berkeley: University of California Press, 1995), p. 44. Bracketed words are my addition. On the accretion of national identity on to native-place identity see Bryna Goodman, *Native Place, City, and Nation: Regional Networks and Identities in Shanghai, 1853–1937* (Berkeley: University of California Press, 1995), pp. 46, 312–13.

23. Shao Qin, "Making political culture: the case of Nantong, 1894–1930," Ph.D. dissertation, Michigan State University, 1994, pp. 226–27, 294–300.

24. Young, "Politics," p. 243; Nathan, "Constitutional republic," p. 259.

25. Schoppa, *Blood Road*, pp. 34–37; Fung, "Center and province," p. 20.

experience in public organization facilitated expansion of new organizations and associations after 1900, and the contingent nature of state authority in local settings carried over into republican contexts.[26]

Yuan Shikai temporarily dampened this expansion, and the unreliable, incomplete statistics from the late 1910s make the timing of recovery unclear.[27] Organizational activity and political expression did rebound, however, and the economic prosperity during the latter 1910s probably contributed to greater political aggressiveness of the hybrid urban-elite of gentry, merchants, professionals and intellectuals. Civic organizations again became expansive vehicles for local participation. *Fatuan*, such as chambers of commerce or educational associations, and private voluntary associations, newspapers and journals not formally authorized by the state might form a (not necessarily united) complex within urban elite society, pulled together by the personal connections and overlapping memberships of those involved and by generally shared goals of modernity and national progress.[28] A weakening political centre did not only mean opportunities for military men. Devolution also provided scope for urban elite public-activism that did not have the same disintegrative force.

Relations between the state and the organizations in the changing urban public arenas were often not competitive, and in this respect were reminiscent of those prevailing in late-imperial local public spheres, existing between official and private domains.[29] However, the situation changed in several ways during the 1900s and 1910s. Once the Qing's prohibition was lifted, a private organizational element was introduced by voluntary associations and the old boundaries between official, communal/public and private were thereby disrupted. Major private associations, like the Red Cross or the YMCA, joined *fatuan* in performing civic functions. They thus became involved in similar negotiatory interactions with local (and sometimes national) officials, but the most prominent organizations also brought with them the stature gained from international connections and their identification with modernity and national purpose.[30]

Services, information and organization provided by civic complexes of *fatuan* and private associations benefited both state and locality. These organizations contributed to integration and infrastructural enhancement usually discussed in terms of officially led modernization and state-

26. Rankin, *Elite Activism*, p. 246; Mary Backus Rankin, "Managed by the people: officials, gentry, and the Foshan Charitable Granary, 1795–1845," *Late Imperial China*, Vol. 15, No. 2 (1994), pp. 41–45. The conceptions of ambivalence and contingency are from Goodman, *Native Place*, p. 129, ch. 4 *passim*.

27. See *Diyi hui Zhongguo nianjian* (*The First China Yearbook*) (Shanghai: Shangwu yinshuguan, 1923), pp. 1543; Jiaowubu zongwuting tongjike (Statistical Section of the Office of General Affairs of the Ministry of Education) (comp.), *1916–1917 Zhonghua minguo diwuci jiaoyu tongji tongbiao* (*Fifth Compilation of Statistical Tables of the Republic of China, 1916–1917*) (Beijing, 1917), p. 63.

28. Schoppa, "Contours of change," p. 778.

29. Rankin, *Elite Activism*, pp. 15–16.

30. Caroline Reeves, "The changing nature of Chinese philanthropy in Late-Qing and Early-Republican China," in Association for Asian Studies (comp.), *Abstracts of the 1995 Annual Meeting* (Ann Arbor, 1995), p. 47; Shirley S. Garrett, "The Chambers of Commerce and the YMCA," in Mark Elvin and G. William Skinner (eds.), *The Chinese City between Two Worlds* (Stanford: Stanford University Press, 1974), pp. 229–230.

building, but at the same time increased their capacities, elaborated their structures and broadened local constituencies. Thus elite civic participation, while neither inherently supportive of or in opposition to the state, enlarged social resources that might be used for either purpose. *Fatuan* might act more like representatives of interest groups than adjuncts of government.[31] These elite organizations also had a potential for mobilizing against government that was essential to the success of the 1911 Revolution and again became a political force in the late 1910s.

The press was the final, and key, element in this civil-elite amalgam. Starting in the 1870s, it spread information, defined issues and facilitated communication between different parts of the country. Neither the political movements culminating in the 1911 Revolution nor those of the early Republic leading into the May Fourth Movement would have occurred without the press. Some idea of its expansion is provided by figures on newspapers and other printed matter transported by the postal service, to which can be added at least as many copies sold locally. In 1908 about 36,000,000 copies were mailed. In 1913 the figure had increased to about 51,500,000. The numbers fell to 39,000,000 in 1915 as Yuan Shikai tightened his hold, but thereafter increased to 47,300,000 in 1916, some 58,800,000 in 1918 and surpassed 91,000,000 in 1920.[32] Not all these publications were concerned with politics or criticized officials, and especially those in the Beijing area were caught between government and the oppositional social movements. Nevertheless, the press as a whole played a vital role in exposing the growing urban audience to political issues and infusing elite participation in local affairs with nationalistic and political purpose.

This locally based societal expansion failed to mature into a full civil society in the far-from-favourable republican environment. Neither provincial regimes, organs of local self-government, assemblies nor the press established secure positions in relation to state power. However, a culture of elite civic participation was developing, with an agenda that was not always the same as that of governmental officials. This culture could be fractious and faction-ridden, but it was also oriented to promoting progressive modern projects to change Chinese identity and strengthen the country, and it emphasized law and legal process.[33] Although civic organizations and activities expanded, their relationships with government deteriorated. The relatively tolerant authoritarianism of the Qing had permitted the beginnings of new civic consciousness and organiza-

31. On the Tianjin Chamber of Commerce, see Zhang Xiaobo, "Merchant associational activism in early twentieth-century China: the Tianjin General Chamber of Commerce, 1904–1928," Ph.D. dissertation, Columbia University, 1995.

32. Ge Gongzhen, *Zhongguo baoxue shi* (*A History of Chinese Journalism*) (Beijing: Sanlian shudian, 1955), pp. 178–181, 230; Andrew Nathan, *Chinese Democracy* (New York: Alfred Knopf, 1985), pp. 145–46.

33. Schoppa, *Blood Road*, p. 35. On this culture in Nantong, see Shao Qin, "Political culture," ch. 7. On creating a different kind of civic society and culture defined by police and the Kuomintang in Shanghai under the Nanjing government, see Frederic Wakeman, Jr., *Policing Shanghai, 1927–1932* (Berkeley: University of California Press, 1995), ch. 4, pp. 242–49.

tion, but these were vulnerable to the repression and military predation that grew during the early Republic. State-determined contexts strongly affected the political potential of civic organization, and uneven repression undermined connections between state and societal leaders without bringing the latter under control. When the centre weakened in the later 1910s, urban civil elites became involved in oppositional protest movements on a scale that surpassed that of the end of the Qing.

*Expanding Student Circles*

The other main participants in protest movements were students, who introduced a radical element into urban-elite activist configurations during the 1900s and 1910s. Student politics and iconoclastic attacks on old society and culture have often been identified with the May Fourth Movement and the 1920s, but historians have also noted student politics at the end of the Qing and have pointed to beginnings of the New Culture Movement in the mid-1910s. Early republican student movements formed a counterpoint to warlordism, and the expansion of student circles at the same time as generals moved into the top of the national government set the stage for confrontations.

Student circles (*xuejie*) arose in Tokyo and Shanghai in the early 1900s, and during 1902–03 a number of students and teachers became involved in radical politics.[34] Henceforth, the image and political import of their circles was avant-garde, radical and nationalistic, even though not all students fitted this profile. During the 1900s and 1910s these circles developed a sense of identity based on new-style education, the social distinction of student status, life-styles in specific areas, national consciousness, and preoccupation with radical or reformist causes. Starting from institutional niches in modern schools and universities, students defined mutual interests and found mutual support in small associations and social groups within larger urban cultural milieus. Shanghai, with its cosmopolitan culture and the protection offered by foreign concessions, remained a primary destination and by 1916 had at least 24 student native-place associations. The circles also spread geographically; enrolment at Beijing University rose steadily from 818 in 1912 to 2,001 in 1918.[35]

A more general increase in schools throughout China underlay the expansion of student circles in the biggest cities. Some graduates of county elementary schools continued their studies at middle schools in provincial capitals, and some progressed still further to metropolitan universities or found ways to support themselves in the student enclaves without formally studying. When open politics revived after Yuan Shikai's death, there was a larger pool of students to become involved in

34. Paula Harrel *Sowing the Seeds of Change: Chinese Students, Japanese Teachers, 1895–1905* (Stanford: Stanford University Press, 1992), chs. 4–7.

35. Chow Tse-tsung, *May Fourth Movement*, p. 49; Goodman, "New culture," p. 85.

patriotic protests and the early stages of the New Culture Movement.[36]

The New Culture Movement has been linked to Western modern and liberal values of science, democracy and individual freedom, but further study suggests that it drew on a larger range of ideas about society, culture and politics. In broader terms, New Culture was both an intellectual and a politically infused social movement, and in these respects the radical and iconoclastic parts of its message were the most salient. Its goals traced back to the last Qing decade, but were reconstrued more adamantly and in different combinations. Thus radical intellectuals before 1911 attacked the Confucian family system, sought personal freedom and saw themselves as standard-bearers leading China into the future. But ferocious attacks on Confucianism in the later 1910s went beyond earlier denunciations, and the exaltation of youth in Chen Duxiu's lead article in the first issue of *New Youth* (*Xin qingnian*) went further in overturning Chinese socio-cultural principles.[37] Specifically woman's issues, too, had been raised at the end of the Qing, but during the 1910s these beginnings acquired new impetus as part of an expanded critique of culture and society.

The growing connection between attacks on Confucian culture and determination to remake society lends credence to the view that anarchism contributed strongly to ideas becoming prevalent in student and intellectual circles in the mid-1910s. There was a conjunction between anarchist convictions that social revolution required cultural remaking and the idea that cultural change required social remaking of familial and other structures. As this conjunction developed through personal rejections of traditional practices, what seems to have been a steady stream of ephemeral, intimate anarchist groups in Guangzhou, Beijing and Shanghai provided refuges and alternative communities for students seeking freedom from family authority.[38]

Concerns for equality and justice, which also related to anarchist agendas, had longer range implications in contributing to the slow coming together of radical intellectuals and urban workers. Workers' problems had been very peripheral to the 1911 radical agenda. Labour organizing begun in 1912–13 was cut off by Yuan Shikai, but strikes increased as the labour force grew along with industrial expansion during and after the First World War. There were 30 in Shanghai between 1909 and 1913 and 86 in 1914–18, mostly after 1916. Social concerns steered anarchist intellectuals, in particular, into labour organizing in Guangzhou and some other cities. Workers, in turn, participated in nationalist demon-

36. The larger numbers of students had still greater political significance from the May Fourth Movement onwards, but the effect in the early Republic warrants more study. On the 1920s see Wen-hsin Yeh, *Provincial Passages: Culture, Space, and the Origins of Chinese Communism* (Berkeley: University of California Press, 1996).

37. Chen Duxiu "Jinggao qingnian" ("A summons to youth"), in Zhongguo shehui kexueyuan jindai shi yanjiusuo (ed.), *Wusi yundong wenxian* (*Materials on the May Fourth Movement*) (Beijing: Sanlian shudian, 1979), pp. 1–7.

38. Arif Dirlik, "The New Culture Movement revisited," *Modern China*, Vol. 11, No. 3 (1985), pp. 265–273, 289–296; Dirlik, *Anarchism*, ch. 2, pp. 126–28; Peter Zarrow, *Anarchism and Political Culture* (New York: Columbia University Press, 1990), pp. 188–194, 210.

strations like the anti-French protests in Tianjin. The way was thus prepared for the Shanghai workers' strikes supporting students during the May Fourth movement.[39]

Diffuse searches for personal and social liberation still intertwined with student commitments to saving China from imperialists, but the political implications were different. Nationalism drew students into coalitions with merchants, professionals, and workers protesting against foreign intrusions and governmental failures to protect China. Nationalistic opposition connected to fear and anger caused by governmental repression, corruption and exactions, and overlapped agendas of urban merchant and professional elites. The search for social justice, on the other hand, would lead some students beyond issues of Confucian familial authority, most relevant to their personal lives, to involvement in labour organization and agitation. In the 1920s, such activities would foster divisive class conflict. In the 1910s, however, anti-imperialism drew students into a broadly resurgent politics of protest.

*Nationalism and the Politics of Protest*

The wielders of governmental power in the early Republic successfully blocked or vitiated formal institutions of political participation, but a new open politics of public opinion, mediated through the press and spread over urban localities, was far more difficult to control. An urban politics of protest arose after 1900, incorporating strengths of societal elites in local organization and dissemination of information. The oppositionist strain in this politics was fed by outrage at governmental failures to withstand foreign encroachment, which, in turn, interacted with anger at official suppression of political participation through parliaments or in local self-government. Particularly after 1911, this politics was also better suited for political opposition than either the old politics of networks, connections and negotiations, or revolutionary uprisings that frightened established elites and suffered from weak organization, poor planning and a scarcity of loyal supporters. Despite governmental efforts, protest politics flourished and impinged strongly on national affairs at the end of the Qing and again in the late 1910s.

The spontaneity of the social impetus and the diffuseness of the movements meant that mobilizations were often reactive and hard to sustain. Nevertheless, possibilities for integration existed and gradually increased over the years. Localities in prosperous cores became less isolated from national politics as men moved back and forth between them, newspapers and the telegraph spread information, and a growing number of national or regional federations formally linked local professional associations.[40] Societal integration might favour extension of

39. Elizabeth Perry, *Shanghai on Strike: The Politics of Chinese Labor* (Stanford: Standord University Press, 1993), pp. 40–44; Dirlik, *Anarchism*, p. 128.

40. Chow Tse-tsung, *May Fourth Movement*, p. 188; Yeh Wenhsin, *Provincial Passages*, pp. 123, 129; R. Keith Schoppa, *Chinese Elites and Political Change: Zhejiang Province in the Twentieth Century* (Cambridge, MA: Harvard University Press, 1983), pp. 5–9, 76, 186–87.

state control, but in the 1900s and 1910s its impetus to social mobilization was more pronounced.

The participants in the two oppositionist streams associated with schools and radical student groups on the one hand, and elite civic organizations and reformist associations on the other, began to develop a repertoire of urban protest during the last Qing decade.[41] Patriotic meetings in Shanghai had stimulated radical journals by 1903. The 1905 boycott to protest against American prohibition of Chinese immigration activated a larger number of merchants and other established elites. Two years later, the 1907 agitation in Jiangsu and Zhejiang provinces against a British loan to the Qing government for a railway between Shanghai and Ningbo indicates that main elements of the oppositionist repertoire had been defined. These included petitions to ministries in Beijing and solicitation of support from sympathetic officials. However, opposition was simultaneously mobilized by publicity through the press and organized through *ad hoc* anti-loan associations and existing local-elite civic organizations. Students joined gentry or organized their own associations. Public support was demonstrated through sometimes large public meetings, a massive fund-raising campaign, and telegrams from local groups within Zhejiang and Jiangsu and from other provincial railway companies.[42] The successful use of similar methods by the Tianjin Chamber of Commerce to block a stamp tax proposed by central officials suggest that such techniques were more common at the end of the Qing than historians have previously thought.[43]

Thus during the 1900s public opinion, publicity and societal mobilizations became a highly visible part of politics. Results were mixed, but officials were put under pressure, and public expression of demands or dissent gave politics an oppositionist cast. The most famous late-Qing example, the provincialist constitutional movement and the three petitions to establish constitutional government, failed. The result, however, was not capitulation by social forces but a hardening of attitudes on both sides leading toward the 1911 Revolution.

Protest politics built upon itself, pulling dissatisfied elites into confrontational demonstrations, politicizing larger numbers of people and involving more segments of society. From the last decades of the 19th century, national consciousness was articulated and spread as people mobilized in response to specific incidents. Such mobilizations crossed regional and occupational lines and crystallized distrust of the govern-

41. The concept of repertoire, implying political theatre, comes from Jeffrey N. Wasserstrom, *Student Protests in Twentieth-Century China: The View from Shanghai* (Stanford: Stanford University Press, 1991), pp. 75–78.

42. Min Tu-ki, "The Soochow-Hangchow-Ningpo railway dispute," in Min Tu-ki, *National Polity and Local Power: The Transformation of Late Imperial China* (Cambridge, MA: Council on East Asian Studies, Harvard University, 1989), pp. 191–207; Rankin, *Elite Activism*, pp. 251–263.

43. Zhang Xiaobo, "Merchant associational activities," pp. 395–400.

ment. The press spread news of foreign incursions and provided new theoretical perspectives incorporating vocabularies of social Darwinism, national sovereignty and national rights. A populist, nationalistic ethics stressed the responsibility of the people (led by elites and redefined as citizens) to become directly involved in a grandiose struggle for survival. Thus the fates of self, family, native place and province all were bound to that of the nation. Conversely, China could be preserved by resistance of "citizens" within their local arenas – a participatory message that might reinforce other causes of societal activism and link group interests to national salvation.[44]

Most importantly, nationalism aroused hostility to governments unable to protect Chinese sovereignty. It thus encouraged provincial constitutionalist movements at the end of the Qing, and furthered the cause of revolutionaries who linked anti-imperialism to anti-Manchuism and republicanism. Different oppositionist agendas interacted in an anti-imperialist, anti-centralizing participatory matrix that nourished hostility to the Qing dynasty and facilitated mobilization to overthrow it.

This interaction of nationalism and opposition to existing governments carried strongly over into the early Republic. Three major events from 1913 to 1918, plus numerous minor incidents and a continual stream of foreign loans, turned public sentiment against imperialists and Beijing powerholders.[45] The Reorganization Loans from an international consortium in 1913 provided for foreign supervision of the Salt Administration to secure repayment. The 1915 Twenty-One Demands gave Japan large economic opportunities in Shandong and political influence through civil and military advisers. Next came the Nishihara loans in 1917–18 and the still more compromising secret 1918 Sino-Japanese Military Mutual Assistance Convention allowing Japan to station troops in northern Manchuria and Outer Mongolia. Despite Yuan Shikai's repression, merchants and professionals in Shanghai organized a boycott in 1915. Students and intellectuals in Japan returned to Shanghai in protest, and students were particularly visible at large public rallies.[46] Accumulating anger burst forth under the weaker governments following Yuan, and nationalistic demonstrations during 1916–18 anticipated the May Fourth Movement.

Protesters against the enlargement of the French concession in Tianjin, led by the chamber of commerce, established a city-wide Coalition for the Preservation of National Rights and Territory in 1916. The protest repertoire expanded to include marches and street demonstrations involving as many as 8,000 people. Participants in the general strike in the

44. Bryna Goodman, "Locality as microcosm of nation," *Modern China*, Vol. 21, No. 4 (1995), pp. 393–400, 403–405.

45. For increasing Japanese economic interests in China, see Shanghai shehui kexueyuan lishi yanjiusuo (Institute of History, Shanghai Academy of Social Sciences) (ed.), *Wusi yundong zai Shanghai shiliao xuanji* (*A Selection of Historical Materials on the May Fourth Movement in Shanghai*) (Shanghai: Renmin chubanshe, 1960), pp. 38–50.

46. Huang Fuqing, "Wusi qianxi liuRi xuesheng de paiRi yongdong" ("The anti-Japanese movement of students studying in Japan on the eve of May Fourth"), *Zhongyang yanjiuyuan jindai shi yanjiusuo jikan*, Vol. 3, No. 1 (1972), p. 117; Chow Tse-tsung, *May Fourth Movement*, p. 79; Wasserstrom, *Student Protests*, pp. 43, 336 n. 41.

French concession included lower-class shop assistants, factory workers and servants. The chamber of commerce demonstrated solidarity with these strikers by raising money to support them, and support also came from other cities in the form of donations and boycotts. This strong response to a relatively small incident was reflected three years later in the militancy of Tianjin elites during the May Fourth Movement.[47]

With the 1918 demonstrations against the secret military agreement, the May Fourth repertoire, including its street theatre, was virtually in place. Chinese students in Japan formed a National Salvation Corps and returned to Beijing and Shanghai to call for demonstrations. Beijing students led the response with a mass march and demonstration in front of the presidential palace. Students elsewhere organized meetings and demonstrations. Merchants in various cities and in the umbrella National Federation of Chambers of Commerce also held meetings and sent telegrams. A riot and attacks on Japanese in the Shanghai working-class suburb of Hongkou indicated the volatile potential of mixing incipient nationalism with emerging political and social awareness of urban workers.[48]

Newly founded associations bridged the short interval to 1919. As at the end of the Qing, nationalism was the catalyst for expansive public movements and reformist/radical coalitions protesting against government policies. The issue of law and order had separated established elites from radicals in 1913, but after the fall of Yuan Shikai there was another convergence as nationalism combined with opposition to the warlord-dominated central government. Nationalism became a catalyst for inclusive social organization and a consistent wedge forcing apart heads of government and leaders of public opinion. Patriotic desires for a strong China seldom rallied support for governments in this period. They came closer to empowering disaffected urban elites, whose discontent extended the reach of local political action into national arenas.

In the second half of the 1910s, expansive protest politics changed the political culture and practice of established elites as well as student groups. Protest movements were exciting, principled moments of social convergence, offering also the relative safety of numbers. They might substitute for the political participation via assemblies and local self-government that societal elites had pursued with difficulty right after the 1911 Revolution. These movements were also ephemeral, however, and this strategy for participation underlines the inability to acquire an effective place in government or guarantees of political rights. Overriding nationalist concerns may have diverted the elite opposition from pursuing such goals as voting rights and legal protections basic to liberal democratic experience in the West. Movement politics were not, in any case, a realistic strategy for inclusion in warlord governments to which local activists had little access.

47. Zhang Xiaobo, "Merchant associational activism," pp. 418–425.

48. Huang Fuqing, "Anti-Japanese movement," pp. 120–138; Chow Tse-tseng, *May Fourth Movement*, pp. 79–82.

Merchants, gentry and professionals were instead brought into a mode of political expression that was hard for them to sustain. They had too many private interests at risk. Moreover, as larger numbers of people from more levels of society were mobilized, established elites dissatisfied with official policies were caught up in confrontational events that they could not control. Unity was difficult when worker allies also pressed economic demands through strikes and radical students supported workers. Well-off, well-established elites easily became unwilling to accept the socially radical implications of protest politics that were temporarily obscured by nationalism. After May Fourth, the existing societal organizations were joined by numerous new associations and publications whose members pursued one or another of the many social and cultural agendas of the 1920s. Protest politics continued to challenge governmental authority, but was too transitory and unstable to weave all these divergent groups into a civil society fabric.

Historians studying early republican politics have often focused on the national governments, revolutionary actions or ideology. Attention to societal organizations and re-evaluation of warlord politics have raised new issues. These in turn invite further exploration of how political initiatives and power were being generated in numerous local arenas and how the bureaucratic centre, military commanders, urban elites and students combined, interacted and recombined. Balances between state power and social autonomy repeatedly shifted from time to time and place to place.

Politics immediately after the 1911 Revolution can be characterized as altered versions of conflicts between centralized bureaucratic state-building and the societal movements for reform, constitutionalism and revolution at the end of the Qing. Societal activists in many different places and with different private and public agendas briefly focused on assemblies as vehicles for participation. Suppression by Yuan Shikai not only effectively ended this stage, but also further damaged shared frameworks and interactive practices that kept violence on the fringe of Qing state–societal disputes until shortly before the Revolution.

When politics revived after Yuan's death, nationalistic mobilizations against weaker Beijing governments again became a major factor in national politics – but with differences. Protest mobilizations of the late 1910s, on the one hand, call attention to growing integration arising from interactions within society rather than from being imposed from the top down. On the other hand, one wonders whether political goals had shifted and narrowed. Did these nationalistic movements of the late 1910s only aim to bring down unpopular officials without seriously trying to establish institutions for continuing participation? If so, to what extent was this because military force constrained public politics and to what extent did it reflect changes in the protest coalition and society? What would be the ultimate effect on local civic efforts and conflicts uninvolved in national politics?[49]

49. Schoppa, "Contours of change," pp. 791–94; Chauncey, "Schoolhouse politics," chs. 3 and 5.

Tracing early republican politics makes clear that the May Fourth Movement was not a sharp break. It seems more like a hinge between the 1910s and the different political directions of the 1920s. Differences partly reflected quantitative increases: more violence, more effective institutionalization of governmental violence and more sustained state-building by the Nanjing government, still more societal organizations, and more people in politics. There were also major reorientations, however. The rather small impact of political parties during the 1910s is striking in contrast to that of the Leninist-style Nationalist and Communist parties in the 1920s. In addition, the rise of open class conflicts and the entry of workers and peasants into political arenas makes clear that politics in the 1910s, although markedly broader than before, still only involved segments of the upper levels of society. The fluid politics of the 1910s would not define the future, but study of this period can increase understanding of the possibilities for political activity and the ranges of state–societal interaction that arose in the brief opportunities during this decade.

# Reflections on China's Late 19th and Early 20th-Century Economy

Loren Brandt

The basic structure of the Republican economy at its pre-1949 peak is not much in dispute.[1] With a population probably in excess of 500 million, the economy was predominantly agrarian: nearly two-thirds of its GNP originated in agriculture, and probably three-quarters of its labour force derived most if not all of their living from farming. There was a small modern sector, comprising parts of manufacturing, transportation, finance and so on, that represented no more than a tenth of GNP and was largely concentrated in the treaty ports. A similar percentage of the population lived in urban areas. It was a relatively commercialized economy, with as much as 40–45 per cent of farm produce making its way primarily into domestic markets. And by most measures, it was also moderately "open." Imports and exports combined totalled about one-eighth of GNP. It was, however, a very poor economy. Per capita GNP in the mid-1930s was only 60 *yuan*, which converting into current U.S. dollars is only $200–250. Purchasing power parity calculations suggest an estimate probably double or even triple this, but by today's standards, this would still rank China amongst the poorer "low-income" countries.[2]

Much more open for debate is what happened to this economy over the course of the late 19th and early 20th century. At the risk of some simplification, conventional wisdom circa the 1970s might be summarized as follows:

- Chinese agriculture experienced enormous difficulty in accommodating modest population growth. Outside the newly settled areas of the north-east, output growth lagged behind population increases and increases in imports were required to feed an expanding urban population.
- Market structure in the countryside was highly uncompetitive, and growth was inhibited by a combination of institutional and political constraints that were not removed until after 1949.
- Development of industry and the modern sector were limited. Like the international economy, their effects were largely confined to the treaty ports and their impact on the rural sector was marginal.

1. This paragraph draws largely on T. C. Liu and K. C. Yeh, *The Economy of the Chinese Mainland: National Income and Economic Development, 1933–1959* (Princeton: Princeton University Press, 1965); Dwight Perkins, "Growth and changing structure of China's twentieth century economy," in Dwight Perkins (ed.), *China's Modern Economy in Historical Perspective* (Stanford: Stanford University Press, 1975); and Liang-lin Hsiao, *China's Foreign Trade Statistics, 1864–1949* (Cambridge, MA: Harvard University Press, 1974).

2. For current comparisons, see World Bank, *World Bank Development Report 1995* (New York: Oxford University Press, 1995).

© The China Quarterly, 1997

- The twin pressures of population growth and commercialization contributed to widening income inequality in the countryside and a growing rural–urban split.
- Economic growth in the late 19th and early 20th century was along the same extensive trajectory as that of the Qing, and marked by neither qualitative nor quantitative improvement in the standard of living.

Over the past ten to 15 years each of these observations has come under careful review and reassessment.[3] This re-examination has been precipitated by a number of factors including the post-1980 scrapping of three decades of socialist planning in the PRC and the implementation of decentralizing market reforms; the economic and political maturation of Taiwan under the Kuomintang (KMT), and the East Asia "miracle" more generally; and an ongoing reassessment of political and economic development during the Qing. Each of these events provides a new angle from which to re-examine and in some cases reinterpret the historical development and evolution of the late 19th and early 20th-century Chinese economy.

The alternative picture being offered is of a spatially-differentiated and uneven growth process that was still sufficient to support an improvement in the standard of living for many Chinese.[4] Although the exact sources of growth are difficult to quantify because of data limitations, the impetus for it was a combination of external and internal factors whose influences spread out from a number of important starting points. Much of the growth was the product of Chinese enterprise, and private sector activity, more generally. As in other parts of Asia, these developments frequently drew on – and were not impeded by – the strengths of China's traditional economy, which was often invigorated and semi transformed in the process. Despite the marked increase in growth, it is obvious that not all the potential of the Chinese economy was tapped, and that a variety of constraints continued to prevent more rapid growth from being achieved. As for inequality, estimates suggest that its level in the 1930s was moderate, and not much higher than current estimates for the 1990s.[5] Trends are much more difficult to assess, but data do not appear to support the view of a long-term deterioration in the distribution of income over the late 19th and early 20th century.

3. Two books that helped precipitate the reassessment are Thomas Rawski, *Economic Growth in Prewar China* (Berkeley: University of California Press, 1990), and Loren Brandt, *Commercialization and Agricultural Development in Central and Eastern China: 1870s–1930s* (New York: Cambridge University Press, 1989). These have been frequently reviewed along with Philip Huang's *The Peasant Family and Rural Development in the Yangzi Delta, 1350–1988* (Stanford: Stanford University Press, 1990), and together were the focus of a series of papers that were subsequently published in *Republican China*, Vol. 18, No. 1 (November 1992), edited by Daniel Little. It remains the case, however, that the amount of work by economists on the Republican period is remarkably thin, and is far outpaced by the work of historians and politician scientists.

4. Rawski, *Economic Growth in Prewar China*, Table 6.11, suggests per capita growth of about 1% over the two decades between 1914–18 and 1931–37. Between the 1890s and 1930s, a conservative estimate for the cumulative per capita growth would be between a quarter and a third.

5. Compare, for example, the estimates in J. Knight and L. Song, "The spatial contribution to income inequality in China," *Cambridge Journal of Economics*, No. 17 (1993), and that

This article focuses on a few issues that relate to this ongoing reassessment of the Chinese economy during roughly the period between the 1890s and 1930s. There are several reasons for this slight departure from the Republican period, 1912–49. First, from the point of view of the Chinese economy, 1912 does not appear to be much of a watershed. It did not mark a sharp break in policy, institutions or external relations with which can be associated *ex-post* the onset of important changes in the economy. For reasons discussed below, the critical turning point is probably several decades earlier. At the same time, economic activity was severely disrupted between 1937 and 1949 by war, and so the mid-1930s are a natural terminal point. Secondly, for issues relating to economic growth and structural change, the quantitative record is simply not good enough to focus on a period that only covers the two and a half decades between 1912 and 1937. Interpretation of trends over this quarter-century is further handicapped by a possible break in the late 1920s and early 1930s caused by a major policy regime shift under the KMT, and external factors including declining terms of trade, a drop in export demand and so on. The third and most important reason for starting the analysis earlier stems from my view that a fundamental alteration in the links between major parts of China and the rest of world dating from the late 19th century make this an important turning point. This also coincides with new rights that foreigners acquired with respect to setting up and operating manufacturing facilities in the treaty ports under the Treaty of Shiminoseki. As elaborated below, these developments also make it much more difficult to provide an explanation for trends in the Chinese economy that tries to span a much longer period.

### *China and the International Economy*

Over the late 19th and early 20th century, China (or major parts) evolved from being a closed (or at best semi-closed) to an open economy. By closed economy is meant one that is cut off from trade and capital flows with the rest of the world. While this was not literally true for much of 19th-century China, trade and capital flows were a very small percentage in the aggregate, and external forces had a limited effect on the real economy. Subsequently, a combination of economic factors, notably falling international transportation and communication costs, and to a lesser extent political forces, led to expanded ties with the rest of the world.[6] These forces were not unique to China but were in fact behind the

---

*footnote continued*

provided by Loren Brandt and Barbara Sands, "Land concentration and income distribution in Republican China," in Thomas Rawski and Lillian Li (eds.), *Chinese History in Economic Perspective* (Berkeley: University of California Press, 1992).

6. Between Asia and continental Europe, for example, the costs of shipping a ton of rice declined by two-thirds between 1870 and 1914, and by an additional half to two-thirds in the 1920s and 1930s relative to the pre-First World War rates. See E. A. V. Angier, *Fifty Years Freight, 1869–1914* (London: Fairplay, 1920), and John McGee, "Ocean freight rate

rapid growth in the international economy and trade flows observed over roughly the same period.

By the turn of the century, external market forces were playing a major role in price determination in key parts of China, and thus indirectly influencing economic activity in countryside and city alike. By the late 1920s, and at its pre-war peak, China's imports and exports combined totalled one-eighth of GNP,[7] and represented 2.3 per cent of total world trade.[8] By this measure, the degree of openness of the Chinese economy in the late 1920s was on par with that estimated for the early 1990s. Foreign direct investment, albeit small in absolute amounts, was still an important conduit for information on new technology and forms of organization, and played an important role in the emerging modern sector. In general, expanded foreign ties introduced new opportunities, technologies and resources into most if not all segments of China's economy. While none of this guarantees growth, these emerging ties have the effect of removing two of the most important *internal* constraints that previously may have been inhibiting the economic growth process: a slow growing primary (read agricultural) sector, and the supply of technology.

In a closed economy, the rate of growth in the modern sector is potentially constrained by the rate at which the primary sector can release labour and feed an expanding non-agricultural population.[9] Thus, productivity increase in the primary sector becomes critical to expansion of the modern sector. The primary sector is also a major source of demand, and therefore a potential drag on the development process through demand-side effects. Imports relax the supply constraint and exports help offset a slow growth of domestic demand, thereby facilitating the movement of labour out of the primary sector and into the modern sector where average productivity is higher. In an analogous manner, an open economy is no longer limited by the pace of domestic technological development and innovation, and growth is largely bounded by the ability of a country to borrow and absorb existing (but new from the perspective of the importing country) technologies and knowledge from outside.

China's new openness shifts attention away from older, highly over-determined questions about internal contradictions and the failure or inability of "internally-generated" forces to give rise to more rapid growth, to questions of absorption, adaptation and assimilation. This is as true for a sector like agriculture as it is for industry. If growth in the

---

*footnote continued*
conferences," in Edward Johnson (ed.), *The Economic Value of the US Merchant Marine* (Evanston, Il: Transportation Center, Northwestern University, 1961).

7. Converting imports and exports into *yuan* from HKT, the total volume of trade in the late 1920s was 3.5 billion *yuan*. GNP in current prices was around 29 billion. The trade ratio declined significantly in the 1930s, a product of increased tariff protection, import substitution and falling export demand. Trade estimates are taken from Liang-lin Hsiao, *China's Foreign Trade Statistics* supplemented with data for Manchuria after 1931.

8. See Nicholas Lardy, *China in the World Economy* (Washington, D.C.: Institute for International Economics, 1994), pp. 2 and 18.

9. For an expression of such a view in the context of China, see Albert Feuerwerker, *The Chinese Economy, ca. 1870–1911* (Ann Arbor: Center for Chinese Studies, 1968), p. 17.

Chinese economy fell below potential during this period, the focus has to be on the difficulties of tapping the benefits afforded to "latecomers" – to use Alexander Gerschenkron's term – of the development process. While technology for the latecomer may not be free, it can be very cheap.[10] Although some of the economic, political and social forces at the root of an earlier technological inertia in China may also have subsequently affected the absorption and assimilation of new knowledge and technology from outside, analytically there are reasons for tackling the question of absorption separately. It is increasingly recognized that technological innovation is a continuum. For a latecomer, it begins with the successful absorption of existing technology from outside, progresses to adaptation and modification, and culminates with original innovation.[11] While there is some overlap, the skills, capabilities and, more generally, institutions required for absorption are much less demanding than those required for original innovation.

Yet being able to limit attention to the 1890s–1930s by no means simplifies the task. Despite more serious data limitations for the Qing, there actually appears to be wider consensus on what happened in the Chinese economy over the three centuries of the dynasty than on developments in the four decades following the Sino-Japanese War of 1895. Underlying this lack of consensus for the later period are problems of data and interpretation.

### *Narrowing the Debate*

Economic history is not all about numbers, but a quantitative assessment of the period provides an extremely important backdrop to the interpretation of how the economy evolved. In the debate, there are actually a few points where there appears to be a consensus about the late 19th and early 20th-century Chinese economy, and much of this relates to the size of the modern sector and its rate of growth in the early 20th century.

The modern sector includes portions of industry, mining, transportation, communications, finance and so on. It is a potentially misleading term and the dichotomy with the traditional sector problematic, but the term modern sector generally refers to that segment of the economy utilizing new (to the importing country) technology and organizational forms borrowed and adapted from the developed world. The ambiguity arises because enterprises frequently combine elements of both the traditional and modern. The dividing line between the two can be fuzzy and semi-arbitrary. Measurement is further handicapped because of differences between countries in the extent to which the more traditional parts of the production process are carried on inside or outside newly emerging firms.

10. Joel Mokyr, *The Lever of Riches* (Oxford: Oxford University Press, 1990), p. 3.

11. See, for example, Richard Nelson, *National Innovation Systems* (New York: Oxford University Press, 1993).

These caveats aside, T. C. Liu and K. C. Yeh in their classic work[12] put the size of the modern industry, transport and communications sectors at 5.9 per cent of GNP between 1931 and 1936, and estimate that growth averaged 6.8 per cent between 1914–18 and 1931–36. The rate of growth of modern industry was 7.7 per cent. Thomas Rawski in his recent reassessment of growth in the inter-war period has modern industry growing modestly faster (8.1 per cent), but transportation and communications slower. The differences more or less cancel out. Altogether, by the 1930s the modern sector represented no more than one-tenth of the economy, but still probably grew on average at about 6 per cent over the preceding three to four decades. This was slightly lower than in Japan, but appears to compare favourably with India.[13]

Moving from the modern sector to the entire non-agricultural sector, larger differences emerge in the estimates. Rawski suggests a slightly higher rate of growth, chiefly because of more rapid growth in the traditional non-agricultural sector. Although performance in this sector is extremely important for how the growth process is viewed and interpreted, from a narrow quantitative perspective these differences are rather minor. First, assessment of economic growth during the late 19th and early 20th century will not be radically altered if in the end it is believed that either the modern or the more broadly defined non-agricultural sector was growing at a rate 1–2 per cent higher than current estimates. Current estimates already suggest respectable sectoral growth rates, especially given the internal and external shocks the economy experienced in the early 20th century. Secondly, modestly higher estimates cannot by themselves alter the reassessment of what was happening to per capita incomes in the aggregate, and much of the current debate is over the aggregate. The current estimate of the size of the agricultural sector – slightly less than two-thirds of GNP in the early 1930s – precludes that. One of the ironies of Rawski's book – and Rawski is fully aware of this – is that his *quantitative* reassessment of growth depends on more rapid growth than previously believed in the one sector in which he has least to say.[14] And thirdly, the important question is: why after the opening up of China in the 1840s did the utilization of new technology take so long to cement and the modern sector take so long to emerge?

Western technology was only introduced in significant quantities after 1895, and modern manufacturing and the rest of the modern sector,

12. Liu and Yeh, *The Economy of the Chinese Mainland.*

13. For Japan, see Takafusa Nakamura, *Economic Growth in Prewar Japan* (New Haven: Yale University Press, 1978). For India, I have not been able to find a breakdown between the traditional and modern sectors. However, between 1913 and 1937, modern manufacturing grew around 5% while all of manufacturing grew slightly more than 3%. Estimates of the growth in manufacturing output are taken from Morris D. Morris, "Growth of large-scale Industry to 1947," and Alan Heston, "National income," both in Vol. 2 of *The Cambridge Economic History of India* (Cambridge: Cambridge University Press, 1983).

14. I emphasize quantitative because Rawski has as much to say about the *qualitative* nature of the growth process, especially the inter-sectoral linkages and externalities, as he does the quantitative. Reviewers have tended to focus on the latter, much to the neglect of the former.

including transportation and finance, are almost exclusively an early 20th-century phenomenon.[15] Economic growth is much more than the development of the modern sector. But, if the modern sector had actually taken serious root 20 years earlier and been able to sustain over this longer period growth rates comparable to those actually achieved over the first three decades of the 20th century, by the mid-1930s the modern sector would have represented nearly a quarter of GNP as opposed to the actual one-tenth. Under this scenario growth in per capita incomes in the early 20th century would not now be a topic of debate. Simple arithmetic illustrates that because with the development process the growth rate in the modern sector is significantly higher than in the traditional, the aggregate growth rate will accelerate as the modern sector increases as a percentage of GNP. With a population that exceeded 450 million by the turn of the century, or more than seven times that of Japan, and an even higher percentage of the population in agriculture to begin with, time becomes an all-important factor in the transformation of a primarily agrarian economy.

Insofar as the transfer of technology to China in textiles and other newly emerging industries was profitable – and estimates suggest, in fact, that it usually was – what combination of forces prevented this transfer from successfully occurring earlier, or from occurring at a more rapid rate? The number of case studies on technology transfer by firms during the last half of the 19th century are minimal, but they generally suggest that the technologies introduced were not economically incompatible with China. That is, they could produce at lower cost than their traditional counterparts and were not crowded out by more efficient indigenous producers as frequently argued. When they failed, the problem appears to lie in the non-economic costs of the transfer, which were frequently tied to China's system of political economy.[16] These costs frequently forced firms to shut down after a few years and discouraged investment by others. While it is probably correct that no potentially profitable industries failed to appear in 19th or 20th-century China because of *official* opposition,[17] opposition more broadly defined appears to have been present, especially before 1895.

15. Foreigners were given the rights to establish manufacturing facilities without government consent in 1895. While foreign established firms were frequently the first to move into a new industry, by the 1920s and 1930s Chinese firms actually dominated most sectors.

16. See, for example, Shannon Brown, "Cakes and oil: technology transfer and Chinese soybean processing, 1860–1895," *Comparative Studies in Society and History*, Vol. 23, No. 3 (July 1979), pp. 550–568; and "The Ewo Filature: a study in the transfer of technology to China in the 19th century," *Technology and Culture*, No. 20 (1979). More recently, business historians have begun to provide new insights into the establishment and dynamics of China's early 20th-century modern sector growth through case studies of Chinese and foreign firms. I should like to thank Sherman Cochran for allowing me to see his unpublished monograph "Adapting to the market: Western, Japanese, and Chinese businesses, 1880–1937."

17. Dwight Perkins, "Government as an obstacle to economic development in China," *Journal of Economic History*, Vol. 27, No. 4 (December 1967).

*Quantitative Assessments of Early 20th-Century Agriculture*

Most of the debate about the quantitative record of the early 20th-century economy ultimately revolves around trends in agriculture. More favourable estimates in the aggregate cannot be made without revisions to existing assessments of the performance of agriculture. Thus, it is valuable to examine the estimates that are most commonly cited, namely Dwight Perkins' for the period between 1914–18 and 1931–36.[18] Perkins estimates that agricultural output increased by 14.8 per cent. This implies an annual rate of 0.81 per cent, or the about same as he estimates for long-term population growth.

In their construction, these estimates are highly problematic. Additional questions are raised by a possible break in the long-term trend that is related to a sharp decline in agriculture's terms of trade in the late 1920s, coupled with a sharp drop in export demand for some key crops. But in defence of Perkins, it must be remembered that these numbers were not constructed for the purpose of estimating growth rates over the early 20th century. Rather, they were part of a more ambitious exercise aimed at looking at *sources of growth* over 600 years. And in this exercise, per capita consumption is assumed to remain constant, which automatically builds in the assumption that output only grew at the same rate as population.

Agricultural growth can occur because of increases in acreage, a rise in crop yields, a shift to higher valued crops and an increase in cropping intensity as measured by the index of multiple cropping. A key assumption in the construction of the estimates for the early 20th century is that yields remained constant. This restricts sources of growth in agriculture to the first, third and fourth factors. Estimated changes in acreage are based on indices constructed by the National Agricultural Research Bureau and Nanjing University in the 1930s and unfortunately it is not known how the actual indices were made. These estimates imply, however, that three-quarters of the growth in cultivated area is in the north-east, with most of the remainder in the south-west. With increases in acreage largely confined to the north-east, Perkins' estimates effectively restrict the potential sources of growth in China proper to only two factors, the shift to higher valued crops and changes in cropping intensity. Of the data he uses, data on cropping patterns probably have the highest margin of error.[19]

With most of the growth over the two decades attributable to increases in cultivated area, his analysis ultimately implies that in China proper

18. Dwight Perkins, *Agricultural Development in China* (Chicago: Aldine, 1969). As far as I know, these are the only serious estimates. An estimate for the 1880s was made by Zhang Zhongli on the basis of Qing land figures and a combination of 19th and early 20th-century data, and later adjusted upwards by Feuerwerker. The odd mixture of data from several periods to derive the estimate undermines its credibility and comparability with other estimates. See Zhang Zhongli, *The Chinese Gentry* (Seattle: University of Washington Press, 1962).

19. These estimates are largely based on data collected by the Ministry of Agriculture and Commerce, which appears to have lacked the necessary manpower to obtain reasonably accurate and consistent estimates.

agriculture grew less than the rate of population growth, implying declining per capita production and consumption.[20] The latter deduction is inconsistent with a host of information on marketing and shipping of major crops such as rice and cotton, the fact that real wages probably did not decline, consumption levels for the 1930s, distribution of income and so on, all of which point to problems either in the assumptions Perkins invokes or in the data he uses. One can also find numerous contradictions between these estimates and alternative ones put together by Xu Daofu, which are equally problematic.[21] If the period is extended to cover the last decade of the 19th and first decade of the 20th century, the margin of error only widens, and the shortcomings of some of the assumptions and of extending Perkins' estimate of the annual growth rate to this longer time interval become more obvious. The bottom line is that the assumption on yields, the margin of error in the acreage estimates and the weakness in the data on cropping percentages leave estimates for 1914–18 and 1931–36, and by extension, the period between the 1890s and 1930s, with a relatively wide margin of error.

In light of current knowledge, a 95 per cent confidence interval for the annual rate of agricultural growth over the late 19th to early 20th century is probably in the region of 0–2 per cent, assuming that population growth was growing at slightly less than 1 per cent per annum. The problem, as shown below, is that this is too wide an interval to be of much use in discriminating alternative hypotheses about agriculture. Moreover, even if a rate of growth could be agreed, the margin of error in the remaining data prevents confident identification of the underlying sources of growth, such as contribution of increases in cultivated or sown area, shifts in cropping patterns, and higher yields. Compounding things, the margin of error in regional estimates is probably even larger.

### *A Standard for Comparison*

By comparison with the rates of growth observed in the late 1970s and early 1980s for Chinese agriculture, and the high rates of GNP growth enjoyed in Asian NICs the last few decades, even an annual growth rate for agriculture as high as 2 per cent still seems terribly low.[22] Is it necessary to bother with refining rates of growth for agriculture? A simple comparison with England in the 18th and 19th century, a period spanning the Industrial Revolution, and pre-Second World War Japan,

20. The data problems are especially severe for the Yangzi region. Perkins' data imply, for example, that rice production, the most important grain crop in the region, declined by 11.5%, and in per capita terms by more than 20%. An increase in grain imports only partially offset this.

21. Daofu Xu, *Zhongguo jindai nongye shengchan ji maoyi tongji ziliao* (*Statistical Materials on Agricultural Production and Trade in Modern Chinese*) (Shanghai: Shanghai People Publishing, 1983).

22. Since the mid-1980s, however, growth rates in agriculture have slipped back to below 3%, and grain production has only increased at an annual rate of 1.3%. Between 1952 and 1978, agricultural output increased 3.2% per annum, but only 2.1% between 1957 and 1978. Over the same period population growth averaged about 2%.

where the role of agriculture in the development process is well documented and often singled out as exemplary, suggests that it is. For additional comparison, Taiwan is included.

*England.* Between 1700 and 1850, grain production grew only 0.7 per cent per annum. Non-grain production grew slightly faster, but in total, agricultural production grew only 0.8 per cent.[23] This increase fell short of the rate of growth in population, and England eventually became a net importer of grain and food products. By the mid 19th century, England was importing more than half its grain.

*Japan.* Between 1890 and 1940, Japanese agriculture, including crop production and sidelines such as sericulture and animal husbandry, grew at an annual rate of 1.5 per cent. Over the same period, population grew 1 per cent.[24] These estimates are potentially misleading and conceal a break in growth rates around the First World War. Before this war, growth averaged 1.9 per cent per annum, but fell to 1.1 per cent in the 1920s and 1930s.[25] Over the entire period, rice production grew only 1 per cent, and total crop production only marginally faster. The most rapidly growing segment was non-crop production, notably sericulture, which averaged slightly below 5 per cent. Agricultural growth in Japan was unable to accommodate population growth, and Japan became increasingly dependent on its colonies as a food source. By the 1930s, rice from the colonies was feeding more than 15 per cent of the population.

*Taiwan.* Between 1905 and 1936, agricultural output grew over 3 per cent per annum. Rice production averaged around 2.5 per cent, while non-grain output grew almost twice as fast. Over the same period, population grew over 50 per cent, or 1.5 per cent per annum.[26] In the first half of the period, growth was largely extensive, and based on significant increases in land, labour and current inputs. Cultivated area nearly doubled. In the second half, growth was primarily intensive, and promoted by nearly a tripling in irrigated area and the adaptation of new high-yielding varieties from Japan.

23. Robert Allen, "Agriculture during the Industrial Revolution," in Roderick Floud and Donald McCloskey (eds.), *Economic History of Britain since 1700, Vol. 1: 1700–1860* (2nd ed.) (Cambridge: Cambridge University Press, 1994), Table 5.1, p. 102.

24. K. Ohkawa and M. Shinohara, *Patterns of Japanese Economic Development* (New Haven: Yale University Press, 1979), especially Tables A16 and A53.

25. Even these figures are slightly misleading. Some portion of the higher growth before the First World War can be attributed to a "one-time" gain in productivity that was associated with the re-integration of Japan during Meiji and the exploitation of previously untapped potential. Also, shortly after the turn of the century, Japan began to protect its agricultural sector and that in the colonies. By the 1920s and 1930s, tariffs on rice from outside the Empire were over 40%. Without the tariffs, growth rates in agriculture would have been significantly lower. See Loren Brandt, "Interwar Japanese agriculture: revisionist views on the impact of the colonial rice policy and the labor surplus hypothesis," *Explorations in Economic History*, No. 30 (July 1993), pp. 259–293.

26. Samuel Ho, *Economic Development of Taiwan* (New Haven: Yale University Press, 1978).

By the standards of the times, and in comparison with two countries that also faced relatively severe land constraints, a sustained growth rate of agricultural output that exceeded population growth by 0.5 per cent or more is respectable. Of course, a simple comparison of growth rates can mask key differences in the underlying development process. In England, for example, the farm labour force declined both in absolute and percentage terms between 1700 and 1850, meaning growth in labour productivity well in excess of output growth. But in Japan the number of individuals and labour supplied per individual in agriculture increased until the First World War before both began to decline. It was only after the war that a more rapidly growing non-agricultural sector finally began to make a modest dent in the absolute size of the farm population. Over the entire period, labour productivity growth was limited to the rate of output growth. In Taiwan, on the other hand, agriculture benefited from restrictions on the flow of resources into industry, and the tariff protection afforded agriculture in the Empire.

There are several lessons here. First, "success" in agriculture is hard to define, and agriculture cannot be evaluated in isolation from developments in the rest of the economy, and the international economy for that matter. The problems of an agricultural sector only growing at the rate of population growth are more pronounced the smaller and/or slower the growth in the non-agricultural sector. Secondly, if growth in excess of population growth is taken as an indicator of success, the problem is that the current margin of error in estimates for China prevent differentiation between the successful and unsuccessful case. When looking at growth in per capita terms, the margin of error in the population figures only further compounds this.[27] And thirdly, the margin of error is only magnified in regional estimates. Given the size and diversity of China, regional estimates are in some respects as important as the national ones.

### *Alternative Indicators*

It is largely because of these kinds of limitations in conventional data that auxiliary data and alternative indicators of the pace of economic growth in China have been used, including wage data, productivity estimates in other sectors, consumption estimates, marketing and trade data, and measures of financial sector development. The use of these kinds of data is not new to debate in historical economics. In the case of China, however, the focus has been almost exclusively on the use of wage data, neglecting other measures of economic change and alternative qualitative features of the growth process.

The potential difficulties with the wage data can be lumped into two categories: problems with the figures themselves and problems with the

27. Peter Schran, "China's demographic evolution, 1850–1953, reconsidered," *The China Quarterly*, No. 75 (September 1978), pp. 638–646, raises doubt about Perkins' estimate of population growth, which are based on late Qing totals. Schran suggests an estimate of 0.5% as opposed to 0.9%.

model used to interpret them. John Buck's nominal wage indices, for example, have been a widely used source of information. Because they were constructed on the basis of villager recall, these indices are often viewed as suspect *a priori*. It is also known that the villages Buck surveyed tended to be more commercialized on average. Other difficulties arise because the wage data must be adjusted for changing prices, which requires construction of a deflator. These are all legitimate concerns.

The logical question that needs to be asked is: how do these problems systematically bias the estimates? Do they impart a systematic positive or negative bias or do they simply imply larger standard errors? The fact that these data are based on villager recall (three well-informed villagers were asked about wage trends) would only tend to increase the standard error of the estimate and should not bias them systematically one way or the other. Most people can recall their wage histories reasonably well, and my more recent survey experience in the Chinese countryside suggests that this includes Chinese farmers. The tendency for these villages to be more commercialized than average is more difficult to assess. If it is believed *a priori* that commercialization tends to increase the demand for labour and thus wages, then data collected in villages in which commercialization is increasing are likely to give positively biased estimates of overall trends. If such a connection between commercialization and wages is not accepted, the bias is harder to handicap, as it is in villages that historically have been highly commercialized. Finally, what about problems in deflating Buck's data?[28] Given that in areas Buck surveyed transportation tended to be better, agriculture was more commercialized on average and prices were likely to be determined in larger markets, how much error is introduced in using a single regional price index as a deflator for a period covering 40 years? For a region like the Changjiang, much of which had been long-blessed with reasonably efficient water transport, one could make the case that the error is fairly modest, and unbiased. For areas in the interior that were newly linked by rail, it is much harder to say,[29] as it is for areas only loosely tied to a major trading terminus.

The purpose here is not to discount the difficulties of using Buck's data. For any kind of data the weakness and biases need to be identified and rigorously evaluated. Moreover, it is necessary to ascertain how trends in these data compare with those implied by other data which do

28. Potential difficulty with some of Buck's data is illustrated by Thomas Wiens' observation that using other data compiled by Buck as a deflator produces real wage behaviour sharply at odds with series Rawski or I present. There are several problems with using Buck's deflator here however. First, they include agricultural and non-agricultural goods, and for purposes of estimating productivity in agriculture, agricultural prices are needed. Secondly, Buck's index for north China is based on data for four localities, three of which are situated in fairly isolated areas of Qinghai, Gansu and Shansi. Thirdly, for all but one of the indices we do not know the weights used in the construction, and moreover, many of the goods would not be in the market basket of a typical farm household. Wiens' observations can be found in "Trends in Late Qing and Republican rural economy: reality or illusion," *Republican China*, Vol. 18, No. 1 (November 1992).

29. The difficulties arise because the introduction of the railway can lead to sharp "one-time" increases as well as decreases in prices through its effect on demand and supply. For example, in a grain deficit area grain prices may fall because of access to new supplies, while prices earned for cash crops may increase.

not suffer from some of the same shortcomings. Miscellaneous wage data are available for the late 19th century, as well as observations for the late 18th and early 19th centuries.[30] These data are not without their own unique problems of interpretation and obviously are limited, but almost without exception suggest a level of real wages (measured in terms of grain, for example) considerably higher for the early 1930s than for the 19th century. Conservatively, the difference is a third, which is in line with estimates of the productivity increase in the handicraft textile sector, and the increase in consumption of cotton cloth.

Equal attention has been given to the model used to interpret the data. And the view of some historians, and economists, for that matter, has been that the value of wage data, including that in the non-agricultural sector, is compromised and undermined by the fact that the neo-classical model does not perfectly hold. Here, I am more sanguine on the issue. As long as wage levels reflect productivity, and adjust to changes in productivity over time, these data remain valuable indicators of productivity change. It is not necessary to believe that rural labour markets function perfectly or that the links between rural and urban labour markets are frictionless in order to be able to make valid historical inferences using the wage data.[31]

In a collaborative effort, I recently analysed data for nearly 600 longer-term (one to 12 months) labour contracts in 1935 covering much of north-east China.[32] The primary purpose in using these data was not in the link between wage levels and productivity *per se*, but rather to analyse a set of credit, incentive and reputation issues intrinsic to these kinds of agency relationships. However, it was found that: cross-sectional differences in wages were a product of labour productivity differentials arising from differences in village factor endowment such as land–labour and draught animal–labour ratio, and land quality; a worker's wages were systematically tied to his own productivity through the effect of experience and skill-level;[33] wages paid to workers in a host of semi-

30. See, for example, Li Wenzhi, *Zhongguo zibenzhuyi mengya wenti taolunqi* (Beijing: Sanlian, 1957), pp. 652–53; Kang Chao, *Man and Land in Chinese History* (Stanford: Stanford University Press, 1986); and "Tenure of land in China and the condition of the rural population," *Journal of the China Branch of the Royal Asiatic Society*, No. 23 (1889), pp. 58–143.

31. Interestingly, in the recent literature on the 19th century U.S. economy there is renewed debate over the urban–rural income gap, and the extent to which the gap is simply a product of measurement error. A comparison of urban and rural wages requires: wage series for comparably skilled workers in the two sectors; correctly valuing all in-kind payments; adjusting wages for differences in the cost of living; and constructing urban and rural deflators. The potential for systematic error is substantial.

32. The data are drawn from contracts covering households in 22 villages in Liaoning, Jilin and Heilongjiang. About half the villages are in Liaoning, and exhibit marked similarity with their north China counterparts. Nearly two-thirds of all contracts are between non-villagers. These contracts, which average over 6 months, cover nearly 85% of all labour hired, which is slightly higher than comparable estimates made for north China villages. See Loren Brandt and Arthur Hosios, "Credit, incentives and reputation," *Journal of Political Economy*, Vol. 104, No. 6 (December 1996).

33. Wages and worker age were positively correlated and increased up to the age of 40 before beginning to decline. The coefficients imply that the wage of a 40-year-old farmhand were almost double those of his counterpart 20 years his junior or senior. Wage premiums were also paid both to more highly skilled farm workers, and certain kinds of non-agricultural workers.

skilled non-agricultural occupations show no premium over wages paid to a typical farmhand; and altogether, and through the effect of the underlying demand and supply for labour, a combination of individual, family and village-level attributes can explain almost two-thirds of the cross-sectional variation in wages.

This is not to suggest that one should infer on the basis of these data that in other parts of China, or that throughout the late 19th and early 20th century, labour markets operated with the same facility. The heterogeneity in China is too great to allow that, and besides, labour markets usually lag behind product and capital markets in the pace of integration. Moreover, because the data are only cross-sectional, their analysis does not help directly in making inferences about historical trends. Yet with limited prospects of revising the agricultural output data within reasonable error margins, and no comparable estimates for the 1890s, the best (and perhaps only) bet for making historical inference is going to be on the basis of the behaviour of a wide variety of auxiliary data. Perkins' data cannot be taken as a benchmark. This means that much more attention needs to given to the data and methodology underlying these alternative indicators, and to their interpretation.[34] And in the latter, a much better grasp of the local institutional setting and how markets functioned will be essential.

### *The Institutional Setting*

The efficiency with which rural markets worked has not only figured prominently in discussions about how to interpret the wage data. In fact, much of the debate over the performance of the Chinese economy has been reduced to differences of opinion over the functioning of markets. This is unfortunate because they are certainly not the *sine qua non* of economic growth. While poorly functioning markets can slow the spread and pace of the growth process, and possibly derail it altogether, they do not have to work perfectly for growth to occur either, as shown by post-reform China. In other words, perfectly functioning markets are neither a sufficient or necessary condition for growth to occur.[35]

34. Differences in the interpretation of cloth consumption data highlight this point. It is generally agreed that cloth consumption increased significantly between the 1890s and 1930s, with estimates ranging between a third and a half. Is the increase related to increases in incomes? Xu Xinwu does not address this question explicitly, but attributes it to an increase in manufactured cloth output and to the fact that manufactured cloth was less durable than handicraft versions. Ignoring problems with Xu's estimate of the percentage of cloth that was manufactured, if durability was the *only* difference between the two type – and I am not suggesting that it is – it should be reflected in lower prices for manufactured cloth. An economic explanation would then attribute the increase in consumption to a falling relative price of manufactured cloth and substitution between the two. No increase in incomes is necessary. An examination of price data for a variety of cloth do not support the underlying claim. An alternative explanation is that the price effects were very small, and that the increase was the product of growing incomes. See Xu Xinwu, "Zhongguo tubu chanxiao guji, 1840–1936," cited in Huang, *The Peasant Family and Rural Development in the Yangzi Delta*.

35. Much of traditional neoclassical economics is narrowly concerned with the efficiency properties of markets, and the static loss of output and welfare arising from market distortions. Static efficiency does not imply higher growth however. In fact, in traditional growth theory, the long-term steady state rate of growth is a function of *exogenous* technological change and

However, they can play an important role, and in the context of late 19th and early 20th-century China, this includes both product and factor markets. The former are critical because they provide households with signals about the returns to alternative activities and information about new opportunities and technologies. Markets, and even integrated national markets, are certainly not products of the late 19th and early 20th century. Historically, parts of China were highly commercialized. But a case can be made that farm household interaction with the market increased over this period.[36] If a major impetus for the (accelerated?) commercialization of the period was indeed external to the rural sector and linked to the nascent modern sector and the international economy, the workings of market institutions and their interaction with political institutions becomes central to how far the effects may have spread. The political dimension is potentially important because of a history of local government intervention in markets in China.[37]

Factor markets, on the other hand, have important efficiency and distributive implications. At one level, they provide a mechanism through which households can offset imbalances in resource endowments, and thus utilize their own resources more efficiently. For a household with landholdings too small to absorb the family's labour supply, hiring out and/or renting-in become important options. If the commercialization process through its effect on the demand for labour and off-farm opportunities was in some sense "labour-using," the ability of small farm households to access the benefits either directly or indirectly depended upon how these markets functioned. In this respect, markets may have distributive implications. Factor markets, especially the credit market, also help insulate household consumption from the effect of idiosyncratic shocks, and thereby provide a mechanism through which households "smooth" (insure) their consumption over time. This also has distributive effects. In addition, the two roles are linked.[38]

---

*footnote continued*

population growth. This explains the interest in new growth theory, and alternatives such as the new institutional economics, which endogenize the growth rate.

36. Again, the data have their limitations, but there are three major factors pointing to an increase in the commercialization of agriculture: a small but important increase in the percentage of the population that was urban and non-agricultural; an increase in the percentage of total acreage in cash crops, which have higher marketing ratios; and as suggested by the experience of crops like cotton, an increase overtime in the percentage of cash crops that was marketed. A comparison of estimates for the 1930s, with an estimate that can be made using Wu Chengming's data for the 1850s also suggest the same thing. See Wu Chengming, "Woguo ban zhimindi ban fengjian guonei shichang," *Lishi yanjiu*, No. 2 (1984).

37. In major upper Changjiang rice markets, for example, provincial officials would frequently try to prevent the flow of rice downriver in times of rising prices. For the early 20th century, Kenneth Pomeranz argues that in parts of Shandong officials tried to block the flow of copper, and the arbitrage of local copper–silver price differentials. The difference between the rice market and the case Pomeranz analyses is that it was nearly impossible to implement a successful blockade of the Hunan rice markets. See Kenneth Pomeranz, *The Making of a Hinterland: State, Society, and Economy in Interior North China, 1853–1937* (Berkeley: University of California Press, 1993).

38. Empirical work suggests that markets are much more successful in their first capacity than the second, i.e. all households are not able to protect themselves perfectly from

An examination of data for the 1930s reveals an enormous diversity across villages and households in the roles of land, labour and credit market institutions in organizing economic activity in the countryside. In some villages, for example, the labour (land) market is thin, and households adjust landholdings to labour endowment through land rental (labour) markets. In other villages, there are active land *and* labour markets, while in others, the role of markets in reallocating land or labour is limited. There is also considerable complexity and sophistication in the contracts[39] underlying these market transactions that confounds simple theorizing. Three examples can be provided, all drawn from north and north-east China.

First, in the region a high percentage of labour hired in agriculture was on longer-term contracts. In these contracts there were marked differences in the timing of the wage payments: sometimes they are at the beginning, sometimes at the end and sometimes in instalments. How can this be explained? Does the design of these contracts reflect potential incentive problems between the two parties, with payments sometimes skewed towards the end (or beginning) to prevent the employee (or employer) from not living up to the terms of the contract? If so, do reputational issues and the fact that the parties are related and/or are from the same village, or that there is a third party present to the contract help to resolve these differences? In general, is contract enforcement a major problem in villages, and does it constrain hiring? Alternatively, does the timing of the payments reflect possible credit constraints, that is, employee (or employer) households cannot borrow in the informal credit market, and are wage payments moved towards the beginning (or end) of the contract as a way to extend credit to those households facing credit market constraints? If the latter, how much credit is extended through this mechanism and how does it compare to credit through the informal market?

Secondly, in China there are contracts in which the rent is fixed in advance but some form of *ex-post* renegotiation occurs. The likelihood of the renegotiation appears to be tied to the quality of the harvest, but the reduction is neither automatic (for any given shock, some households in a village benefit while others do not) nor uniform. Moreover, the *ex-ante* rent (agreed in January or February) appears to reflect the likelihood of renegotiation in the event of a bad harvest and potential access to credit. In other words, those households that were more likely to receive rent reductions paid higher rents, suggesting a form of implicit insurance. This interpretation can be contrasted with traditional interpretations of rent-reduction in times of a poor harvest in the context of a "moral" economy.

Thirdly, in addition to credit extended through labour contracts, credit was extended in villages in the form of zero and positive interest-rate loans. On average, and at any given time, a half or more of all households were involved in these contracts, with lending activity more widely

*footnote continued*
idiosyncratic exogenous shocks through the use of markets and non-market institutions. The source of these differences and their possible implications has yet to be explored.

39. I use the term contract loosely here and allow it to include both implicit and explicit contracts, verbal as well as written.

dispersed across households than generally assumed. Across villages, there are marked differences in the composition of the two types of contract. There are also differences across households in their "portfolio" of contracts: some households borrow (or lend) only at positive rates; others only participate at zero rates, and others use a combination of the two types of loan. How are the two related? What determines access to zero interest loans? Is it only between relatives or villagers? Is some kind of reciprocity involved, and are these loans only for certain kinds of uses? Are zero interest rate loans, in fact, a form of insurance *cum* credit? How does a household's current asset position influence credit access and the terms of loans, that is interest rate, repayment period, use of collateral? Is credit in the interest-bearing segment price or quantity rationed? How are these contracts enforced and is default a major issue? How does market development and the appearance of new financial intermediaries influence the role of these two types of credit?

The degree of complexity and diversity in these contracts is certainly not unique to the 1930s, nor to the north and north-east. However, these features suggest a much richer institutional environment than earlier acknowledged in the literature, and raise a host of more general and difficult questions about contractual relationships, economic organization, growth and distribution in the Chinese countryside that deserve more careful investigation. What was the role of these institutions in resource allocation? How did markets interact with and possibly complement non-market institutions such as reciprocal insurance in resource allocation? How well did the markets perform in this capacity and how far did they extend? Within markets, was contract enforcement a problem? If so, did relational ties, or possibly social or cultural norms, resolve these difficulties and thus facilitate wider market exchange? Were there problems in property rights and if so, what effect did this have on incentives, resource use and market exchange? What was the source of local diversity observed in contracts and organization? Is the diversity a product of custom or highly idiosyncratic local features, or is there an economic explanation for much of it? In these differences are there clues about the longer-term evolution of the rural Chinese economy, and the impact of external developments on economic organization? More generally, what implication did these institutions have for resource allocation, productivity, growth and welfare in rural China?

### *Markets, Involution and Technology*

The overriding question is: is there, in how markets may have functioned and in the economic organization of the countryside, an explanation for the level of development observed in the 1930s, or does the problem lie elsewhere? In two influential books, Phillip Huang makes a bold link between market institutions and economic growth.[40] He invokes

40. Philip Huang, *The Peasant Economy and Social Change in North China* (Stanford: Stanford University Press, 1985) and *The Peasant Family and Rural Development in the Yangzi Delta*.

the metaphor of involutionary growth to explain the failure of China's rural economy to grow more rapidly over a long period. Under involutionary growth, an elaboration of existing institutional patterns effectively inhibits the economic growth process. Central to the problem in the pre-1949 period are imperfections in rural markets and the perpetuation of the small family farm.

Huang argues that market imperfections, including social constraints on the hiring of women and children, gave smaller farm households "competitive" advantages over larger managerial farms in agriculture and alternative forms of organization in a host of non-agricultural sidelines such as textiles. The argument in its more general form is not new, and has been made before.[41] In both agriculture and industry, smaller farm households effectively crowded out their larger "capitalist" counterparts, which in other countries were reportedly the source of technological innovation, higher rates of investment and higher growth, and thus superior performance. Market imperfections and thus the "familization" of production in which farming and sidelines were tightly integrated were at the centre of China's failure to grow more rapidly. Regardless of how rapidly agriculture grew in the late 19th and early 20th century, there are several analytical issues that need to be addressed: how the modern and traditional sectors interact in the context of an open economy: the behaviour of China's factor markets; and how the process of technological change and innovation is conceptualized.

*The interaction of the modern and traditional sectors in an open economy.* In a closed economy, an emerging modern sector must compete with the rural sector for resources and markets, but this is not necessarily so in an open economy. Integration with the international economy eliminates important constraints on either the demand or the supply side previously imposed by the traditional sector. The pace of technological change is now largely dictated by the rate at which the economy can absorb existing technologies and knowledge outside the country, and learning by doing plays a major role in the growth process. Under these conditions, the failure of the modern sector to appear and grow more rapidly can primarily be attributed either to difficulties in absorbing the new technologies, or to the possibility that at locally prevailing costs of labour and capital, domestic firms cannot compete with their international counterparts. Rudimentary calculations suggest that the latter was not the case.

The potential impact of the traditional sector on the modern sector through demand-side linkages remains important,[42] but it does not make

41. Much earlier, Kang Chao, *The Development of Cotton Textile Production in China* (Cambridge, MA: Harvard University Press, 1977), made a related argument about development in the textile industry.

42. Despite access to export markets, domestic demand, much of it originating in the rural sector, remains extremely important. And in this regard, it does not matter if the growth of rural incomes is coming from an increase in working days or productivity per day. It all has the same effect on demand.

sense to talk about a modern sector being "squeezed" by the traditional sector on the supply side in this context. In fact, if industry organized all or in-part through the family enterprise can produce at lower costs than modern firms, presumably the same opportunities for growth through export expansion would apply for them as well. Thomas Smith in his classic work on pre-Meiji Japan argues that the organization of much of non-agricultural production in the context of the family was invaluable in Japan's shift from a traditional to modern economy.[43] These numerous by-employments, Smith contends, were geared towards the markets rather than household consumption and were part of an elaborate division of labour at the intra- and inter-county level. In the late 19th and early 20th century, this continued to be used to Japan's advantage in the organization of sericulture, which grew more than 5 cent per annum. A similar observation can be made about Taiwan, where a putting-out/sub-contracting system involving rural households persists to this day for some sectors in light industry. The economic veracity of the family as a production unit cannot explain an open economy's failure to grow more rapidly. It can actually be a big plus.

*Markets, organization and inequality.* If it is assumed that labour markets functioned poorly and that the larger farms faced higher implicit costs for labour, this puts them at a serious competitive disadvantage vis-à-vis smaller farms, and stymies their development. In the commercialized areas there was typically an active land rental market. On average, a third or more of all farm land in China was rented-in, with the percentage in more commercialized areas even higher. As long as land could be rented in or out, any differences in factor proportions or intensity arising from imperfections in the labour market could be offset through the land rental market. It takes differences in at least two input markets to generate differences in factor intensities across households. The possibility of renting-in land effectively wipes out any "advantage" of smaller farms and leads to a wage-rental ratio identical to that observed if the labour market was perfect. The fact that larger farms were not larger suggests that other economic forces were at work.[44]

There is an even more serious problem. Some observers note that women and children participated in the labour market only marginally, and conclude that it must be the product of discrimination. An alternative and observationally equivalent explanation is that households allocate their labour optimally and that the combined returns to farming and non-farming activity (including home production, which is unobserved)

43. Thomas Smith, "Farm family by-employments in pre-industrial Japan," *Journal of Economic History*, Vol. 29, No. 4 (December 1969).

44. The most likely explanation concerns the monitoring costs of labour. In north and north-east China, for example, most larger farms were, in fact, extended families that typically had two or three adult males involved in farming operations. This helped to reduce some of the monitoring costs of hired hands, but there were limits. One of the advantages of the family farm is the "self-monitoring" of family labour. Traditional technology did not confer any obvious advantages on size, nor were there organizational advantages.

in the household for women and children are higher than they are off the farm; thus, no hiring out.

Drawing on a unique data set for north-east China, Dwayne Benjamin and I analysed the economic contribution of women and their labour supply decisions to farming.[45] In the north-east, as is true in most other regions of China, women do not hire out; however, in the sample there is considerable diversity among villages and households in the number of women who worked in agriculture. Are these patterns a product of some form of discrimination, or is the allocation of female labour between the market, working in agriculture on the farm, and non-agricultural work on the farm, based on productivity considerations? Moreover, are there in the land rental market residual effects of labour market discrimination? Because the land rental market provides a way for households to offset imbalances in resource endowments, discrimination against women and children should spill over to it. Households with "surplus" women should adjust in the land market, implying that the demographic effects of women and children relative to men on the household's demand for land rental would be out of line with their productivity.

Several results are of interest. First, the economic contribution of a woman measured in *yuan* is as great as a man's. The contribution is both direct (working on the farm or in other income-generating sidelines), and indirect, which captures the influence of a female on labour supply decisions of other family members. Having an additional woman in the household effectively releases someone from non-income earning home production, and thus allows an increase in labour supply to income generating activity. Secondly, the magnitude of the direct contribution was positively correlated with the degree of market development. In areas in which farm households faced significant opportunities for off-farm sales, the direct contribution of a woman was as great as that of a man, while in less commercialized areas it was indistinguishable from zero (that is, not that the contribution was zero, only that the directly observable contribution was small). In the more commercialized areas, men were more likely to be observed working off the farm, and more women were involved in family farming. And thirdly, the effects of an additional male and female on the household's demand for land and size of farming operations are consistent with their relative productivity in farming.[46]

These results are indicative of complex family labour supply decisions, and suggest that the allocation of time within the farm household was more influenced by the productivity of women than was the product of economic or market discrimination. This is not to infer that *social*

45. See Dwayne Benjamin and Loren Brandt, "Markets, discrimination, and the economic contribution of women in China: historical evidence," *Economic Development and Cultural Change*, Vol. 44, No. 1 (October 1995).

46. From regression analysis, the following are the effects of an additional male or female on the household's net demand for land (measured by the amount of land the household cultivates). The effect of an additional male (or female) aged 13–17 was to increase the amount of land farmed by 4.92 (0.09) *mu*; for age 18–55 the corresponding figures were 10.42 (7.66) *mu*; and for age over 55, 8.98 (5.46) *mu*. These results are consistent with estimates of labour productivity.

discrimination was not a problem: social or cultural norms may dictate a gender-based division of labour within the household. Taking this as given, the allocation of labour within the household can still be based solely on productivity considerations, with returns to a woman's labour higher inside the household than outside.

In separate work, Benjamin and I analysed the influence of market structure and land inequality on income distribution, and the returns to land.[47] In the 22 villages surveyed there was enormous variability in the role of land and labour markets in organizing agriculture and sizeable differences in the level of income inequality. If markets are perfect, that is, the neo-classical benchmark, returns to factors (primarily land and labour) will be more-or-less constant across households within a village, and household incomes are solely a product of factor returns and endowments; similarly, income distribution depends only on factor returns, that is wages and land rents, the distribution of endowments, and a few covariance terms. For example, income inequality will be decreasing in the level of wages, but increasing in the rental rate and the inequality of land.

Factor market imperfections lead to deviations from this benchmark. Problems in the land and labour market, for example, may mean that land-poor households cannot hire out all the labour they want at the prevailing wage rate, or adjust through land rental. At the household level, the shadow price of labour (the value that the household puts on an additional unit of its labour) will be less than the market wage, and a household's income will be lower than that predicted on the basis of its endowment and prevailing factor market returns. At the village level, because a household's shadow price of labour will be positively correlated with its landholdings, the distribution of land will have a disproportional effect on income distribution.

There is no good metric of how well factor markets work, but it is known how much land and labour were exchanged in the market in these villages. A reasonable assumption is that the level of exchange is positively correlated with the ability of the market to function. Tests carried out at both the village and household levels show that while the distribution of endowments and factor returns have the predicted effects, markets do matter for inequality. Not unexpectedly, this is not a perfect neo-classical world. But contrary to some views common in the development and historical literature, markets are income-levelling: that is, in those villages in which factor markets are more active, including the land rental market and markets for agricultural and non-agricultural labour, and which are located more favourably relative to the major commercial centre in the county, household income is nearer to that predicted by the neo-classical model and actual income inequality is lower. Conversely, in those areas in which factor markets are not well developed, deviations from the neo-classical model are larger, income inequality is higher, and

47. Dwayne Benjamin and Loren Brandt, "Land, factor markets, and income inequality in rural China: historical evidence," *Explorations in Economic History*, forthcoming.

land is found to have a disproportionate effect on income distribution.[48]

If the more commercialized areas are defined to be those in which market exchange is greatest, it is exactly in these areas of rural north and north-east China where markets perform best, households are less constrained in their choices and allocative distortions caused by market imperfections are smallest. I hesitate to generalize, but this is one result that may carry over easily to other regions of China as well. In establishing this link between economic organization and income distribution, it still remains to explain the underlying diversity observed in the organization of agriculture.

*Sources of technological innovation in agriculture.* While technological invention and innovation are frequently the product of non-economic forces, they are also influenced by both demand and supply. Demand pressures induce agents to look for more cost-effective ways of producing, or alternatively, of producing more from a given set of inputs. These pressures are presumably always present to some degree. Sometimes the resulting changes in technology are neutral, in that they reduce input requirements uniformly; but other times the changes are biased, and are skewed towards economizing on the use of a particularly scarce resource, such as land or natural resources (Japan), or labour (U.S.), while reducing overall costs.[49] Supply forces include the current state of scientific knowledge, the prevailing level of technical skills, the structure of the incentives facing suppliers and the attributes of locally available raw materials, all of which affect the costs-side of the innovation process.

The experiences of Japan, Taiwan, Korea, other countries of Asia and some parts of North America now provide a much better picture of the motive forces of technological innovation in agriculture and some of the ingredients of successful technology transfer. Regardless of how rapidly agriculture was growing in China in the late 19th and early 20th centuries, herein lies the key to either faster growth or sustained growth throughout the 20th century.

The early Green Revolutions in Asia entailed the development of a technology that was easily divisible. In other words, it could be utilized

48. These results also provide some empirical support for a heuristic argument offered in an earlier paper with Barbara Sands. We argued that with the impact of commercialization on inequality via its effect on asset distribution ambiguous, commercialization may have actually helped to reduce inequality because of its positive effect on wages and the levelling effect of wages on distribution, and increased factor market activity. While the links between late 19th and early 20th-century commercialization and wages remain open to debate, empirically it appears to be true that higher wages and expanded opportunities in land and labour markets are associated with lower inequality, *ceterus paribus*. See Loren Brandt and Barbara Sands, "Beyond Malthus and Ricardo: economic growth, land concentration, and income distribution in early twentieth century China," *Journal of Economic History*, Vol. 50, No. 4 (December 1990).

49. A major consequence of poorly functioning factor markets is that they may distort the direction and path of technological change. In an economy with poorly functioning labour markets and wages well in excess of market clearing levels, employers are motivated to move along a path of labour-saving, capital-using technological change, and to demand innovation in the same direction.

effectively by farms of all sizes, and did not confer cost advantages on larger farms. This meant that the benefits were also fairly uniformly distributed across farm size categories, the distribution of which is very similar to what is observed for China in the 1930s. Central to the development were the selection and later breeding of new fertilizer-responsive varieties. In Japan, for example, the percentage of acreage under new improved rice varieties increased from 1.5 in 1890 to 61.9 by 1940, and Japanese seed development went through three generations. In these efforts, especially for the last two generations of seeds, government expenditure on research and development and extension were extremely important. By the 1930s, annual expenditure on R&D averaged between 6 and 7 per cent of agricultural output. Much of the R&D in seed improvement drew on the well-established principles of pure-line selection and only later shifted to hybridization, which benefited from advances in the West in plant physiology and genetics. Taiwan and Korea, on the other hand, benefited significantly from investment by the colonial government in R&D on the adaptation of Japanese high-yielding rice varieties for local conditions. In Taiwan, related work on new high-yielding varieties of sugarcane were also carried out.

New hybrids required complementary inputs of water and fertilizer. In the inter-war period, total expenditure on land improvement projects in Japan exceeded 3 billion yen, an increasing percentage of which was publicly financed. During this period, "improved" acreage increased by more than 50 per cent, or by a third of total paddy land. In Taiwan, capital investment in irrigation, about half of which was by the colonial government, increased nearly six-fold in real terms, and irrigated acreage expanded by 60 per cent. In the 1930s, similar investments in Korea were important.

The distinction is occasionally overdrawn, but in contrast to the path of technological development in the United States and the West, which entailed the development of a mechanical technology, in Japan and Asia a bio-technology emerged. While the new mechanical technology facilitated the substitution of power and machinery for labour, the new biological technology, which entailed increases in the complementary inputs of chemical fertilizer and water, was land-saving, and could be either labour-saving or using. In Japan, although the new technology was technically "labour-saving," the total demand for labour increased. The number of days worked per individual in agriculture increased throughout much of the late 19th and early 20th century. This contributed to rising income in the rural sector, which was a major source of demand for the products of the non-agricultural sector. Total demand for labour also increased significantly in Taiwan and Korea. In Japan, rapid increases in the use of labour-saving machinery, primarily in the form of small gasoline or electric-powered engines for pumping and threshing, and powered hullers, did not occur until the 1950s. This helped to ease serious *labour* constraints in Japanese agriculture inherited from before the Second World War, and paved the road for rapid increases in productivity in the post-war period.

A brief review of the experience of other Asian economies reveals the important contribution of state investment to agriculture growth. R&D, irrigation, drainage, water control and even rural education are either in full or in part public goods, and expenditure on them will usually be under-provided by private agents.[50] Yet government involvement was not strictly financial. Co-ordination problems with respect to investment or the adoption of new varieties at the local level can also be important, and frequently require some form of government intervention. The Arable Land Replotment Act of 1899 in Japan, for example, made participation in irrigation projects at the district level mandatory if they were supported by two-thirds or more of landowners owning two-thirds or more of the land. Similarly, associations of land-improvement projects in Japan were given legal status, and thus allowed to borrow from newly emerging financial institutions.

The more general question that needs to be asked is why these actions were taken in some settings and not in others. Why are some governments able to internalize the positive externality related to the investment in these areas, and either directly or indirectly help mobilize and funnel the necessary resources to such activities? By all indications, the potential returns to these expenditures were fairly high, and far exceeded either the costs of capital or the rates of return in industry. Anthony Tang's lower bound estimate for the rate of return to combined education and research expenditure in agriculture for pre-Second World War Japan is 35 per cent.[51] How does it come to be that the allocation of public resources reflects the demands and needs of a rural constituency? What is the nature of the political institutions that provide political actors incentives to commit resources to agriculture? What is the nature of the interaction between the public and private sectors that fosters the positive dynamic observed in Japan, but never got off the ground in China, or at best, was severely limited in the late 19th and early 20th century?

Differences of opinion appear to exist over the extent of progress made in China's agricultural research establishments in the 1930s.[52] But even those sympathetic to the most favourable assessment would conclude that the immediate effect of these efforts in terms of growth was very modest, and that most of the benefits coming from the research were probably not reaped until the 1950s. What can be said with certainty, however, is that both the research agenda of the 1930s and the path of technological development in agriculture ultimately observed in China in the post-1949

50. The logic here is very simple. Public goods have two key features: they are non-rivalrous, meaning that the marginal costs of providing them to an additional consumer are zero; and they are non-exclusive, meaning that people cannot be excluded from consuming them. Under these conditions, private agents will supply a level of the goods below that socially optimal.

51. Anthony Tang, "Research and education in Japanese economic development, 1880–1938," *Economic Studies Quarterly*, Vol. 13, Nos. 2 and 3 (1963).

52. Contrast, for example, the view offered by Randall Stross in *The Stubborn Earth* (Berkeley: University of California Press, 1986), with T. H. Shen's more positive assessment in Paul Sih (ed.), *The Strenuous Decade: China's Nation-Building Efforts, 1927–1937* (New York: St John's University Press, 1970).

period parallel that observed in Japan and the colonies. Over the last four decades, technical change, much in the form of new HYV, has been the source of between half and two-thirds of agricultural growth.[53] Unfortunately, over three-quarters of this period, the returns to the new technology were largely offset by inefficiencies inherent to the collectives and the anti-market bias of the Chinese leadership.[54]

These observations about the experience of China's Asian counterparts suggest the following conclusions regarding technological development in Chinese agriculture. First, the problem in the agricultural sector was not a lack of demand for technological innovation. Innovations that increased output from existing resources and economized on land, the scarce resource, would have been valued by farmers of *all* sizes because they were income-increasing. The constraint was on the supply side. The key innovation was the fertilizer-responsive varieties which were the product of pure line breeding and later hybridization programmes. These were not likely to emerge as the product of private entrepreneurial efforts, and required co-ordinated public efforts in R&D, including experimentation and testing, as well as investment in other complementary areas. This R&D did not entail basic research, but rather was adaptive, and could draw on existing knowledge and experience.

Secondly, successive regimes in China failed to internalize the returns to investment in agriculture, and thus direct and encourage such things as spending on R&D and investment in water control. Investment in the latter was a necessary ingredient to maximize the advantages of the new technology. Similarly, political institutions failed to provide the voice for a rural constituency, which might have helped push the state to commit more resources to agriculture. In the early 20th century under the KMT, as well as in the post-1949 period, the rural sector was largely ignored, and government investment in agriculture has been abysmally low.[55]

Thirdly, the experiences of Taiwan and Japan indicate that education and institutional innovation at the local level were also important to absorption and exploitation of the new technology. In Taiwan, for example, farmers' and irrigation associations were important from the early 20th century on, as they were in Japan even earlier. These institutions, by facilitating dissemination of information and local co-ordination, promoted the adoption of new varieties and techniques. In Taiwan, these

53. See, for example, Bruce Stone and Scott Rozelle, *Foodcrop Production Variability in China* (London: The School of Oriental and African Studies, Research Notes and Monograph Series, Vol. 9, 1995), and Jikun Huang and Scott Rozelle, "Technological change: rediscovering the engine of productivity growth in China," *Journal of Development Economics*, No. 49 (1996).

54. Nicholas Lardy, *Agriculture in China's Economic Development* (Cambridge: Cambridge University Press, 1983).

55. In Chinese history, there are numerous occasions in which such systems were financed using a combination of public and private funds. In Japan, a combination of public and private finance was also used, although public funding became more important later after the First World War. See, for example, Peter Perdue, *Exhausting the Earth: State and Peasant in Hunan, 1500–1850* (Cambridge, MA: Harvard University Press, 1987). For data on public funding, see Yujiro Hayami and Saburo Yamada, *The Agricultural Development of Japan: A Century's Perspective* (Tokyo: University of Tokyo Press, 1991).

institutions began largely at the initiative of the colonial government, while in Japan their evolution is more complex. What are the links between this kind of institutional development and economic organization? Although it is tempting to argue that a homogeneous rural community made up almost entirely of owner-cultivators would have been the most conducive, there are too many counter-examples, including pre-war Japan and the United States, which show that this is not necessarily the case.

And finally, these innovations would have not only helped increase farmers' income, but would have had important backward linkages to industry through an increased demand for current inputs such as chemical fertilizer, and would have increased consumer demand as well. In other words, investment in agriculture would have had even higher results for economic growth.

*Conclusion*

At a minimum, the ongoing reassessment of the late 19th and early 20th-century Chinese economy has succeeded in directing some badly-needed attention to this critical period. Definitive conclusions have yet to be drawn. Thus the purpose of this article has been selective: rather than summarize the ongoing debate, it has highlighted a number of issues that are central to any interpretation and assessment.

Above all, assessment and theorizing about the late 19th and early 20th-century economy remain seriously hampered by severe data problems for the agricultural sector. The margin of error in estimates is uncomfortably big. Given that agriculture in successfully modernizing economies had never previously grown more than 1.5 to 2 per cent per annum, these data cannot be used to differentiate competing claims about growth in the aggregate, let alone at the regional level. Based on a wide variety of auxiliary information, my own view remains that agriculture grew more rapidly than population over this period, and that the assessment of the level of agricultural output in the late 19th century has been unduly optimistic. Indeed, if agriculture and the Chinese economy grew only as rapidly as population growth between the 1890s and 1930s, this gives the paradoxical result that the level of development and the standard of living in Japan and China were more or less the same during the 1880s and 1890s. This is hard to reconcile with the much higher degree of urbanization and the proportion of the population in non-agricultural activity in Japan in early to mid-Meiji, and what is known more generally about economic development during Tokugawa. Having said that, considerably more work needs to be done on providing better estimates for the period, or justifying the existing ones.

The constraint on Chinese agriculture is not likely to be found in the nature of rural factor market institutions. There is still much to learn about these institutions. However, while the markets may not have functioned perfectly, they appear to have been fairly flexible and, in the more commercialized areas, reasonably successful in promoting an efficient resource allocation and in helping to alleviate inequality. The experience of Japan and other land-scarce economies suggests that the major constraint on technological innovation, and thus growth in agriculture, was not with the demand for innovation, but rather on the supply side of the equation. This directs attention to the anaemic efforts of the state in directing resources into the required areas, and in facilitating related investment by resolving a host of co-ordination and incentive issues at the local level through either the legislative process or the legal system. The reasons for this institutional failure and the lack of support and group action for larger public investment will only be found through a more careful examination of the political economy dimensions of the problem, and China's changing political institutions at the national and local level.

Data problems aside, the interpretation of what happens in the agricultural sector must be in light of developments in the non-agricultural sector, as shown by the differences in the experiences of England and Japan. The development process entails a massive reallocation of labour out of agriculture and into the non-agricultural sector in which average productivity is higher. In England, this occurred over several centuries, with the percentage of the population in agriculture already less than half the labour force in the 1700s. This had important implications for the growth in labour productivity in agriculture over the next century and a half. In China, however, around 85 per cent of the labor force was still in agriculture on the eve of the appearance of a modern sector, while in Japan it was nearer to three-quarters. One implication of this is that it would take considerable time and growth before the non-agricultural sector began to siphon off an increasing percentage of the labour force, and even longer before the agricultural labour force began to decline in absolute terms. In addition, because the potential for growth and actual growth in the modernizing non-agricultural sector were so much greater than in agriculture, over the course of the early 20th century rates of growth in the aggregate were likely to accelerate as the modern sector grew in absolute size.

This last observation directs attention once again to the role of technology transfer to China. The opening-up of China should have helped to resolve some of constraints on the supply side, and provide China with access to new technology and knowledge essential to more rapid economic growth (that is, "new" from the perspective of China). This process began in manufacturing, transportation and finance around the turn of the century, but only with long delays. The fact that there was not a more immediate effect highlights one of the shortcomings in earlier work which sees the opening to the West as a panacea. While this technology itself may have had fairly low costs, its successful absorption, adaptation and assimilation required the development of a new complement of administrative, organization and technical skills that were in short supply, and a host of new institutions more generally. Herein lies the most difficult part of the development process, and the one about which we probably know the least.

# Civil Society and Urban Change in Republican China*

Marie-Claire Bergère

From the 1950s to the 1970s, historians' approach to Republican China was informed by a predominant concern for Revolution. Scholarly priorities were focused on the early history of the Chinese Communist Party and on the socio-economic analysis of the countryside where the Chinese revolution had achieved its first success. Few publications were devoted to urban China. The Maoist regime until its end was seen to maintain a strong anti-urban stance. Great ex-treaty port cities were condemned for their past co-operation with foreign imperialism. In the West, the Republican era was often perceived as a confused interregnum between the Qing dynasty and the Communist Empire. And more than a few historians shared the views of their Chinese colleagues and featured big cities of the 1920s and 1930s as outposts of foreign economic exploitation and political oppression, as citadels of cultural arrogance.[1]

Perspectives changed after the reversal of Chinese policy in 1978 and the opening of the country to foreign investments and technology. The ideal of Revolution gave way to "modernization fever." There was a growing feeling that Deng Xiaoping and the reformists were taking up the job that had been left unfinished in 1949. The Republican era was more and more perceived as the starting point of a forceful modernization drive, as a time of economic and cultural innovation and creativity to which contemporaries should turn for inspiration.

As the role of cities in the economic system was rehabilitated, a review of precedents became part of Chinese historians' agenda. The issues with which Shanghai or Beijing residents and municipal governments had been grappling with in the 1920s and the 1930s were not so different from those faced by present-day urban society: the retreat and/or sprawl of state power, corruption, the proliferation of new economic and social organizations, livelihood, public order, cultural representations and so on. In China the revival of Republican urban history resulted from political choice: from the adoption by the party/state leadership of a new reformist line. Historians did not initiate this move, but they took advantage of it and enthusiastically endorsed the consequent reorientation of their research by the reappropriation and legitimation of China's urban past.

Their achievements during these last 15 years have been impressive.[2] Documents have been collected and compiled (most conspicuously the

*I wish to thank Frederic Wakeman and Yeh Wen-hsin for their comments on an earlier draft of this article. I am also grateful to Bryna Goodman, Lucien Bianco and Yves Chevrier for their criticisms and suggestions.

1. Rhoads Murphey, *The Outsiders: The Western Experience in China* (Ann Arbor: University of Michigan Press, 1977).

2. For a brief presentation of these achievements, see Xiong Yuezhi, "Zhongguo chengshi shi yanjiu gaikuang (1979–1994)" ("General view of the research on urban history in China"), unpublished manuscript, Shanghai Academy of Social Sciences, Institute of History, 1995.

© The China Quarterly, 1997

new local gazetteers, *difangzhi*), archives have been organized and opened, books have been published on the development of various cities (Tianjin, Wuhan, Chongqing and, most of all, Shanghai), as well as monographs contributing new and reliable knowledge about topics such as urban population, chambers of commerce, emigrant communities, religious organizations and cultural activities. In analysing the development of Chinese cities during the 19th and 20th centuries most Chinese authors break away from previous interpretive frameworks based upon the concept of class conflict, although they generally retain an essentially Marxist approach emphasizing the role of economic and social transformations as moving forces of history.

By the middle of the 1980s Chinese historians were devoting much attention to the question of foreign concessions. The issue was the subject of intense debate at a conference organized by the Institute of History of the Shanghai Academy of Social Sciences in 1988. The ambivalent influence (*shuang yingxiang*) of foreign concessions upon China's development had become a generally accepted idea among Chinese historians. They carried over their usual perspectives of national and political history into the new-found field of urban studies, and the foreign presence in treaty-ports was mainly considered through its implications for the national status of China. However the perspectives of social and local history were not ignored. For example much attention was devoted to the study of Shanghai culture (*Hai pai*) and of its role in the construction of an urban identity and of nationalism.[3]

The parallel development of Western research on modern China's urban history was supported and stimulated by these Chinese achievements. As archives opened and academic contacts intensified, Chinese and foreign scholars using approximatively the same materials discussed issues of common interest and became familiar with their respective explanatory frameworks. There were mutual borrowings of topics and concepts. But Chinese and Western approaches remained distinct. Even though Chinese scholars were alerted to Western concern with civil society,[4] they did not take up this theme as a major part of their work.

In the West the ambiguity and complexity of the opposition between state and society lies at the heart of academic research on China (as well as on other countries and cultural areas). This theme appears as a central one for understanding the growth and transformation of Chinese cities, as they accelerated during the Republican era, and for asserting the relevance of such historical developments to the present-day situation. Because the problem of the emergence of civil society appears as a mainly Western concern, this presentation is focused on research carried on outside China. This is not to mean that Chinese research is less important, but it has to be evaluated with reference to different categories of analysis.

3. Among many other examples, see: "Wenhua bian" ("Section on culture"), in Zhang Zhongli (ed.), *Jindai Shanghai chengshi yanjiu* (*Research on Modern Shanghai*) (Shanghai: Renmin chubanshe, 1990).

4. Ma Shu-yun, "The Chinese discourse on civil society," *The China Quarterly*, No. 137 (March 1994), pp. 180–193.

These considerations reveal the preliminary problem of the legitimacy of such a presentation. Do concepts generated from European historical experience help towards a better understanding of the Chinese past? There may be a risk of substituting a Western view of China for Chinese reality, substituting orientalism for the Orient, as Edward Said warned a decade ago.[5] These are questions that must be kept in mind while reviewing the achievements of Western research and the pros and the cons of a civil society approach of urban change in Republican China.

Two sets of causes may explain why this approach has become so popular with Western specialists. The first concerns methodology. By the 1980s, at a time when these specialists were reorientating their research toward modern urban history, the disciplinary field of social sciences was being transformed. In the late 1960s and the 1970s, the issues and methods of European social history had been redefined. Under the influence of E. P. Thompson and Natalie Davis, the emphasis shifted from socio-economic factors to the cultural analysis of popular behaviour.[6] Building upon the work done by the *Annales* school and its study of *mentalités*, the "new social historians" often relied on the methods and concepts of anthropology whose influence was "chiefly felt ... in an emphasis upon ... value-systems and upon rituals ... upon symbolic expression of authority, control and hegemony."[7] Clifford Geertz is among those whose influence is more often acknowledged. His *Interpretations of Culture* taught historians how to read "the symbolic content of action, interpret it as sign."[8]

As communist systems of Eastern Europe declined and then suddenly collapsed, political institutions more and more appeared as devoid of meaning, ideologies faded out, and capital and labour were no longer considered motive forces of growth. Post-modernism was a huge enterprise of deconstruction. Historical evolution was seen as governed by an immaterial principle: culture, understood in its broadest sense as the way of life in a given civilization. The existence of extra-cultural (economic, social) dimensions of experience was denied. Social reality was determined by the representations of social world themselves. The central task of the new social/cultural historians was to decipher meanings rather than look out for causes and search for explanatory laws.

Patterns of life and systems of representation were apprehended from below and described as autonomous activities, free from state interference and tutelage. Anthropologists often consider such activities as attributes of "civil society." Mayfair Mei-hui Yang, for example, conceived the

5. Edward Saïd, *Orientalism* (New York: Random House, 1979).

6. E. P. Thompson, *The Making of the English Working Class* (London: Gollancz, 1963); Natalie Zemon Davis, *Society and Culture in Early Modern France* (Stanford: Stanford University Press, 1975).

7. E. P. Thompson, "Folklore, anthropology, and social history," *Indian Historical Review*, Vol. 3 (1977), pp. 247–266, as quoted in Lynn Hunt (ed.), *The New Cultural History* (Berkeley: University of California Press, 1989), pp. 53–54.

8. Cf. Clifford Geertz, *The Interpretations of Cultures* (New York: 1973) and Hunt, *The New Cultural History*, pp. 74–75.

emergence of civil society as "the resuscitation of a society's own non-state structure of integration."[9] Given the amorphous nature of the concept and its various usages in Western intellectual history, it was not illegitimate to borrow it to identify a sphere of social organization enjoying more or less autonomy from the state, distinct from the political sphere, and not necessarily endowed with civic activism. But one may well ask whether "civil society" represents a useful category for historians, when understood in this broad sense, and what the difference is between such "civil society" and society.[10] Seen from the methodological angle, the concept was not used as a paradigm. But it signalled a new approach to social history, based upon cultural anthropology. It was used as a key to the hitherto little explored field of Chinese urban society.

The second set of causes which made "civil society" such a popular concept with China specialists reflects the political and ideological choices of academics who as specialists and as citizens had been confronted with the 1989 tragedy of Tiananmen. Many of them, at first, viewed this tragedy as the result of the Reform decade (1978–88), during which Chinese society had enjoyed a growing autonomy in terms of economic and personal freedoms. They identified a momentum towards a fully fledged civil society (endowed with civic activism) and ascribed the ultimate failure of the Chinese democratic movement to the weakness of this incipient civil society.[11] After the Tiananmen massacre, they thought that if in a not too distant future China were going to break away from its tradition of autocratic rule and bureaucratic control, a reconfiguration of state and societal power would have to take place which eventually could be helped by the re-emergence of pre-existing elements of elite and popular political participation. Their search for a Chinese civil society was stimulated by the publication in 1989 of the English translation of Jürgen Habermas's *The Structural Transformation of the Public Sphere*.[12] For historical evidence, they considered the urban society of Late Imperial and Republican China in which several historians had identified some of those institutions and groups which in Europe had been associated with the rise of civic activism.

Different definitions – methodological or political/ideological – of civil society opened up different lines of inquiry into Chinese urban society, the achievements and limitations of which are now considered.

9. Mayfair Mei-hui Yang, *Gift, Favors and Banquets: The Art of Social Relationships in China* (Ithaca: Cornell University Press, 1994), p. 287. However, one should note that Yang prefers not to apply this interpretive framework to an understanding of China.

10. See remarks by Gordon White, "Prospects for civil society in China. A case study of Xiaoshan City," *The Australian Journal of Chinese Affairs*, Vol. 29 (January 1993), pp. 63–68.

11. For such an approach, one may see Tony Saich (ed.), *The Chinese People's Movement: Perspectives on Spring 1989* (Armonk: M. E. Sharpe, 1990); or Arthur Rosenbaum (ed.), *State and Society in China: The Consequences of Reform* (Boulder: Westview Press, 1992).

12. Jürgen Habermas, *The Structural Transformation of the Public Sphere: An Inquiry into a Category of Bourgeois Society* (Cambridge, MA: MIT Press, 1989).

*Civil Society and the Ethno-Cultural Approach of Chinese Urban Society*

Following this approach and relying on interviews and archival sources, the younger generation of China social historians produced a number of first-rate studies. This article cannot do justice to them all, and will simply describe the new picture of urban society and its functioning which is emerging from their works. First, a word a caution is needed: most of these studies are focused on Shanghai. The reasons why Shanghai has become, according to Marilyn Levine's ironic remark, "a subsphere of sinology"[13] are still to be elucidated. But it is obvious that conclusions drawn from the history of the great port city may not apply to other Chinese urban centres. One, may note, however, that in several cases where evidence is provided, these conclusions do apply.[14]

It has been common knowledge that pre-1949 Chinese urban society was extremely diversified, cosmopolitan and multi-layered. Now a more complete understanding of these social groups and communities is being constructed. Because of the rapid development of a modern economic sector in big treaty ports during the early decades of the century, much attention was drawn to workers and capitalists directly associated with industrialization and modernization. As research topics, they displaced the proletariat and the bourgeoisie whose role as revolutionary agents was previously emphasized. Whereas Jean Chesneaux in his pioneering book *The Chinese Labor Movement, 1919–1927*[15] mainly studied the politicization and revolutionary struggles of the Shanghai working class, Emily Honig and Gail Hershatter were more interested in workers' daily life patterns and social (horizontal) relations, at home and in their workshop.[16] They inquired about the sexual division of labour, the role of women in the workforce, the protection afforded to workers by traditional mutual aid societies, religious brotherhoods and sisterhoods, and the intervention of the criminal underworld in mediating labour disputes. Following and extending E. P. Thompson's assumptions, they described workers as "a multitude of individuals with a multitude of experiences."[17] Elizabeth Perry's more recent volume displays the same concern for workers' culture and consciousness and for the various features such as geographical origins, educational background and gender that structure the workers' milieu.[18]

13. See Marilyn Levine's review of Christian Henriot's book, *Shanghai 1927–1937, Municipal Power, Locality and Modernization* (Berkeley: University of California Press, 1993), in *China Review International*, Vol. 2, No. 1 (Spring 1995), pp. 109–111.

14. See Ming Chan's review of Elizabeth Perry's book, *Shanghai on Strike. The Politics of Chinese Labor* (Stanford: Stanford University Press, 1993), in *China Review International*, Vol. 1, No. 1 (Spring 1994), p. 208: "The picture she presents and the conclusion she draws are valid for more than Republican Shanghai. Considerable similarities and parallel developmental patterns can be found in the case of North China (Tianjin), Central China (Hunan) and, to a lesser extent, Guangdong."

15. Jean Chesneaux, *The Chinese Labor Movement, 1919–1927* (Stanford: Stanford University Press, 1969).

16. Emily Honig, *Sisters and Strangers. Women in the Shanghai Cotton Mills, 1919–1949* (Stanford: Stanford University Press, 1986); Gail Hershatter, *The Workers of Tianjin, 1900–1949* (Stanford: Stanford University Press, 1986).

17. Thompson, *The Making of the English Working Class*, p. 11.

18. Perry, *Shanghai on Strike*.

Earlier studies dealing with urban merchants and entrepreneurs more often than not dealt with their economic activities, political role and relations with foreigners.[19] Later, Yen-P'ing Hao, Marie-Claire Bergère and, much more extensively, William Rowe and Bryna Goodman dealt with these cultural and societal problems now considered so important.[20]

Intellectuals and students had also been given a prominent place in previous writings on early 20th-century China. They were featured as playing a central role in the May Fourth Movement, the anti-Japanese campaigns, and the foundation and rise of the Chinese Communist Party.[21] But until the publication of Yeh Wen-hsin's book *The Alienated Academy*, no one had looked at "these faces in the crowd."[22] Yeh no longer addressed the old problem of changing values brought about by Westernization, from the angle of intellectual history. Her analysis was based on the study of campus culture "which stemmed from a profound sense of alienation." She contrasted the youth culture of the May Fourth period, "committed to the regeneration of the social values," with the culture of the 1930s, "permeated with a sense of fatigue, weariness, skepticism ...."[23] The despondency and disillusionment of students, and their passive withdrawal into melancholy and aesthicism are explored through the study of life styles, sexual and ethical behaviour, and personal and familial relationships.

Even when dealing with students' political protests, Jeffrey Wasserstrom takes these youths' intellectual commitments to nationalism and democracy for granted.[24] He turns away from ideological and political analysis, and addresses new issues such as how students could translate their anger into effective collective action, which "implicit rules" shaped their behaviour and how daily patterns of campus activities

19. Wellington K. Chan, *Merchants, Mandarins, and Modern Enterprise in Late Ch'ing China* (Cambridge, MA: Harvard University Press, 1977); Parks M. Coble, *The Shanghai Capitalists and the Nationalist Government, 1927–1937* (Cambridge, MA: Harvard University Press, 1980); Joseph Fewsmith, *Party, State, and Local Elites in Republican China; Merchant Organizations and Politics in Shanghai, 1890–1930* (Honolulu: University of Hawaii Press, 1985); Susan Mann, *Local Merchants and the Chinese Bureaucracy, 1750–1950* (Stanford: Stanford University Press, 1987).

20. Hao Yen-p'ing, *The Comprador in Nineteenth Century China, Bridge Between East and West* (Cambridge, MA: Harvard University Press, 1970) (esp. ch. 8: "Non-economic activities of the compradors"); Marie-Claire Bergère, *The Golden Age of the Chinese Bourgeoisie, 1917–1937* (Cambridge: Cambridge University Press, 1989) (esp. ch. 3: "The new entrepreneurs in the city"; and ch. 4: "The social structure of the new bourgeoisie"); William Rowe, *Hankow: Commerce and Society in a Chinese City, 1796–1889* (Stanford: Stanford University Press, 1984), and *Hankow: Conflict and Community in a Chinese City, 1796–1895* (Stanford: Stanford University Press, 1989); Bryna Goodman, *Native Place, City, and Nation. Regional Networks and Identities in Shanghai, 1853–1937* (Berkeley: University of California Press, 1995).

21. Chow Tse-tsung, *The May Fourth Movement: Intellectual Revolution in Modern China* (Cambridge, MA: Harvard University Press, 1960; John Israel, *Student Nationalism in China, 1927–1937* (Stanford: Stanford University Press, 1976).

22. Yeh Wen-hsin, *The Alienated Academy; Culture and Politics in Republican China, 1919–1937* (Cambridge, MA: Council on East Asian Studies, Harvard University, 1990), p. xi.

23. *Ibid.* pp. 5, 253.

24. Jeffrey Wasserstrom, *Student Protests in Twentieth-Century China. The View from Shanghai* (Stanford: Stanford University Press, 1991), p. 9.

contributed to their successful mobilization. Social history is seen as reflecting political culture. And Wasserstrom concludes that the borrowing of state rituals and of pre-existing formal structures by radical student movements posed a very serious symbolic threat to power-holders whose legitimacy was thus called into question.

Workers, merchants and intellectuals are well-established social categories whose study has been completely transformed by resorting to the ethno-cultural approach. This approach also allowed some new social categories to emerge as fields of enquiry. Special attention was paid to the experience of non-elite groups which had hitherto been excluded from the historical narrative, such as prostitutes, a topic long considered demeaning. Inspired by Alain Corbin's pathbreaking research on French prostitutes,[25] Christian Henriot devoted his *thèse d'État* to the study of prostitution in 19th and 20th-century Shanghai.[26] The choice of such a topic reflects historians' new interest in the more "private" forms of social life: sexual practices, illness, and the criminal and floating population of the hitherto unrecognized drop-outs and underdogs. Some of Henriot's best chapters describe the hierarchical characterization and variety of Shanghai prostitutes, and the cultural specific patterns of their behaviour: the courtesans' elegant ways of life in the late 19th century or the etiquette governing their relationships with their patrons. In later chapters the anthropological essays which deal with the lower class of prostitutes emphasize the growing commercialization of sexual intercourse as Shanghai's population increased and local traditional elites were displaced by new migrants.

Seen from the vantage point of the Public Security Bureau, organized crime represented a lesser threat to the Kuomintang regime than Chang Kai-shek's political enemies. The Shanghai police force was the instrument of institutionalized coercion which characterizes the modern state. Police confrontation with the city underworld and the outlawed opposition members gave rise to many dramatic episodes brought to light by Wakeman.[27] Explorations of this social underworld greatly contribute to the understanding of urban history. Martin Brian's book on the Green Gang is essential reading on the working of Shanghai society and the nature of the Chinese and foreign political systems operated in the city.[28]

Last, but not least, foreign presence is no longer understood through the exclusive study of extraterritorial rights, economic exploitation and political oppression. Beside the social elites who staffed the Shanghai Municipal Council and managed the International Settlement, historians

25. Alain Corbin, *Women for Hire. Prostitution and Sexuality in France after 1850* (Cambridge, MA: Harvard University Press, 1990).

26. Christian Henriot, *Belles de Shanghai. Prostitution et sexualité en Chine aux XIXe–XXe siècles* (Paris: CNRS Editions, 1997).

27. Frederic Wakeman, Jr., *Policing Shanghai, 1927–1937* (Berkeley: University of California Press, 1995), and *The Shanghai Badlands. Wartime Terrorism and Urban Crime 1937–1941* (Cambridge: Cambridge University Press, 1996).

28. Brian Gerard Martin, *The Shanghai Green Gang. Politics and Organized Crime 1919–1937* (Berkeley: University of California Press, 1996).

have now become interested in "small Treaty Port people," those Shanghailanders who refused to adapt to changing times and were responsible for the bad images of the foreign community and of the "Shanghai mind" which prevailed during the 1930s in the European home societies of expatriates as well as in China.[29]

Images are important whatever their relations with actual practices. The perceptions and misperceptions which they reflect contribute to the making of history. Such is the myth of the "Dogs and Chinese not admitted" sign which was allegedly posted at the entrance of the Bund Park, near the British Consulate. Although the exclusion of Chinese residents from the public parks of Shanghai foreign concessions was real enough until 1928, there is no evidence of such an outrageous wording. But the legend is well entrenched in both Chinese and Western imaginations and remains a potent symbol of imperialist social and cultural arrogance. The perception which is conveyed remains valid even if the Shanghai foreign community was more heterogenous and divided along class lines than is suggested by this symbolic representation.[30] The ongoing research on British residents (including those of lower social status), Jewish refugees and White Russians will certainly help to delineate the inner structures of the Western imperialist outposts which so deeply influenced Chinese urban development in the first half of this century.[31] The cultural/ethnological approach casts a different perspective on an older set of problems. The divisions that fragmented urban society in Republican China are no longer identified only with colonial prejudices, the socio-professional hierarchy or the hierarchy of wealth. They are considered as reflections of various cultural practices: oppositions between generations or between men and women, provincial affiliations and so on.

This reassessment of Chinese social realities is also linked with the investigation of new topics which is the hallmark of the neo-culturalist historians. The proliferation of new areas of inquiry has led to a "remapping" of China and to a deep alteration of the field of Chinese Republican history.[32] As far as urban society is concerned, attention given to the body (sexuality, illness) or to commercial advertising singularly broadened historians' perception and comprehension of social practices. Acknowledging the increasing sexualization of urban culture, Frank Dikötter analysed the numerous sexual discourses produced by the new print industry of Republican China. He described the appropriation of sex by science as part of a modernizing drive which led to the replacement

29. Robert A. Bickers, "Changing British attitudes to China and the Chinese, 1928–1931," unpublished Ph.D. thesis, University of London, 1992.

30. Robert A. Bickers and Jeffrey Wasserstrom, "Shanghai's 'dogs and Chinese not admitted' sign: legend, history, and contemporary symbol," *The China Quarterly*, No. 142 (June 1995), pp. 444–466.

31. Research on British residents is carried on by Robert A. Bickers. Françoise Kreissler is preparing a thèse de Doctorat d'État on the Jewish refugees from Central Europe in Shanghai during the Sino-Japanese war.

32. Cf. Gail Hershatter, Emily Honig, Jonathan N. Lipman and Randall Stross (eds.), *Remapping China. Fissures in Historical Terrain* (Stanford: Stanford University Press, 1996).

of Confucian philosophy by human biology "as the epistomological foundation for social order."[33] In organizing the Cornell's Third Luce Seminar on Shanghai, "Inventing Nanjing Road: commercial culture in Shanghai," Sherman Cochran drew attention to the consumption of images (posters, photographs, advertisements, vignettes in the mass press) and of slogans (broadcast or printed) which shaped fantasies and identities and encouraged the new cultural practices.[34]

The new social historians accomplished a great deal. They substituted life for abstractions, individuals for classes, and social consciousness for mechanical reactions to outside political incentives. The picture of urban society which emerges from their research is infinitely more precise, vivid and complex than previous sketches drawn from theoretical (mostly Marxist) assumptions. They reveal a fragmented society, residents divided along lines of ethnic (provincial) identity, with no common language, food, religious cults or professional associations; "a patchwork of sojourners"[35] whose activities develop along specific networks based on primordial solidarities such as native-place, lineage, occupation, neighbourhood or secret societies membership. Overlapping affiliations alleviate this fragmentation and make this polynuclear structure of Chinese urban society into an imbricated whole. Could this process transcend sojourners' parochialism and provide a basis for a shared identity upon which urban social autonomy and political initiative could be developed? For historians this is a most important question. But at this point they are confronted with some drawbacks of the methodological approach they borrowed from anthropologists who admittedly are more interested in the study of internal structures.

A feature of this "new" social history is its underestimation of historical chronology. As economic and social relations are themselves considered products of cultural mediations, it would be pointless to look for any causal relationship between the historical context and "discursive objects." Even though, in the view of "new" social historians, Chinese culture is no longer to be understood as an immutable force, as reified structures and symbols operating through collective consciousness to shape historical process, cultural analysis may still be "as static as any structuralism."[36] In any case, it does not lead to the same chronological framework as the one offered by traditional political narrative. It pays more attention to long-term evolutions and emphasizes structural continuities. Seen from the vantage point of social history, the dates of 1911 and 1949, generally accepted as markers of the Republican period, are not

33. Cf. Frank Dikötter, *Sex, Culture and Modernity in China. Medical Science and the Construction of Sexual Identities in the Early Republican Period* (London: Hurst & Co., 1995), p. 9.

34. This conference took place on 20–22 July 1995 at Cornell University. The conference volume, edited by Sherman Cochran, is to be published in 1997.

35. Frederic Wakeman, Jr. and Wen-hsin Yeh (eds.), *Shanghai Sojourners* (Berkeley: University of California, Institute of East Asian Studies, Center for Chinese Studies, 1992), p. 5.

36. Aletta Biersack, "Local knowledge, local history: Geertz and beyond," in Hunt, *The New Cultural History*, pp. 72–96, quotation p. 80.

very significant. "History is defined by its appreciation of process, not by chronological stelae."[37]

In the field of urban studies, many authors trespassed across the old chronological boundaries. For example Bryna Goodman studied the history of Shanghai guilds *huiguan* over the course of a century from the Late Imperial to the Republican periods,[38] and Jeffrey Wasserstrom, after studying student protest in the Republican era, invaded the most recent period and investigated the rebirth of the May Fourth Tradition in the 1980s.[39] But there is no firm proposition for any alternative periodization as can be seen from the various dates selected as starting points (1853, 1900, 1911, 1919) or as terms (1937, 1945, 1949, 1989) in recently published monographs. Characterized by the persistance of traditional elements in a changing culture, or more accurately by a constant flux of interactions and overlaps of various knowledges, the evolution of urban society in Republican China is presented as a result of deep historical shifts taking place "below the surface of political events beyond the cycles of social and economic change."[40] How should this new social history be integrated with the historical context and the global perspectives to be found in the old-fashioned narrative? In fact it often appears quite disconnected from the flow of historic events.[41]

Such seems to be the case for the pioneering studies published in the mid-1980s, such as those by Emily Honig and Gail Hershatter. While pursuing their research on Shanghai and Tianjin workers, both authors ignored the concept of working-class, let alone the history of the Chinese labour movement. Hershatter had to be "convinced" by editors to add a final chapter – "The shaping of working-class protest" – to a monograph which dealt exclusively with cultural practices.[42] This welcome addition seems not to have modified the author's basic assumption that "much violence in the mills, subsequently labelled 'class-struggle,' might be more accurately characterised as gang warfare."[43] Such a depoliticized approach raises the problem of how to reconcile the portrait of these self-contained and self-organized groups of individuals with Chinese workers' militancy as recorded in the history of strikes and of the revolutionary movement.

37. Randall Stross, "Field notes from the present," in Hershatter *et al.*, *Remapping China*, pp. 261–274, quotation p. 264.

38. Cf. Goodman, *Native Place, City and Nation.*

39. Cf. Wasserstrom, *Student Protest*; and Jeffrey Wasserstrom and Liu Xinyong, "Student associations and mass movements," in Deborah Davis *et al.* (eds.), *Urban Spaces in Contemporary China. The Potential for Autonomy and Community in post-Mao China* (Cambridge: Cambridge University Press, 1995), pp. 362–393.

40. Dikötter, *Sex, Culture and Modernity*, p. 13.

41. According to Christian Henriot (*Belles de Shanghai*, p. 24), this kind of "timeless" analysis led Gail Hershatter to confuse 19th and 20th-century categories of Shanghai prostitutes and to blurr historical perspectives in her otherwise very interesting studies: "The hierarchy of Shanghai prostitution, 1870–1949," *Modern China*, Vol. 15, No. 4 (October 1989), pp. 463–498; and "Prostitution and the market in early twentieth-century Shanghai," in Rubie S. Watson and Patricia Buckley Ebrey (eds.), *Marriage and Inequality in Chinese Society* (Berkeley: University of California Press, 1991), pp. 256–285.

42. Hershatter, *The Workers of Tianjin*, p. viii.

43. *Ibid.* p. 175.

Struggling to reconcile these contradictions, Emily Honig suggests a very interesting interpretation: "Patterns of localism and traditional hierarchical loyalties are perhaps not as antithetical to working-class consciousness as many ... have assumed."[44] This point, on which she did not much elaborate, was taken up later by other analysts. In *Shanghai on Strike*, published in 1993, Elizabeth Perry acknowledges the deep divisions by gender, age, ethnicity and skill of Shanghai workers, but forcefully argues that "the fragmentation of labor can provide a basis for political influential working-class action."[45] This view is partially endorsed by Alain Roux who considers that the fragmented nature of Chinese labour did not prevent workers' militancy but confined it to the limited space of the workshop or at best of the factory, thus undercutting the political influence of the Chinese working-class.[46]

The integration of cultural and anthropological analysis within a precise historical/chronological framework now seems to be a common concern for modern China specialists. Bryna Goodman, for example, describes how opium trade in mid-19th-century Shanghai narrowed distinctions between respectable merchants and gang smugglers, all hailing from Guangdong, and how the Small Sword uprising (1853–55) reflected the centrality of native-place associations channelling both social control and social disorder.[47] The cultural/anthropological method, however, seems to have an inherent tendency for a disconnected approach of various aspects of social history and a predisposition to build each aspect into a separate field of study: that of women's studies, for example. In Gail Hershatter's and Emily Honig's writings there is some suggestion that the stories of Shanghai prostitutes or female cotton-mill workers present an interest of their own, distinct from what they contribute to the global history of Chinese society. This endorsement of particularism hardly incorporates a concern for interaction and dynamics of power and change.

Moreover, when used in an underdeveloped historiographical field, such as modern China where there is no established corpus of general knowledge to rely on, the history of culture remains shorn of all assumptions – even implicit ones – about culture's relationship to context. It is true that many new social historians have endorsed Foucault's critique against any understanding of culture as reflective of social reality. They consider every practice – economic, social or political – as the product of historically contingent discourses. But even as they maintain that reality is linked with and part of representation, they may retain a kind of implicit, underlying materialism based upon their knowledge of the historical record that they contemptuously call the "high" historical narrative. When such a narrative does not exist or is still very fragmen-

44. Honig, *Sisters and Strangers*, p. 248.

45. Perry, *Shanghai on Strike*, p. 2.

46. Alain Roux, *Le Shanghai ouvrier des années trente* (Paris: l'Harmattan, 1993), pp. 308–310.

47. Goodman, *Native-Place, City, and Nation*, ch. 2: "Foreign imperialism, immigration and disorder: Opium War aftermath and the Small Sword Uprising of 1853."

tary, as is the case for Chinese Republican history, there is no antidote to the nihilistic subjectivism induced by the anthropological (and linguistic) models after which new social/cultural history has been patterned. In 1930s' Shanghai, Chinese advertisers made women the main targets of their broadcast or printed announcements and young "shopping wives" appeared as the queens of Nanjing Road's commercial world. This may have created some aspirations to women's liberation but can it be concluded that female urban residents were liberated women? Without a clear understanding of the general (and more specifically economic) context, which admittedly is still not available, it is difficult to analyse the impact of the advertising trade.[48] If some kind of distinction is not drawn between reality and the way reality is perceived, the content of social history cannot but be dissolved.

Implicit rules and symbolic representations provide valuable clues and interpretive frameworks. But does history amount to no more than the interplay of images reflected by various mirrors? If it were so, how would one confront the fact that so many Chinese urban residents died from hunger, misery, epidemics, terrorist attacks or war injuries during the Republican era? After reading Jeffrey Wasserstrom's bright analysis of student protest, I still remain of the opinion that the intellectuals' special status within Chinese society goes further than the highly organized nature of campus daily life and the availability of a symbolic repertoire to account for students' successful collective action; and that the reasons for the working out of a powerful alliance between the students' movement and part of the bureaucratic apparatus in 1989 cannot be apprehended without fully understanding the unfolding of factional struggles between top leaders.[49]

In the neoculturalists' approach to Chinese society the concept of "civil society" is not explicitly articulated as a framing concept of analysis. Whenever the term is used, it just refers to society and "civil" is redundant. Using this term, however, emphasizes the autonomy enjoyed by various social organizations vis-à-vis state power and draws attention to the inner working of these organizations. It helps to delineate self-sustained social movements fuelled by symbolic repertories of protest. But explicit articulation with the overall – political and economic – context is too often missing. Furthermore, given the lesser development of modern China historiography, whole parts of this context are still ignored or neglected. When "new" social historians attempt to integrate their analyses into a global framework, they more often than not have to rely on general and vague categories such as modernization or Westernization. They rightly insist that Chinese urban society often coped with historical change through an adjustment process taking place within pre-existing structures. Such a sophisticated analysis, however, seems

48. This point was forcefully argued by William Kirby at the Cornell Third Luce Seminar on Shanghai, "Inventing Nanjing Road: commercial culture in Shanghai, 1864–1949," 20–22 July 1995, Cornell University.

49. Wasserstrom, *Student Protests*, p. 15; Wasserstrom and Liu Xinyong, "Student association and mass movements."

quite dissonant with the absence of consensus about the nature of historical changes at work within Chinese modernizing society. New social/cultural historians provide precious building blocks, but the construction is still to be completed. China historians' agenda cannot be exactly the same as that of Western Europe specialists: it still calls for the study of chronology, events, personalities, political institutions, economic evolutions and intellectual trends.

### *Civil Society and the Political Interpretive Framework of Republican Urban History*

Whereas the neoculturalists' approach towards Chinese society reflects methodological concerns which are shared by historians all over the world,[50] the search for a civic, politically active "civil society" has opened up a more specifically American line of inquiry into the nature of Chinese social process. This is a recent development and may be an ephemeral one. When in early 1989 I was revising the English version of *The Golden Age of the Chinese Bourgeoisie* a problem arose about how to translate *société civile*. There was no ready rendition of this term, I was told. "Civil society" would not be understood by British or American audiences. The translator finally opted for "autonomous society" and added an explanatory note![51]

After the 1989 Tiananmen massacre, the problem of whether China had or has had a civil society became a central issue among American sinologists. For China-watchers and social scientists the existence of civil society appeared as the consequence of economic liberalization and the precondition of political democratization. For historians, the debate highlighted the pre-existing set of problems linked with state–societal relations and invited comparisons with Western modern history. Among the early and most authoritative writings published on these topics, those by Mark Elvin, William Rowe and Mary Rankin respectively appeared in 1969, 1984 and 1986.[52] They all focused upon Late Imperial China and none referred to Habermas's theories, even when identifying "distinct elements of protodemocratic behaviour"[53] or "non-administrative structures of social and political power,"[54] or explicitly dealing with "the public sphere of institutionalised collective activities" managed by local elites and providing "an intermediate arena where state and society met."[55] These analyses were later integrated into an Habermasian framework.

50. Cf. Review of the 18th International Congress of Historical Sciences, "L'histoire s'est arrêtée à Montreal," *Le Monde*, 8 September 1995, "Le Monde de Livres," p. viii.

51. Bergère, *The Golden Age*, p. 7

52. Mark Elvin, "The gentry democracy in Chinese Shanghai, 1905–1914," in Jack Gray (ed.), *Modern China's Search for a Political Form* (Oxford: Oxford University Press, 1969); Mary Rankin, *Elite Activism and Political Transformation in China: Zhejiang Province, 1865–1911* (Stanford: Stanford University Press, 1986); Rowe, *Hankow: Commerce and Society*.

53. Elvin, "The gentry democracy," p. 42.

54. Rowe, *Hankow: Commerce and Society*, p. 9.

55. Rankin, *Elite Activism*, p. 16.

This *a posteriori* theoretical alignment was made either by the authors themselves (Mary Rankin, William Rowe),[56] or by their critics such as Frederic Wakeman.[57] The heated debate which these works provoked was not when they were first published, but several years later, after Habermas's book had been translated into English and at a time when the terms "civil society" and "public sphere" had come to prominence in the general discourse about social and political change in post-Maoist China. What does such a delay signal? Could it be that the target of criticism was the Habermasian flavour of these writings (and consequently their implicit meaning for present-day political debate over China's mid-term perspectives) rather than their sheer historical analytical content?

In the course of these polemics, studies of Republican China were not mentioned as often as these of Late Imperial China: they were less numerous, some of them produced outside the United States. Moreover the Republican institutional and social context may appear less conducive to the formation of a civil society than the Late Imperial environment, when big cities were on their way to achieving partial autonomy and local elites took advantage of their tradition of self-management to address a wider range of political and national problems. After 1911, as modernization and urbanization accelerated, as revolutionary ideologies and mass movements changed the rules of the political game, the role of local elites was challenged by new power holders and seekers such as warlords, political party leaders and gang bosses. This could not but affect the elite institutions and ideology which had sustained the rise of late Qing activism. Was the scope of this local activism threatened or enlarged by the decline of traditional elites?

Arguments go both ways. The continuity and domination of these elites may be seen in the wider range of public activities they were engaged in, in the development of many individual careers which continued after the revolutionary break of 1911, well into the 1920s and 1930s. It may also be seen in the co-operation between old and new elites and the cooptation of new elites into traditional institutions. On the other hand, was not the Republican context of political disruptions, revolutionary struggles, foreign invasion and reinforced social control less conducive than the self-limiting and declining power of the state imperial bureaucracy to the kind of institutionalized political participation which is the hallmark of civil society?

Fragmented evidence is provided by recent research. Within Republican society a range of elements have been identified which are generally considered as constitutive of civil society. First and foremost was the emergence or remodelling of all kinds of voluntary organizations: native-place as well as commercial, professional, educational, political, patriotic,

56. Mary Rankin, "The origins of a Chinese public sphere: local elites and community affairs in the Late Imperial Period," *Etudes chinoises*, Vol. 9, No. 2, pp. 13–60; William Rowe, "The Public Sphere in Modern China," *Modern China*, Vol. 16, No. 3, pp. 309–329.

57. Frederic Wakeman, "Civil society and public sphere debate," *Modern China*, Vol. 19, No. 2 (April 1993), pp. 108–138.

philanthropic or criminal associations. The Cotton Millowners' Association and the Modern Bankers' Association were both established in 1918 as local Shanghaiese or Pekingese institutions and later evolved into national organizations.[58] Although founded in 1904, the Shanghai (Chinese) General Chamber of Commerce adopted a new look after 1920 when elections brought forward a team of younger, less conservative directors.[59] All these modern or half-modern institutions perceived their role as the defence of corporate, public or state interests. Their activities were oriented by a concern for economic growth, social progress and national development.[60] In 1921 bankers, through their associations, put pressure upon the Beijing government to compel it "to clean up public finance." According to a contemporary foreign observer, their action bore "a portent deeper than its influence in financial affairs. It is an assertion of part of the populace ... toward its rulers which spells democracy."[61] Some time later, Shanghai Chinese business circles, led by the General Chamber of Commerce, advocated a complete recasting of the state system and supported the convocation of a National Convention. As this convention did not bring the constitutional renewal which had been hoped for, the General Chamber of Commerce attempted to substitute merchant power (a committee drawn from its own membership) for the crumbling central government.[62] In spite of its immediate failure, this move deserves attention as it represented the transposition of merchants' traditional management of community crises to a nation-wide scale.

Many of the old-style study, educational or agricultural societies which had appeared at the turn of the century survived the Revolution. Some of them blossomed into more specialized institutions. Established in 1905 by reformist gentry-leaders and Shanghai entrepreneurs, the Jiangsu Provincial Educational Association later gave birth to the Chinese Society for Vocational Education which expressed the alliance between old notables and Shanghai new industrial elites.[63] Not much is known about professional associations which flourished during the inter-war period, but they are under investigation.[64] More attention has been devoted to secret societies, gangs and criminal associations.[65]

The intensification of political debate and of political participation which took place during the Republican period may also be considered as underpinning the emergence of a public sphere, as has been forcefully put

58. Bergère, *The Golden Age*, pp. 132–134. Marie-Claire Bergère, "The Shanghai Bankers' Association, 1915–1927. Modernization and the institutionalization of local solidarities," in Wakeman and Yeh, *Shanghai Sojourners*, pp. 15–34.

59. Bergère, *The Golden Age*, pp. 222–225.

60. *Ibid.* p. 225.

61. *Ibid.* p. 223.

62. *Ibid.* p. 225.

63. Xiao Xiaohong, "La Société générale d'Éducation du Jiangsu et les problèmes de la modernisation, 1905–1914," thèse de l'Institut National des Langues et Civilisations Orientales (presented in June 1997).

64. Cf. for example, Nathalie Delalande, "Une culture d'ingénieur. Origine de l'architecture moderne de Shanghai," Mémoire de DEA d'histoire de l'architecture, Université de Paris I, September 1994, 2 vols., pp. 128 ff.

65. Martin, *The Shanghai Green Gang*.

forward by David Strand.[66] Gentry, merchants and urban middle-class opinion no longer depended on official power. The changing urban landscape offered new forums for discussions such as restaurants, bathhouses and public parks in which citizens – including non-elite ones – could gather and develop a growing awareness of public issues. According to Strand's analysis, the vitality of public life in a partially modernized city like Beijing is to be explained by the synthesis of old and new political practices and their mutually supportive roles. The sphere of public discussion was no longer limited to the realm of professional/regional associations (*fatuan*). It vastly expanded as nationalist mass demonstrations such as the May Thirtieth movement invited the participation of all citizens. "Politics was no longer the exclusive preserve of elite mediation and government institution."[67] This enlargement of political arena is shown by the increasing number of city-wide marches in 1925.

Modernization helped to enhance social communication. Hundreds of newspapers were published in main cities across the country. In the wake of the May Fourth Movement most of them started using vernacular Chinese. They reached larger audiences than the 19th-century influential *Shenbao* ever did. There were "mosquitoes" papers oriented towards social gossip and major papers covering national politics. The latter admittedly tended to be read only by urban elites. But there were some intermediate publications which engaged in "serious commentaries on contemporary affairs" while remaining "very popular middle-brow journals of diversion." Such was the *Shenghuo zhoukan* (*Life Weekly*) which addressed an audience of lower middle-class young professionals and petty urbanites – clerks, school-teachers, shopkeepers – and forged among them "a distinct sense of social reference that might lead them to look beyond the confines of their immediate work-places and neighbourhoods."[68]

Do such elements add up to a civil society? For David Strand, there is no doubt that "by the end of the twenties, a major proportion of city people in China had reached a level of political consciousness commensurate with their formal status as citizens of a Republic."[69] Mass mobilization proceeded through the co-operation and interlocking activities of various social organizations (merchant and craft guilds, student unions, provincial clubs and so on) which endowed public protest with some measure of formal legitimacy. But "this incorporation of groups that in

66. David Strand, *Rickshaw Beijing. City People and Politics in the 1920's* (Berkeley: University of California Press, 1989).

67. *Ibid.* p. 197.

68. Wen-hsin Yeh, "Progressive journalism and Shanghai's petty urbanites. Zou Taofen and the *Life Weekly*, 1926–1945," in Wakeman and Yeh, *Shanghai Sojourners*, p. 195. On the building up of a "national network of authors, readers and distributors of iconoclastic journals" after the May Fourth Movement, cf. Wen-hsin Yeh, "Print capitalism and the rise of radical policies in Shanghai in the 1920's," paper prepared for "Urban Progress, Business Development and the Modernization of China," Conference at the SASS, Shanghai, 17–20 August 1993, pp. 14–15.

69. Strand, *Rickshaw Beijing*, p. 284.

many cases were elitist or inclusive" could not entail a reorganization of urban society. "Mass politics was not a solvent capable of breaking down barriers based on status, native place, ... so much as it was an opportunity to display these divisions in public."[70] Should the conclusion be that in Republican cities there was a public sphere but no civil society? Some historians even argue against the emergence of a public sphere. According to Frederic Wakeman, social fragmentation could not nurture the development of a public spirit shared by urbanites. Chinese urban residents remained chiefly sojourners, transients from other provinces with no sense of common interest and identity. The existence of numerous social organizations reflected and increased this fragmentation. It stimulated the development of corporatism more than that of public spirit.[71] Native-place associations fostered divided loyalties and their inherent parochialism worked against the development of civic consciousness.

An additional line of argument militating against the identification of a civil society in Republican China's cities concerns state–societal relations. For Frederic Wakeman, there was a constant "growth of autocratic power from the late Qing's 'New Laws' through the Nanjing decade's failed second revolution to the spectacular disorder of the dictatorship of proletariat." "The lamentable durability of governmentalized autocracy," as described in *Policing China 1927–1937*, did not allow for the assertion of local elites' political power (let alone the influence of popular masses).[72]

Against these views, it can be argued that, during the early part of the Republican period, state authority was not reinforced but nearly disappeared when the warlords took over (1917–27). According to Marie-Claire Bergère, the success of the Shanghai bourgeoisie at the time of its Golden Age is largely to be explained by the decline of central power which led to a partial lifting of bureaucratic constraints and favoured the rise of autonomous social forces. However Pransejit Duara came to an opposite conclusion when he observed that in the early 20th century "state involution" led to the reign of local bullies and to social atrophy. Duara's conclusions are drawn from the study of rural cases. They may not apply to the urban context which had already been transformed by economic modernization and cultural Westernization.[73]

In fact there is still no clear picture of Chinese Republican society. But the debate about civil society certainly stimulated reflection and research. As a result, analysis has been made more sophisticated. An example of growing sophistication is Elizabeth Perry's and Ellen Fuller's essay "China's Long March to democracy" whose main themes have been endorsed by Jeffrey Wasserstrom.[74] For these authors the problem is not

70. *Ibid.* p. 196.
71. Wakeman and Yeh, *Shanghai Sojourners*, p. 6.
72. Wakeman, *Policing Shanghai, 1927–1937*, pp. xvii, 291.
73. Pransenjit Duara, *Culture, Power and the State. Rural North China, 1900–1942* (Stanford: Stanford University Press, 1988).
74. Elizabeth Perry and Ellen Fuller, "China's Long March to democracy," *World Policy Journal* (Autumn 1991), pp. 663–685; Wasserstrom, "Student associations and mass movements."

one of an uncompleted historical process (why the enlargement of political participation did not entail the formation of an institutionalized civil society) but one of cultural specificity: how a civil society with Chinese characteristics was established, different from its Western counterpart. Perry, Fuller and Wasserstrom had observed that in China mass mobilization played a fundamental role in the formation and manifestation of public opinion. Consequently Chinese civil society as a distinct entity, counterpoised to the state, could be best apprehended through these nation-wide protest movements which from the 1920s to the 1940s erupted in Chinese cities. They were the most spectacular expression of urbanites' participation in politics: crowds of students, teachers, journalists, workers, shopkeepers and merchants marching through the streets and holding meetings at cross-roads. Non-adherents to cultural relativism would not, however, consider these demonstrations as symptoms of an expanding civil society for at least two reasons.

First, these mass movements were hardly accompanied by any institutionalization of social protest. They were punctual efforts aiming at specific goals. Their organizing or co-ordinating committees were generally disbanded after the end of the movement: they did not evolve into permanent representative organs in charge of negotiating with state power whenever important issues were at stake. The enlarged political participation to which these movements gave rise was episodic and was not underpinned by the establishment of organizations generally associated with civil society. Secondly, in Chinese cities, mass mobilization was closely associated with the surge of nationalist fervour which focused on the creation of a strong state guaranteeing national unity and prosperity. This statist stance, which led the Shanghai bourgeoisie to rally to Chiang Kai-shek in 1927 and liberal intellectuals to accommodate a large measure of interventionism, runs against the principles of social autonomy which lay at the foundation of civil society.[75]

Another example of sophisticated and perceptive analysis is to be found in Bryna Goodman's *Native Place, City, and Nation.* While recognizing the persistant native-place segmentation of Shanghai's urban community through the Republican period, Goodman convincingly argues that native-place sentiment nevertheless played a crucial role in the construction of urban nationalism and civic consciousness. The emergence of such a consciousness did not call for the displacement of native-place identity: it developed through a process of accretion of identities, through the adoption and accommodation of modern elements by Chinese traditional culture.[76]

A further important point made by Bryna Goodman bears upon the state's and society's respective influence. As others did before, Goodman rejects or transcends the binary opposition between state and society, a

75. This problem is briefly addressed in Philip H. Kuhn, "Civil society and constitutional development," paper prepared for the American-European Symposium on "State and Society in East Asian Tradition," Paris, 29–31 May 1991.

76. Goodman, *Native Place, City and Nation*, pp. 45–46.

construct which was built after Western experience.[77] She readily acknowledges that native-place associations were targets of state control, especially after 1927, when they became increasingly subject to official regulations: they had to register, restructure according to governmental directives and follow Kuomintang rhetoric. (One may add that during the Nanjing decade, such was the case for all social organizations such as chambers of commerce, professional associations and workers' unions.)[78] But this policy resulted less in state control than in interpenetration and overlapping between state and native-place associations. Goodman's arguments run parallel to those of William Rowe who observes that in Late Imperial China "organizational autonomy ... is not an all-or-nothing issue" and that "the balance between autonomy and state control ... was the result of a process of continual negotiation."[79] Similarly, during the Republican era, native-place associations proceeded according to "modes of public manoeuvering ... which were neither fully autonomous nor state-controlled"[80] but helped them to create a civic ground and an independant basis of self-legitimation.

Such a line of analysis had been previously tackled, although in a less systematic way, by Alain Roux who described the interpenetration of Shanghai workers' unions and state apparatus in 1928–32, insisting that the Nationalist policy could not be considered only repressive but that it allowed for workers' authentic revendications and struggles.[81] Christian Henriot also drew attention to the fact that after 1927 the Chinese bourgeoisie was not as completely emasculated as previous historians had suggested.[82] As members of the Provisional Municipal Council, part of the banking and industrial elites were able to retain their influence over local politics and to hold their opinions vis-à-vis government and party officials.

All these analyses point towards a different and much more complex state–societal relationship than is suggested by the Habermasian concepts of public sphere and civil society. The Habermasian construct has proved itself a useful analytic device. But now what is called for is a reconceptualization of the relationship between state and society in Republican China and more generally in modern and contemporary China, and the creation of new interpretive frameworks drawn from the Chinese experience itself. These problems have already been addressed in most recent works such as those by Goodman, Perry and Yang.[83] It is to be expected

77. For a criticism of this construct, cf. Philip C. Huang, "Public sphere/civil society in China? A third realm between state and society," *Modern China*, Vol. 19, No. 2 (April 1993), pp. 216–240.

78. Bergère, *The Golden Age*, p. 61; Coble, *The Shanghai Capitalists*.

79. William Rowe, "Civil society in Late Imperial China," *Modern China*, Vol. 19, No. 2 (April 1993), pp. 107–148.

80. Goodman, *Native Place, City and Nation*, p. 302.

81. Alain Roux, *Grèves et Politique à Shanghai. Les Désillusions* (Paris, Editions EHESS, 1995), partie III, "La paradoxale vitalité du mouvement ouvrier."

82. Henriot, *Shanghai 1927–1937*, pp. 81–82, 283–84.

83. Goodman, *Native Place, City and Nation*; Perry, *Shanghai on Strike*; Yang, *Gifts, Favors and Banquets*.

that, in this new stage of research and analysis, debate will be no less intense than during the previous "Habermasian" phase. Almost everyone will acknowledge the important role played by historical and cultural specificities in China's modernizing process: external (Western) influences triggered or interfered with a series of evolutions which were shaped and appropriated by indigenous forces. But how should the result be evaluated? Should there be a search for Chinese variants (of the public sphere, of civil society) to be compared with Western models and thus with a theoretical universal validity? Mary Rankin leads in this direction when she describes a Chinese public sphere different "from the public sphere of Europe in being bounded by local arenas, defined by the practices ... of management ... oriented more to collective interest than to individual property rights ...."[84] Bryna Goodman seems to borrow the same idea, when in the introduction of her book she asserts that "elements of 'traditional' culture [i.e. native-place organizations] helped facilitate and structure the process of radical transformation we associate with modernity."[85]

Is the answer to go a step further and search for the emergence of a specific Chinese modernity that has its roots in Chinese culture and its historical transformations (many of them predating the exposure of the country to foreign intercourse)? Is a plurality of modernities to be substituted for the appropriation of Western modernity by the local context, as an interpretive framework?[86] Such a cultural relativism may better accommodate the historical experiences of the many societies of the global world. But as it deprives both concepts of civil society and modernity of their original content – a Western one – it takes away their meaning and relevance.[87]

84. Rankin, "The origins of a Chinese public sphere," p. 55.

85. Goodman, *Native Place, City and Nation*, p. 40.

86. This concept of multicultural modernities has been put forward by authors such as Tani E. Barlow who, as editor of the magazine *Positions*, argues that "East Asian representations are neither disfigured nor unsuccessful replications of any prior ... concept from another place or time.... Asian modernities perform their own recoding of the discourses of modernity ...." *Positions. East Asia Cultures Critique*, Vol. 1, No. 1 (Spring 1993), p. vi. It has also been put forward by Dikötter, attempting to trace "the emergence of a plurality of intertwined modernities" (*Sex, Culture and Modernity*, p. 12). Bryna Goodman's view of the problem has been shifting. As expressed in the conclusion of her book *Native Place, City and Nation*, p. 311 (where she proposed to rethink "the idea of a public sphere" as a "developing public realm ... specific to China"), it is more relativistic than the one to be found some 300 pages earlier in the introduction of the same book (p. 40).

87. The implications of cultural relativism on Chinese modern studies and more generally on contemporary social sciences are critically assessed by Yves Chevrier, "La question de la société civile, la Chine et le chat du Cheshire," *Études chinoises*, Vol. XIV, No. 2 (Autumn 1995), pp. 153–251.

# The Evolution of Republican Government*

Julia C. Strauss

The topic of government and administration in the Republican period (1911–49) has attracted periodic bursts of scholarly attention in the first three decades of the post-1950 period. Some of these works focused on the weakness of political institutions in the early Republic,[1] several were sympathetic to the state-building efforts of the Kuomintang (KMT),[2] and the remainder were overtly or covertly negative in their assessment of Republican, particularly KMT, government.[3] Whether sympathetic to Republican-era government or not, this scholarship was largely informed by a constellation of three factors: the deep Cold War era divisions between left and right in the United States as to how the spread of Communism in Asia should be accounted for and dealt with, the lack of research access in China itself, and, perhaps most important, what might be called "the prismatic event of 1949," when the Republican government was militarily defeated in the civil war, driven into exile on a small island, and replaced with a self-consciously revolutionary government which vigorously attempted to recreate and transform state and society. It is little wonder that this abrupt terminus of the Republican period slanted many of the questions implicitly posed in post–1949 scholarship towards explaining the Republic's demise on mainland China. At best, the efforts and strategies of the Kuomintang were considered to have long-term promise until seriously undercut by the Japanese invasion in July 1937; at worst, the entire Republican period was relegated to the status of a transitional period that gave way before the inevitable primacy of "bottom-up" revolution.

Insofar as a commonly accepted view of Republican era government emerged, it was a mostly critical one. The two most influential and

*I would like to extend special thanks to William Kirby and R. Bin Wong for their helpful comments on earlier versions of this article.

1. K. S. Lieuw, *Struggle for Democracy: Sung Chiao-jen and the 1911 Revolution* (Berkeley: University of California Press, 1971), esp. pp. 127–201, and Ernest Young, *The Presidency of Yuan Shih-k'ai* (Ann Arbor: University of Michigan Press, 1977) are the best examples.

2. For a relatively sympathetic view of the KMT's state-building efforts (as well as the role of Western financial and technical knowledge in aiding those efforts), see Arthur Young, *China's Nation Building Effort: The Financial and Economic Record, 1927–37* (Stanford: Hoover Institution Press, 1971), Arthur Young, *China and the Helping Hand, 1937–45*, (Cambridge, MA: Harvard University Press, 1963). Another somewhat later sympathetic view is expressed in Maria Hsia Chang, " 'Facism' and Modern China," *The China Quarterly*, No. 79 (September 1979).

3. For critical views, see Ch'ien Tuan-sheng, *The Government and Politics of China* (Cambridge, MA: Harvard University Press, 1950), Lloyd Eastman, *The Abortive Revolution: China Under Nationalist Rule, 1927–37* (Cambridge, MA: Harvard University Press, 1974), and Tien Hung-mao, *Government and Politics in Kuomintang China, 1927–37* (Stanford: Stanford University Press, 1972).

© The China Quarterly, 1997

widely read works, Lloyd Eastman's *The Abortive Revolution* and Hung-mao Tien's *Government and Politics in Kuomintang China*, both dating from the early 1970s, stress the multiple weaknesses of the KMT Party and the government that it set up in 1927–28. Both these books single out phenomena that were widely seen to be prevalent in the 1930s and 1940s: endemic factionalism within the Kuomintang, the lack of an effective examination system or pro-actively functioning bureaucracy, the absence of the means or will to penetrate into the countryside and re-order rural relations, as well as the loss of revolutionary fervour and the increasing militarization of the regime. The conventional analysis of Republican government, as set out by Eastman and Tien, suggests at least implicitly that the seeds of Republican demise were planted long before the events of 1949. In this view, the Republic gave way to the People's Republic because it was institutionally weak, with its weaknesses variously illustrated by what it failed to accomplish in the 1930s and 1940s, contemporary critical opinion in the 1930s and 1940s, and of course, the harsh reality of ultimate defeat and exile in 1949.

However, in working backwards from 1949, this conventional view ignores much that is common sense in any kind of comparative perspective. After all, most political systems exhibit fairly large gaps between what politicians say ought to be accomplished and what in fact is accomplished; serious criticism of either individuals or policy in the government is an inevitable feature of any regime with a less than totally controlled press; and all political systems produce informal groups (and the line that differentiates between tightly organized faction and informal groupings is, at best, ill-demarcated). When one turns to the governments of developing countries, many have a strong military component, are invaded with personalistic networks of various sorts, are institutionally weak, and have no particular correlation between civil service examinations and political stability. Further, the vast majority, even those who at some point in their political consolidation call themselves revolutionary, have neither the capacity nor the interest in radically restructuring rural relations.[4]

Intellectual and political trends in the 1980s, dramatically culminating in the end of the Cold War with the collapse of the Leninist regimes of Eastern Europe and the Soviet Union, have prompted a substantial requestioning of basic assumptions about China's 20th-century revolution. Scholars have increasingly gained access to archival materials that have made it possible to conduct intensive research on Republican China, and this research has revealed substantial continuities in the pre- and

4. An analysis of the widespread phenomenon of penetration of the state by society in developing countries can be found in Joel Migdal, (Princeton: Princeton University Press, 1988). An impressive example of a state with many parallels to Republican China is Atatürk's Turkey in the 1920s and 1930s: like Chiang Kai-shek, Atatürk proclaimed himself the head of an anti-imperialist movement of national liberation, and like the KMT in the 1930s, the Republican People's Party attempted to build a strong central state from the top down in urban areas, with little capacity and still less interest in radically restructuring the life of the Anatolian peasantry.

post-1949 periods. As in addition the People's Republic has renounced its earlier radical vision of revolution, and the post-1986 political liberalization in Taiwan proceeds, the year 1949 increasingly seems to be less of the all-encompassing prism through which all perspectives on the preceding Republican period are necessarily and inevitably refracted.

Research on Republican-era government and administration is now beginning to shift away from explaining the outcome of the civil war in terms of the KMT regime's undeniable weaknesses, and towards evaluating what Republican governments attempted to do, given the context and constraints of their own times, to overcome those weaknesses.[5] Current work has just begun to scratch the surface, and many basic questions about Republican-era government, particularly those concerning the relations between the different levels of central, provincial and local government, remain unanswered. This article concentrates on central government in the Republican period and develops three preliminary themes: that despite changes in regime, Republican-era governments were characterized by a surprising consistency in terms of basic agenda and constraints on action; that this agenda pushed all Republican-era governments to attempt to build institutional capacity rapidly; and that to this end, Republican-era governments experimented widely and intensively with models drawn from elsewhere, recombined these models with long-standing Chinese norms of statecraft and governance and produced a wide variety of new hybrids – often only partially reconcilable – in different sectors of the central government.

## *Executive Agendas and Institutional Weaknesses*

Despite obvious and important changes in regime and government organization – from presidential dictatorship in the 1910s, to the Beiyang governments of the 1920s, to the ascendancy of the KMT Party and its National Government in the late 1920s and 1930s – the executives of Republican-era governments were characterized by a quite remarkable consistency in agendas and goals. They were also constrained in achieving those goals by an equally consistent set of structural constraints. Government in the Republican era inherited substantially intact the late Qing *xinzheng* (New Government) agenda which held that China depended on a vigorous central state to lead the way out of international

5. This shift in emphasis began in the early to mid-1980s, with the publication of William Kirby's *Germany and Republican China* (Stanford: Stanford University Press, 1984). Preliminary research on my forthcoming book, *Strong Institutions in Weak Polities: Personnel Policies and State Building in China, 1927–40* (Oxford: Oxford University Press, 1998) was conducted in 1987–89. At present there is a significant cadre of graduate students from programmes in history and political science at Harvard, Berkeley, and Washington University, St. Louis who are in some stage of writing or research on Ph.D. dissertations that address such different aspects of Republican government as constitution-drafting, the KMT's efforts to combat low-level corruption, and water conservancy. Even within the People's Republic, scholars are also beginning to reconsider the Republican period in a more sympathetic light: Nanjing University Press began publication of *Minguo yanjiu* (*Studies on Republican China*) with an editorial board of members from China and abroad, in summer 1995.

weakness and underdevelopment and into strength and power. The *xinzheng* programme set a new template for the evolution of a "modern" Chinese state: first by replacing the imperial Six Boards with modern-style ministries, and secondly by systematically drawing up plans to project central government power much further than ever before into the provinces.[6]

Although the *xinzheng* and subsequent Republican-era centralizers claimed to adhere to the principle of mechanisms through which those at local levels could have input into the decision-making process or manage their own affairs, throughout the Republican period, consultative bodies, representative institutions and regularized channels of articulation from below were minor strains in the dominant theme of centrally ordained statism and national unity.[7] The vast majority of those with executive power were socially conservative military men, and the socializing effects of a career in the military plus the structural predisposition of all executives to want more discretionary power made them even more consistent in their collective distaste for all forms of political participation and expression that they could not directly control.

Virtually all executives in the Republican period also conflated their own personal reach with central government power, and in turn central government power with the good of the country as a whole; conversely, any identifiable group or interest that in any way acted as a brake on the executive's policies was excoriated as subversive of the greater good of the nation. Thus in the 1910s Yuan Shikai dissolved the National Assembly and for a time succeeded in abolishing provincial assemblies as well, characterizing them as the preserve of selfish individuals. In the 1920s, a long line of Beiyang warlords periodically packed what remained of the National Assembly to draft constitutions that would legitimize their rule while they hurled epithets at each other as being detrimental to national unity. Finally, in the 1930s and 1940s Chiang

6. The *xinzheng* era, important as it is for the subsequent evolution of the 20th-century Chinese state, remains crucially understudied. Some of the more important works on this period include: Mary C. Wright, *China in Revolution: The First Phase, 1900–11* (New Haven: Yale University Press, 1968); Ernest Young, *The Presidency of Yuan Shih-k'ai* (Ann Arbor: University of Michigan Press, 1977), chs. 1–2; Esther Morrisson, "The modernization of the Confucian bureaucracy," unpublished dissertation, Radcliffe College, 1959; and Paul Hickey, "Fee taking, salary reform and the structure of state power in late Qing China, 1909–11," *Modern China*, Vol. 17, No. 3, pp. 389–417.

7. There was much about the *xinzheng* reform package that was either ambivalent or unclear, and this lack of clarity particularly stood out in the delicate issue of relative degrees of centralization and decentralization, an issue that continued to reverberate through the remainder of the 20th century. The late Qing *xinzheng* reforms allowed for the creation of provincial assemblies and even drew up a schedule for the gradual implementation of constitutional monarchy. Yuan Shikai, while hostile to any body that he could not directly control, toward the end of his life seemed quite desperate to make links with any source of popular support and launched a doomed monarchical revival, and the Chiang Kai-shek regime, while no less suspicious, allowed the existence of a Legislative Yuan and National Assembly, and paid at least lip service to the idea of village self-government. On the *xinzheng* constitutional programme, see Morrisson, "The modernization of the Confucian bureaucracy." On Yuan Shikai, see Ernest Young, "Yuan Shikai as a conservative modernizer," in Charlotte Furth, *The Limits of Change: Essays on Conservatism in Modern China* (Cambridge, MA: Harvard University Press, 1976), pp. 171–190.

Kai-shek became near hysterical about the continued existence of Communists who not only challenged his government from within the body politic of China but, even more seriously, posed an alternate and highly threatening model of "bottom-up" mobilization.[8]

For Republican-era central governments, the primary ordering principle was rapidly to build and project central state and bureaucratic power in order to create a viable and legitimate form of civil government. Subsidiary components of this larger agenda that remained virtually unchanged throughout the Yuan Shikai, Beiyang and KMT regimes included: promoting administrative and fiscal centralization, rationalization and standardization; the central state attempting to set the standard in programmes for modern education and industrial development; and – civilianizing imperatives to the contrary – militarily crushing open opposition whenever it was feasible to do so and opting for inclusion and co-optation when it was not.

Unfortunately for the evolution of post-1911 government in China, while the last years of the Qing bequeathed a largely unaltered agenda for central government action and state-building, it also passed on a complex of very serious structural weaknesses. These were exacerbated by the political volatility of the early Republic, which made the goals doubly difficult to realize in practice. In spite of the standing desire of all central government actors to promote centralization, unity and civil legitimacy, central state capacity was extremely limited with respect to the key issues of taxation and personnel, and the project of building civilian institutions was consistently undercut by the twin phenomena of internal division and external military pressure. Internally weak and fragmented government institutions in turn led to short-term horizons and political expedience, and the continued existence of armed challengers within China and aggressive imperialism from without mandated the continued importance of the military within government decision-making. To a greater rather than to a lesser extent, weak central projective capacity, internal divisions and external military pressure remained constraining and constant features throughout the Republican period.

During the last years of the Qing, the rate of real taxation in many parts of China had increased because of the proliferation of locally imposed surtaxes and sub-bureaucratic offices while the quotas remitted to the central government remained unchanged. This situation worsened after the 1911 Revolution, when provinces refused to remit anything at all to the central government. Although Yuan Shikai briefly got tax receipts coming into the capital in 1914, things so deteriorated after his death that during the Beiyang period, insofar as the central government had any revenues at all, they were provided via the remission of the remainder of salt tax funds collected by customs and Sino-foreign tax collecting

8. Young, *The Presidency of Yuan Shih-k'ai*, pp. 148–155. On warlord actions in the capital, see Chien Tuan-sheng, *The Government and Politics of China*, pp. 65–76, and on the structural systems behind warlord behaviour, see Ch'i Hsi-sheng, *Warlord Politics in China, 1916–28* (Stanford: Stanford University Press, 1976), pp. 185–195.

agencies that were independent organizations but nominally supervised by the central government in the 1910s and 1920s.[9]

The issue of government personnel was more subtle, but no less intractable. For centuries prior to the establishment of the Republic, those in state service in China had to strike a balance that could accommodate the inherent tensions between two sets of claims: the Confucian bureaucracy's demand that the individual in its employ be responsive to its standardized and impersonal rules and regulations while in office, versus the more enduring claims of the individual's friends and family to provide for them and "be sensitive to human feelings" (*gan renqing*). If left unchecked this latter set of pressures could easily lead to rampant corruption. Although real levels and subjective perceptions of corruption as a problem in the late imperial state certainly varied widely, some combination of "good institutions" through formal and bureaucratic sanctions of deviance, and normative socialization into behaviour as "good men" was the recognized way of keeping the tensions between a depersonalized bureaucracy and the particularism of society in some sort of balance.[10] In terms of institutions, the existence of Confucian civil service exams as the primary route into the bureaucracy cut off one obvious way of providing patronage. Years of studying the Confucian ethics may have pre-disposed individuals to be "good men," but clearly "good institutions" were also necessary to maintain an equilibrium between particularist interest and impartial law.

By the early Republic, however, neither of these components obtained. The Confucian civil service examinations, viewed by progressives as hopelessly archaic and a brake on progress, had been abolished in 1904–05, but nothing convincing had been instituted as a replacement.[11] Although all Republican regimes repeatedly professed their desire to recruit talent through the institution of modern civil service examinations to create a technically competent and pro-active government, the short-term pressures to provide patronage and buy off recalcitrant subordinates and would-be allies repeatedly stymied the

9. Young, *The Presidency of Yuan Shih-k'ai*, pp. 164–167. On the creation of the Sino-Foreign Salt Inspectorate and the revenues it remitted to the Beiyang governments, see S. A. M. Adshead, *The Modernization of the Chinese Salt Administration, 1900–1920* (Cambridge, MA: Harvard University Press, 1970), pp. 61–117. Prasenjit Duara in *Culture, Power and the State: Rural North China, 1900–42* (Stanford: Stanford University Press, 1988), pp. 59–85, also suggests that the very late imperial and Republican proliferation of local tax bureaus and *tankuan* led to significant increases in the rate of real taxation, virtually none of which was passed up to the central government.

10. The relative weights of the perceived importance of "good institutions" and "good men" in late imperial Chinese statecraft varied substantially, and is a vast topic in its own right. For views in English, see Benjamin Schwartz, *The World of Thought in Ancient China* (Cambridge, MA: Harvard University Press, 1985), pp. 102–105 for a discussion of the importance of "good men." For the importance of "good institutions," see Madeleine Zelin's excellent study of the rationalizing fiscal reforms of the Yongzheng Emperor, *The Magistrate's Tael: Rationalizing Fiscal Reform in 18th Century China* (Berkeley: University of California Press, 1984).

11. Wolfgang Franke, *The Reform and Abolition of the Traditional Chinese Examination System* (Cambridge, MA: Harvard Monographs, 1960) and Benjamin Elman, "Delegitimation and decanonization: the trap of civil service examination reform, 1860–1910," paper prepared for the First International Conference of Ch'ing Intellectual History, National Chung-shan University, Kaohsiung, Taiwan, 19–21 November 1993.

re-institutionalization of norms of objectivity and impartiality, however attractive they remained in principle. Fairly consistent foreign pressure, combined with distressing levels of domestic militarization, made the operations and institutions of civil Republican government even more problematic. Clearly, in this highly unfavourable environment of fragmented organizations, ambiguous loyalties, internal divisions, slender resources and external pressures, what the central governments of Republican China needed was, in effect, an "institutional breakthrough" – some means by which to climb out of this morass of weakness and begin to implement a vision of centrally led institution building and development while standing up to external pressure.[12]

Over the course of the Republican period, there were two analytically distinct methods or "logics" by which government elites worked to build institutional capacity. The first was to try to create a new set of "good institutions" for government and administration. "Good" was now redefined to be impersonal Weberian bureaucracy, characterized by objectively oriented, efficient, rule-based technocracy, with a *de facto* division of labour between politicians who set policy and bureaucrats who implemented it, and a sharp legal distinction between office and office-holder as the "most rational known means of exercising authority."[13] The second "logic," which arose with the reorganization of the KMT and the expansion of revolutionary sentiment in the mid-1920s, used long-standing beliefs in the importance of "good men." In this conception, "good men" were the raw materials who would effect institutional breakthroughs via a controlled mobilization whereby political leadership would arouse the pre-existing values and commitments of those below towards collective ends, and, where "correct" values and norms were lacking, would inculcate those norms.

### *Attempting Institutional Breakthroughs: Pre-1927 Visions and Implementation of Statist Technocracy*

Although the full-fledged articulation of the vision of "government as statist technocracy responsive to the executive" did not occur until the emergence of a group of Kuomintang administrative reformers in the mid-1930s, there can be little doubt that in embryo very similar principles animated both the Yuan Shikai and Beiyang governments of the 1910s

12. For the idea of an "institutional breakthrough," I slightly adapt Kenneth Jowitt's concept of a "revolutionary breakthrough" for the early developmental stage of Leninist systems. In contrast to "revolutionary breakthroughs," which are highly specific to Leninist regimes attempting to consolidate and carry out a "heroic" programme of modernization through collectivization and transformation of the basic units of society, "institutional breakthroughs" are more generic, and can be directed towards any number of different ends (including socially quite conservative ones). However, both revolutionary and institutional breakthroughs are sought after by executive elites wherever institutions are weak and fragmented. See Kenneth Jowitt, *Revolutionary Breakthroughs and National Development: The Case of Romania* (Berkeley: University of California Press, 1971), pp. 94–95.

13. This list of attributes is drawn from Max Weber, *Economy and Society* (Berkeley: University of California Press, 1978), pp. 223–26.

and 1920s. In his short tenure between 1912 and 1916, Yuan Shikai devoted a considerable amount of attention to attempting to create "good institutions" by regularizing, standardizing and establishing executive control over the government bureaucracy while pushing it in the direction of "objective" technocracy. Yuan established a new system of rank classifications and procedures for promotion in the civil bureaucracy as a whole. He drew up draft regulations to re-institute nation-wide open civil service examinations that assessed a combination of literacy in Chinese and knowledge of technical subjects as the preferred "regular path" into the bureaucracy, which was then followed by a provisional assignment to a ministry and two-year probationary period of intensive training. And Yuan consistently wooed to his administration "men of talent" who had been educated either abroad or domestically in modern subjects.[14]

There is some evidence to suggest substantial continuity of these policies in the central Beiyang governments into the early 1920s. The first nation-wide post-imperial civil service examinations were held in 1916, shortly after Yuan Shikai's death, and were identical in form to those he proposed the year before. The Beiyang Ministry of Finance, at least in its earliest years, seems to have continued in the way outlined by Yuan Shikai: in 1917 it assigned some 35 examinees who had passed the national civil service exams to a two-year probationary appointment. Until the early 1920s, when large numbers of staff began to be regularly replaced with those from outside, the Ministry of Finance probably retained many of the Yuan Shikai regime "men of talent" who had some mix of credentials in the "modern" subjects of government, economics and law, and practical experience in local, provincial or central government financial administration.[15]

Although the Yuan Shikai and early Beiyang government push towards central government technocracy, standardization, rationalization, examination and training systems provided a powerful model that continued to influence parts of the National Government once the KMT came to power in the late 1920s, it did not in its own time effect an institutional breakthrough, as it had no means by which to project its authority much beyond Beijing into highly unstable and militarized provincial and local environments. Taxes from the provinces simply did not come in and government regulations had little meaning. During the Beiyang period the central government of China operated as a head without a body, fiscally kept alive (as noted above) by regular transfusions of the surpluses remitted by quasi-government tax collection agencies that it did not control, and loans from Western banks.[16]

14. This discussion draws on my article, "Symbol and reflection of the reconstituting state: the Examination Yuan in the 1930s," *Modern China*, Vol. 20, No. 2 (April 1994). Many of the original details can be found in Qian Shipu (ed.), *Beiyang zhengfu shiqide zhengzhi zhidu* (*The Political System of the Beiyang Government Period*) (Beijing: Zhonghua shuju, 1984).

15. This segment is based on details in ch. 5 of Strauss, *Strong Institutions in Weak Polities*, with the original documentation from the No. 2 Historical Archives, files 1027/176 (2), 1027/179, 1027/181, and 1027/188 (1).

16. The fact that the Beiyang government in Beijing was the officially recognized central government of China meant that control of it provided automatic access to a range of financial

*Generating Institutional Breakthroughs: The Sino-Foreign Salt Inspectorate "Model" and After*

Ironically, the very weakness of the early Republican government brought about the creation of a quasi-government organization that became one of the more powerful models of a statist technocracy and, in the critical sphere of tax collection, did generate an institutional breakthrough. When the Yuan Shikai government went to the Western banking establishment to conclude a large Reorganization Loan to refinance outstanding debts and consolidate the regime in 1913, the price demanded was that the salt gabelle be reorganized administratively so that an efficiently collected salt tax could service the debt on the loan. The result was a new tax-collecting agency nominally under the supervision of the Republican central government, the Sino-Foreign Salt Inspectorate (*Yanwu jihe zongsuo*). The Inspectorate was explicitly modelled on the customs administration and, by extension, on other British colonial bureaucracies: it was a hybrid, prefectural tax-collecting agency, jointly staffed by foreign and Chinese personnel, in which all orders and documents were co-signed by foreign and Chinese staff of equal rank. However the preponderant influence in establishing the core values and methods of operation of the Inspectorate for its turbulent history was that of its first foreign Chief Inspector, Sir Richard Dane.[17]

The programme of the Salt Inspectorate was to standardize, simplify, bureaucratize and establish direct control over China's far-flung and heterogenous salt works and taxation arrangements by replacing a centuries-old patchwork of indirect control via official monopolies with the principle of "tax directly levied at source" (*jiuchang zhengshui*). Obviously, such reforms would engender the resistance of everyone who stood to lose by them: salt merchants, local-level governments who had long added surtaxes to the salt gabelle, local smugglers, and corrupt salt tax officials from pre-existing administrations. Yet in spite of resistance and a quite hostile environment in which to carry out these reforms, the Salt Inspectorate was astonishingly successful by almost any measure: in the first full year of its operations, net salt tax receipts nearly quintupled from $11,471,000 in 1913 to $60,410,000 in 1914, and gradually increased thereafter to a pre-KMT era high of $85,789,000 in 1922.[18] Much to the surprise of everyone, the Salt Inspectorate not only produced enough each year to service the Reorganization Loan debt to the foreign

---

*footnote continued*
resources not available elsewhere (primarily customs and salt surpluses as well as the possibility of foreign loans). This ironically increased the attractiveness of the city and rump central government administration as a target for warlord depradations during the 1920s.

17. The analysis in this and the following section of the Salt Inspectorate presents an overview of ch. 3, "Effective institution building: the case of the Sino-Foreign Salt Inspectorate," in Strauss, *Strong Institutions in Weak Polities*. See also S. A. M Adshead, *The Modernization of the Salt Administration, 1900–20* (Cambridge, MA: Harvard University Press, 1970), especially ch. 4.

18. These figures are taken from Kwei Chungshu (ed.), *The Chinese Year Book, 1935–36* (Shanghai: Commercial Press, 1936), p. 1298. The currency in which these figures were calculated was the standard silver dollar.

banks: it even produced enough to remit a substantial annual remainder to the central government.

It was able to do so by effective pursuit of a two-pronged strategy of internal and external bureaucratization. It generated the capacity to implement its programmes in part because of non-replicable factors of serendipity, astute leadership and the extreme weakness of the Chinese central government at the time when it came into existence: a few months into his tenure, Dane managed to expand the authority of the Inspectorate to include not only collecting the tax but also authorizing the transfer of revenues to the banks and the Chinese government, and taking over the power of audit in the district offices. This extraordinary amount of authority was then translated into organizational capital in terms of institutional bureaucratization: the funds it collected gave the Inspectorate the financial means by which to insulate itself from the highly hostile surrounding atmosphere, whereby it promptly established a civil service system entirely separate from that of the rest of the Chinese government. The system had different classification grades, substantially higher salaries, rigorous enforcement of the principle of entry exclusively by examination into the lowest three grades, promotion based largely on seniority and to a lesser degree on performance, frequent internal audit and review, and absolutely regular tours of rotation between districts for all regular staff.[19]

Both the foreigners and the Chinese who worked for the Inspectorate believed that its separate civil service system was at the heart of its success. All the available evidence indicates that once thus buffered from the claims of friends and family, socialized into the bureaucratic and performance-oriented norms of the organization, and given a stable source of income with every prospect of long-term employment, staff did commit themselves and their careers to the Inspectorate. For those who worked for it, the Inspectorate stood out as an unusually impartial and *fair* organization.[20]

Such internal insulation, combined with the Inspectorate's external implementation of rationalizing reforms and its success (relative to all other organizations of the time), was mutually reinforcing, and on more than one occasion enabled district offices of the Inspectorate literally to *buy* their continued existence through *ad hoc* negotiations with warlords during the turbulent 1920s. The ultimate example of this came in 1927–28. After the National Revolutionary Army forcibly closed down all the district offices in its path and the KMT regime abolished the Inspectorate as an unsavoury vestige of imperialist domination, the Salt Inspectorate was able to negotiate its revival by styling itself as an impersonal, efficient organization of Weberian bureaucrats that could serve any political master, including the KMT. By accepting its incorporation into the National Government under the Ministry of Finance, the Salt Inspectorate was revived as a still semi-autonomous administration

19. *Yanwu renshi guize* (*Regulations on Salt Affairs Personnel*), Ministry of Finance, n.d. (c. 1948). Interviews with: Zhong Liangzhe, Taipei, Taiwan, 20 January 1989; Lin Jiyong, Tainan, Taiwan, 24 January 1989; Chen Guisheng, Taipei, Taiwan, 16 January 1989.

20. Interviews, Chen Guisheng, Taipei, Taiwan, 16 January 1989; and Zhou Weiliang, Tainan, Taiwan, 24 January 1989.

with substantial control over internal operations and personnel. Had it not consistently "produced the goods" in terms of efficient and non-corrupt tax collection, it is extremely unlikely that it would have survived the 1920s; but had it not so successfully insulated itself from the external pressures around the norms of fairness, depersonalization, performance and Weberian technocracy, it is unlikely that it would have had such an impressive record in terms of external performance. Thus internal and external strategies of bureaucratization were mutually reinforcing: "good institutions," buttressed by external and measurable high performance, enabled staff to behave as "good (albeit technocratic) men."

The Inspectorate's anomalous foreign adviser presence as well as its early virtual independence of any wing of the Chinese government might well have limited its usefulness as a "model" for the rest of the government: certainly, no self-respecting Chinese government with the power to prevent it was going to invite foreigners to have co-equal authority with Chinese nationals.[21] In 1927–28, the Inspectorate was saved by its previous record in tax extraction and the KMT's need for revenue, and indeed throughout the 1930s it provided the National Government with between one-fifth and one-quarter of its total income.[22] But in the 1930s, as a semi-autonomous agency under the Ministry of Finance, its systems and results gained the admiration of a substantial segment of finance technocrats and administrative reformers. Song Ziwen spoke glowingly of the Inspectorate on several public occasions,[23] and despite ambivalence on the part of KMT elites who oscillated between "wanting to use the Inspectorate and control it,"[24] it was allowed in fact to expand in influence and operations as part of the Ministry of Finance right up to the outbreak of the Sino-Japanese War. Perhaps more importantly, other organizations in the National Government admired and attempted to emulate the "Inspectorate model" in the 1930s. For example, the Consolidated Tax Administration, another prefectural tax agency under the Ministry of Finance *without* the anomalous foreign adviser presence, quite self-consciously set out to replicate Inspectorate-style policies (through centralization, standardization and simplification of tax rates, and dispatching staff to levy tax at the site of production) and strategic internal insulation (by attempting to set up a semi-separate personnel system). Significantly, the Consolidated Tax Administration also exhibited quite impressive jumps in efficient and effective tax collection in its early years. Its contributions to government income steadily increased over the Nanjing

21. In fact, when the National Government was established in 1927–28, political leaders varied quite dramatically between wishing to abolish the Inspectorate as a tool of imperialism insulting to China's sovereignty and desperately needing access to the funds that the Inspectorate could reliably supply.

22. These figures are taken from the table "Distribution of revenues" in Young, *China's Nation Building Effort*, p. 73. In 1929, the Inspectorate only contributed 9% of the central government's revenues, but by 1930 the figure was up to 25.2%.

23. Song Ziwen (T. V. Soong), "1931 annual financial report," reproduced in *China Year Book, 1933* (Shanghai: Kelley and Walsh, 1933), p. 338.

24. Liu Foding, interview, Tianjin, 24 June 1988.

Decade, supplying 11 per cent of the funds in 1929, rising to 22.2 per cent in 1937.[25]

This "logic" of rapidly building government capacity through the creation of strong, rule-based, efficient and "objectively oriented" technocratically based institutions coalesced in a number of important pockets of Republican government: in finance and tax, in water conservancy, in the national personnel policy articulated by the Examination Yuan and Ministry of Personnel, in the National Resource Council and, from the middle of the 1930s, through the activities and writings of a group of administrative reformers headed by Gan Naiguang of the Ministry of the Interior.[26] There was support and justification for the model from the positive elements of the example of hybrid colonial administrations like the Salt Inspectorate and the Customs Administration, as well as from specially convened commissions and foreign advisers from Germany, Britain and the United States, and from the newly coalescing field of American public administration.

The model assumed that it was possible to separate technical "facts" from political "values,"[27] clearly distinguish "politics" and "administration," and appropriately divide responsibility between bureaucrats and political leadership, resulting in a situation in which technically proficient and objectively oriented bureaucrats would "speak truth" to political "power."[28] Political leaders would then make appropriate decisions and transmit these decisions to the bureaucrats for implementation. It completely sidestepped sensitive questions that became increasingly important in the 1920s regarding political participation, mobilization and power from below. This "logic" implicitly held the government of Republican China to be a potentially efficient mechanism of unification and standardization from above, thus making it an attractive proposition for the socially conservative political executives interested in expanding and projecting state power while maintaining control. And, in sectors where the goods being provided (like tax revenues) were critical to the government's continued survival, politicians in the party-state were to a greater rather than a lesser degree inclined to allow the technocrats, particularly below the top levels of the organization, an arena for technocratic quasi-autonomy, at least during the 1930s.

25. Young, *China's Nation Building Effort*, "Distribution of revenues from 1929–37," p. 73.

26. For the National Resource Council, see William C. Kirby "Continuity and change in Modern China: economic planning on the mainland and on Taiwan, 1943–58," *Australian Journal of Chinese Affairs*, No. 58 (July 1990), pp. 121–141. On water conservancy, David Pietz has an excellent dissertation in progress; on the Ministry of Personnel, particularly its attempt to "objectify and depersonalize" the criteria for advancement and promotion in the civil bureaucracy, see Strauss, "Symbol and reflection of the reconstituting state," and on the activities of technocratically oriented administrative reformers, see Julia Strauss, "The cult of administrative efficiency: myth and statecraft in the Republic of China," unpublished paper presented at the Association for Asian Studies Annual Meeting, 25–28 March 1993, Los Angeles.

27. For the original formulation of this "fact/value" dichotomy, see Herbert Simon, *Administrative Behavior*, 2nd ed. (New York: Macmillan, 1961), pp. 4–8.

28. Aaron Wildavsky, *Speaking Truth to Power: The Art and Craft of Policy Analysis* (Boston: Little, Brown, 1979).

Despite the attractiveness of this statist/technocratic model, the conditions for building functionally oriented, rule-based, proactive institutions could not be replicated uniformly throughout the Republican era government. Weberian government presumed agreement in the political leadership as to policy, and further, it was expensive. When political leadership was deeply divided as to basic orientations and goals (as with education), it was impossible to establish objective measures for technocratic performance. If leadership for other reasons suddenly reversed its earlier *de facto* practice of non-interference in the internal workings of the organization (as happened across the board during the Sino-Japanese War), there was little that technocrats could do to resist, however much they may have disagreed with the thrust of these changes. And if the organization's goals far outstripped its capacity in terms of available resources (as became the case for even previously successful technically based units during the Sino-Japanese War), at best, no institutional breakthrough was possible. At worst, the unit in question slipped into inactivity and became vulnerable to the pressures of patronage.

### *Generating Institutional Breakthroughs: Controlled Mobilization and the Sunist Legacy*

Another "logic" of attempting to generate institutional breakthroughs existed from at least the mid-1920s on. This orientation, while not denying the need for a unitary central government or of technically competent individuals in government service, focused on mobilizing commitments and support from below while maintaining direction and control from above as the route out of ineffective weakness and into strength and modernity. The ideas elaborated by Sun Yat-sen in the Three Principles of the People and Five Power Government were animated by a syncretic mixture of Chinese nationalism, admiration for Western-style constitutional democracy and classic division of powers, and populist belief in social justice and the desirability of mass participation in local self-government.[29] With the KMT's acceptance of Soviet advisers, its reorganization and incorporation of the Chinese Communist Party in 1923 and its establishment of the Whampoa military academy to train a corps of revolutionary officers in 1924, a heavy Leninist component was added to this mix. The adoption of Leninist norms and tactics meant the KMT began to style itself as a combat revolutionary party entrusted with the fundamentally heroic dual task of consolidating the country militarily while also teaching the people appropriate commitments, values and behaviour in preparation for eventual self-government.[30]

29. Sun Yat-sen, *Three Principles of the People* and *Fundamentals of National Reconstruction* (Taipei: China Cultural Service, 1953), Chinese and English text.

30. I take the idea of a "combat/heroic Party" from Ken Jowitt, who uses the term to describe Leninist parties of all types. See Kenneth Jowitt, "The Leninist phenomenon," reproduced in *New World Disorder: The Leninist Extinction* (Berkeley: University of California Press, 1992). There were of course significant differences in the methods of the KMT and the Chinese Communist Party: the former shied away from violent social revolution

Political tutelage into correct values and behaviour began, so to speak, at home, in the KMT Party and the National Revolutionary Army itself. As the captured documents of Soviet advisers from the mid-1920s make abundantly clear, transforming a motley collection of poorly trained and badly equipped military units into a National Revolutionary Army capable of launching a military drive to reunify the country on a limited budget was a far from easy matter. With limited "objective" means, attention was turned to the "subjective" creation of revolutionary commitments: post-entry socialization into appropriate knowledge and revolutionary norms through political education for both officers and enlisted men was felt to be every bit as important as the "harder" aspects of military training.[31] And certainly at Whampoa Military Academy, political study and the commitments which proper indoctrination was presumed to generate from below were a very strong presence. When combined with anti-imperialist struggle and fervent nationalism, political study at Whampoa in particular created a set of utopian ideals of self-sacrifice, hard work, plain living, revolutionary discipline, unquestioning obedience to superiors and "taking risks to attack difficulties, making use of little to win more" (*yao maoxian fannan, yishao shengduo*) – in short, relying on the internal commitments and orientations of "good men" to become revolutionary heroes and create institutional breakthroughs despite unpromising objective circumstances. Tempered by a militarist rhetoric stressing obedience, discipline and control, this combat/heroic theme was endlessly repeated by the KMT Party and to a lesser extent the National Government in the 1930s and 1940s to anchor legitimacy (particularly the legitimacy of party and military organizations) – a phenomenon that would be repeated a generation later, in an even stronger form, with the Chinese Communists and their idealization of the Yan'an period.[32]

## *The Kuomintang Regime: Agendas, Constraints and Strategies*

While setting out an appealing programme, Sun's ideas for a phased process of national reconstruction and eventual five-power government

*footnote continued*
and class struggle while the latter embraced it. But both were definitively stamped by Leninist principles of discipline and mobilizing the heroic commitments of those from below, as well as a faith in the party to effect an institutional breakthrough by transforming beliefs.

31. C. Martin Wilbur and Julie Lien-ying How, *Missionaries of Revolution: Soviet Advisors and Nationalist China* (Cambridge, MA: Harvard University Press, 1989), Document 29 "The training of the National Revolutionary Army for war," Document 37 "Political work in the National Revolutionary Army," Document 39, "Program of political lessons for enlisted personnel" and Document 40 "How to carry on the political education of officers" are full of examples.

32. See Chiang Kai-shek, "Gemingjun teshu de jingshen he zhanshu" ("The National Revolutionary Army's special esprit and military techniques"), speech given at Whampoa on 9 November 1924, and "Junshi jiaoyu zhi yaozhi yu junji de genyuan" ("The basic principles of military education and the origin of military discipline"), speech given at Whampoa on 14 April 1925, in Zhang Qijun (ed.), *Xian zongtong jianggong chuanji*, Vol. 1 (Taipei: Wenhua daxue and Zhonghua xueshuyuan, 1984), pp. 475–481 and 493–96.

were full of ambivalences, and were at best unclear as to how inconsistencies ought to be resolved in practice. The *Fundamentals of National Reconstruction* (*Jianguo dagang*) was vague on such important issues as the appropriate distribution of power between centre and localities, division of power within the central government, how long the period of political tutelage should last and who would have the authority to declare it at an end. Perhaps most important, the *Fundamentals* did not specifically mention either the KMT or the National People's Army, and seemed to assume implicitly that both could be subsumed under "the government."

Once the KMT established the National Government as an inclusivist regime that defined itself in opposition to social revolution and class struggle in 1927–28, the central government largely picked up the agenda of the preceding Yuan Shikai and Beiyang regimes, despite its explicit self-legitimation as the standard bearer of Sun's vision. Although preserved in vestigial form, the parts of the Sunist legacy that stressed division of powers from above and self-government from below were systematically marginalized in favour of "top-down," centralized military and administrative reintegration and control. In accordance with Sun Yat-sen's blueprint, the National Government promulgated a constitution and a series of Organic Laws in the late 1920s and early 1930s and formally established a Five Yuan system that was explicitly modelled on American-style division of power.

But in practice, all the government Yuan save the Executive remained weak organizations throughout the remainder of the Republican era. The Legislative Yuan sat, but merely rubber-stamped legislation drafted elsewhere in the government; the Control Yuan had formal power of audit and impeachment, but its procedures were slow and it proved to be politically impossible to charge those high in the party-state with malfeasance in office; the Examination Yuan periodically held open civil service examinations, but appointment of personnel, formally examined or not, rested largely with the ministries themselves. To confuse matters even further, the regime, particularly at higher levels in the KMT, government and military, was permeated with overlapping jurisdictions and unclear lines of authority. In theory the KMT Party and the National Government were closely connected but identifiably separate entities with their own hierarchies and channels of information and command: one did not have to be a KMT Party member to serve in the National Government, and orders issued to subordinate organizations in the civil bureaucracy went through the relevant Yuan (typically the Executive Yuan). In practice, political decision-makers at the apex of party, state and military organizations were a small group of individuals with simultaneous and overlapping appointments in the KMT Party Central Executive Committee,[33] as heads of important government bodies and/or in the military.[34] In real

33. The term in Chinese is Zhongyang zhixing weiyuanhui, which can also be translated as "Politburo" or, more loosely, "Central Executive Committee."

34. The nature of the one-party government, and the dual roles that much of the senior leaders played have led to an understandable tendency in much of the English-language literature to conflate the Party with the National Government as the "KMT Government" or KMT "Party-state." The two were closely related, particularly at the very top, but were

terms, whether orders and laws were issued in the name of the KMT Party, the National Government or from an "extraordinary" military committee, the locus of decision-making authority increasingly slid to the Military Affairs Commission headed by Chiang Kai-shek as the twin pressures of continuing internal division and external aggression made it possible for the military to justify its continued dominance of domestic politics and the lion's share of the annual budget.

Military and fiscal weakness, combined with the KMT Party's genuine belief in the organic unity of the Chinese people and a pathological fear of open divisions, dictated an inclusivist and co-optive strategy towards all those who could in any way be formally incorporated into the National Government, up to and including nominally reconstructed warlords, old Beiyang bureaucrats, business and landed interests, and the Shanghai underworld. This strategy presumed that rapid formal unification was infinitely preferable to continued division, and that those thus brought in would eventually be co-opted under the veneer of the formal authority of the state. Despite, or perhaps because of, its co-option of so many different groups (many of which imported their pre-existing networks into the National Government in the late 1920s) the KMT regime looked upon all forms of open political participation that it did not directly control or sanction with a great deal of suspicion.

Although the KMT regime had a much stronger base with which to work – and in fact it was able to project its authority into at least one important region of China (which was significantly more than the Beiyang governments had managed to accomplish) – the post-1927 Republican government was at least as much in need of a set of institutional breakthroughs as the Yuan Shikai and Beiyang regimes. The pre-1927 period offered two basic strategies: the Weberian technocratic bureaucracy of the Inspectorate, or the Soviet inspired Whampoa legacy of "controlled mobilization" via revolutionary indoctrination. For the 20 years between 1928 and 1949 the regime oscillated between these two strategies, attempted to reproduce elements of each in different sectors, and, when seriously troubled during the Sino-Japanese war, began to collapse the two together into one drive to generate an institutional breakthrough under rapidly deteriorating conditions.

### *The Ambiguity of Xunlian*

*Xunlian* (training) and the activities clustered around it were closely associated with the rise and expansion of the KMT Party and the National Revolutionary Army. The term itself was inherently ambiguous: it either simply referred to "drill and exercises for military personnel" or meant "education with the purpose of acquiring a certain style of behaviour or technical knowledge," usually implemented through short-term courses with fixed objectives. This gave rise to a continuum of *xunlian*,

---

*footnote continued*
analytically and organizationally separate, particularly for middle and lower levels of the government bureaucracy.

with military or technical training at one end and inculcation of party or militarily determined styles of behaviour at the other, although in practice the two could be combined (as indeed they were at Whampoa and in the National Revolutionary Army in the 1920s).[35]

During the 1930s, the term *xunlian* came to be commonly used to refer to two quite different phenomena. The first, which explicitly hearkened back to its institutional origins in the Whampoa model of controlled mobilization, referred to a series of short-term training courses largely centred on the military with the announced objectives of rapid acquisition of technical military skills *and* indoctrination into the "revolutionary" norms of loyalty and obedience to the central military leadership. The most important post-Whampoa *xunlian* sessions were held at Lushan in 1933, in preparation for extermination campaigns against the Communists, at Emeishan in 1935, specifically to have the military commanders of non-central government troops from the south-west undergo training with the presumptively more loyal central government troops, and at Lushan again on the eve of the Sino-Japanese War in July 1937, this time with an eye towards mobilizing a broader base of anti-Japanese patriotic resistance, and therefore including figures in KMT Party and, to a lesser degree, government organizations.[36] Military cum Party *xunlian* in the 1930s was geared to some combination of military training and political indoctrination, with the political indoctrination component probably the more important of the two.

But at exactly the same time, the term *xunlian* came to refer to training in the sense of "on-the-job acquisition of technical skills" in which a programme of political indoctrination did not largely figure. During the 1930s, technically trained personnel were in short supply, and individual ministries (usually the relevant sub-division of the organization where the lack of trained personnel was felt most keenly) such as the taxation sub-units of the Ministry of Finance and the telecommunications wing of the Ministry of Communications set up *ad hoc* programmes to fill the gaps. The curricula of these training courses varied from organization to organization, and most were short term (from a few months to a year). Although they indirectly incorporated some amount of loyalty training by requiring one course on Party principles (*dangyi*), the bulk of these courses focused on practical or applied work (*yewu gongzuo*). For the Ministry of Communications, this meant courses in telegraph study, electromagnetics, electrical engineering, mathematics, geography, accounting, surveying and English language; for the Ministry of Finance,

35. This section is drawn from my article, "Wartime stress and Guomindang response: *xunlian* as a means to statebuilding," delivered at the Annual Meeting of the Association for Asian Studies, 11–14 April 1996, Honolulu, Hawaii.

36. Liu Xianyun, who was then a relatively low level *ganshi*, was on site for the 1937 *xunlian* session, and attested that while the majority of the individuals undergoing *xunlian* were from the KMT Party and military, there was "some number" of high level non-party civilians involved with either education or cultural activities who were in attendance. Interview, Taipei, 17 May 1995. See also Wang Dongyuan, in speech given on 9 December 1939 in which he reviewed the previous occasions of *xunlian*, reproduced in *Ganbu xunlian wenti* (*Questions on the Training of Cadres*) (Chongqing: Zhongyang xunlianban di wuqi jiangyan lu, 1939). See esp. pp. 8–13.

there were courses in economics, statistics and the Ministry of Finance's regulations.[37] In practice this suggested the creation and strengthening of a Weberian managerial technocracy.

*The Sino-Japanese War and Strategies of Institution-Building*

The disastrous military defeats in the autumn of 1937 resulted in the National Government's loss of its economic heartland and political base, and the eventual relocation to Chongqing as wartime capital substantially weakened central government strength. Wartime emergency powers were increasingly concentrated in Chiang Kai-shek, but decrees without governmental and administrative capacity for implementation counted for little. Wartime conditions (loss of the central government's traditional fiscal and political base, relocation in an area where it had very little pre-existing control, and lessened influence vis-à-vis provincial military commanders) set off an increasingly desperate search to augment government capacity rapidly, which took three forms: hyperexpansion of the government, an obsession with control from above, and the collapsing of the two previously quite distinct forms of *xunlian* into one throughout all levels of the government.

Although there are no good figures on exactly how large the National Government bureaucracy was in the pre-1937 period, all the indirect evidence points to an enormous expansion during the Sino-Japanese War, by a factor of at least four to five, and perhaps much more.[38] Some of this growth took place in already established units, some in military administration, but the vast majority was through the wartime proliferation of government administrations set up to manage the economy from the top, establish a grain procurement system, enforce (or attempt to enforce) government monopolies on key commodities, and extract tax in areas where central government projective power was practically non-existent.[39]

Given that precipitous decline in terms of objective resources was accompanied by simultaneous hyper-growth in the size and scope of government organizations, the regime turned to what it did have in terms of establishing control and mobilizing commitments: normative appeals

37. *Jiaotong bu nianjian* (*Ministry of Communications Yearbook*) (Nanjing: Jiaotong bu, 1935), pp. 106–113 and *Caizheng bu nianjian* (Nanjing: Caizheng bu, 1935), pp. 67–69 and 72–73.

38. As one suggestive example, the Ministry of Personnel, which before 1937 was an exceptionally small organization with under 100 staff, quintupled in size. Documents published by the Examination Yuan in the early 1950s state explicitly that the Ministry of Personnel grew five-fold over the course of the Sino-Japanese War. See See Niu Yongzhen (ed.), *Xingxianhou kaoshiyuan chengli sanzhounian jiantao huiyi tekan* (*Special Publication: The Examination Yuan's Self-Criticism Meeting on the Third-Year Anniversary of the Implementation of the Constitution*), published by the Kaoshiyuan Secretariat, 1951, p. 11. It is a reasonable hypothesis that other organizations may have grown even more quickly, as it became very common to make *daili* (acting) appointments that escaped registry and scrutiny with the Ministry of Personnel.

39. Lloyd Eastman, "Nationalist China during the Sino-Japanese War, 1937–45," in Lloyd E. Eastman *et al.*, *The Nationalist Era in China, 1927–49* (Cambridge: Cambridge University Press, 1991, 1993), pp. 155–56, 165–67. For the range of monopoly control the wartime government attempted to institute on products as diverse as matches, salt, sugar and tobacco see *Kangzhan shiqi zhuanmai shiliao* (*Historical Materials on Monopolies During the Sino-Japanese War*) (Taipei: Guoshiguan, 1992).

to Chinese patriotism as it styled itself the saviour of the Chinese nation. The twin processes of establishing control and attempting to generate commitment from below was carried out by a revival and dramatic expansion of the scope of *xunlian* that touched virtually everyone in government service during the war years. In late 1938, a Central Training Corps (*Zhongxuntuan*) was established, to which army officers and then, increasingly, senior and mid-level government bureaucrats were dispatched as detachés for one-month training courses that exclusively stressed militarization and political indoctrination.

The Central Training Corps' leadership believed that the problems of the nation could be largely located in the internal orientation of the individual: most Chinese were "physically weak, passive, lacking in spiritual vigour, with non-orderly habits and lax collective organization."[40] *Xunlian* was a means by which to unify the nation and save it from extinction. As such, its intermediate goals aimed at nothing less than to "completely militarize the daily behaviour of everyone, in order to realize the militarization of society," and create orderliness and vigorous collective organization by indoctrinating trainees with military goals and values prior to their acceptance into the KMT Party (for those who were not already party members). The training programme therefore consisted of four intensive weeks of leader worship, mornings of lectures to educate people as to "correct" wartime government policies, afternoons on the drill ground, evenings of political study with small group discussion, and the keeping of a daily journal to "measure" the individual's progress in assimilating the values and norms the regime wished to inculcate.[41]

It is estimated that between 1938 and 1945 the *Zhongxuntuan* trained around 30,000 – a not insubstantial number.[42] However, given its limited reach, the new wartime imperative of the political leadership to "thoroughly militarize and politicize" state and society led it to enjoin units elsewhere in the government to set up and run their own *xunlian* courses on the Central Training Corps model under the loose supervision of a Central Training Committee (*Zhongyang xunlianhui*).[43] In the central government, organizations as diverse as the Ministry of the Interior, the Ministry of Finance and the Examination Yuan set up

40. Wang Dongyuan, *Zenyang shixing xunshi?* (*How Should Training Instruction be Implemented?*), pamphlet (Chongqing: Zhongyang xunliantuan, 1940), p. 8.

41. For the mechanics of *xunlian*, see *ibid*. For critical views of those who underwent the training session, see Liu Yaozhang, "Guomindang zhongxuntuan de lailong qumai" ("The origins and development of the KMT's Central Training Corps"), *Wenshi ziliao xuanji* (*Selected Materials on Civil History*) No. 74; Cai Duan (ed.), *Zhongguo renmin zhengzhi xieshang huiyi quanguo weiyuanhui wenshi ziliao yanjiu weiyuanhui* (Beijing: Wenshi ziliao chubanshe, 1981) pp. 1–21; and Zhao Puju, "Zhongyang xunliantuan genggai" ("A synopsis of the Central Training Corps"), pp. 23–41, in same.

42. Liu Yaozhang, *ibid*., p. 2.

43. *Tongyi gedi xunlian jiguan banfa quanguo ge xunlian liguan xunlian gangling* (*An Outline for the Unification of Each Region's Organization and Methods for Training*) (Chongqing: Guomindang zhongyang zhixing weiyuanhui xunlian weiyuanhui, January 1940), pp. 1–3.

*xunlian* courses, with the process replicated at the provincial and sub-provincial level for military cadres, county chiefs and KMT Party personnel.[44] Although much more research needs to be done to ascertain the degree to which these *xunlian* sessions replaced pre-existing technocratic orientations (for central ministries like the Ministry of Finance), provided an arena for factional politics (at all levels), or met their goals, it is clear that for at least those sessions run by the Examination Yuan and the Ministry of Finance, by the early 1940s the two previously distinct streams of *xunlian* began to merge into one. Course curricula, while maintaining a substantial *yewu* (functional/practical) component also included a minimum of two hours a day military drill as well as the inevitable lectures on "correct" government policy through the importation of party ideologues like Chen Lifu, as well as small group discussions.[45]

In terms of institution-building, the attempt to increase commitments from below while maintaining control from above through *xunlian* was in the short term a relatively cheap and easy way of boosting morale and moulding large numbers of people into support for wartime leadership. Instead of exclusively relying on long years of professional or technical training (that China could in any case ill afford on the scale that was necessary), ideological *xunlian* was quick and inexpensive, and connected to ideas long held by Chinese elites – that the "natural good" and "natural trainability" of the individual could, with proper training and self-cultivation, be channelled towards positive, collectivist ends.

Unfortunately for the KMT political leadership, government expansion during the war years had the net effect of undercutting both the Weberian/technocratic and heroic/control strategies, as government organizations were flooded with young, untrained and inexperienced personnel. On the state-society axis, the proliferation of government organizations during the Sino-Japanese war did not translate into the government's ability to restructure and reorder society and economy from above; and within the state itself, the unrestrained incorporation of everyone and anyone not a Communist into the government undercut both technocratic quality con-

44. For a partial listing of the names of the non Central Training Corps *xunlian* organizations that sprang up during the first years of the Sino-Japanese War, see Wang Dongyuan, *Ganbu xunlian wenti*, pp. 4–5.

45. Although this probably varied from case to case, it appears that at least some individual organizations subtly fought to maintain their technocratic *yewu* orientations to the greatest degree possible given the extraordinary politicization and militarization of the war years. For example, the Examination Yuan, while in form following the schedule of activities laid out by the Central Training Institute model, in practice modified the contents of many of the lectures and the orientation of the small group discussions to focus on the practical problems of personnel administration under wartime conditions. This information comes from a long document entitled *Di'si renshi xingzheng renyuan xunlian ban de baogao* (*The Fourth Personnel Administration Personnel Training Report*), which was written in February 1942. This report, which runs to nearly 100 pages, reviews the previous *xunlian* sessions held by the Examination Yuan, and can be found in Guoshiguan microfilm reel No. 20000000A 0313/8050.01–01, pp. 1155 and *passim*. The degree to which other organizations did the same is an empirical question that awaits further research. However, whatever the quiet resistance, the trend to conflate military cum political *xunlian* with functionally oriented technocratic *xunlian* during the Sino-Japanese War is clear.

trol and the *xunlian* effort to generate heroic commitments while maintaining discipline and control, as the movement spread out in ever widening circles from its original constituency in the central KMT Party and military.

*Strategies for Institutional Breakthroughs and Avenues for Future Research*

Both the Weberian/technocratic and the normative/heroic approaches of generating institutional breakthroughs had advantages and serious drawbacks. The advantage of Weberian technocracy lay in its orientation towards the objective: with criteria for performance (as well as indicators of corruption) clearly established it was possible to depersonalize administration and suppress rent-seeking. However, strategies of bureaucratization were both precarious and costly: a steady supply of technically competent individuals was not easy to procure and was expensive to retain, insulating boundaries were difficult to draw and maintain, and the entire enterprise was dependent on the good will of the political leadership to trust a semi-autonomous technocracy, listen to its advice and not interfere too much in its internal operations. In some government organizations during the 1930s these conditions were met, but even the most steady and well-bureaucratized experienced serious de-institutionalization during the prolonged crisis of the Sino-Japanese War.

The advantage of the *xunlian* strategy and its attempt to generate normative commitments from below lay in its practical feasibility in times of limited resources and in the way it appealed to deeply held norms about the values of "good men" leading to "good institutions." Normative appeals had at least the potential to be cheap and cost-effective (a "poor man's approach to institution building"). This strategy had two main problems. First, finding an objectively "knowable" basis for determining individual commitments and internal values was notoriously slippery, and could easily lend itself to politicization and personalization; secondly, establishing and maintaining boundaries to differentiate the committed from the uncommitted proved increasingly difficult to maintain over time. When the strategy moved beyond its natural constituency to encompass those who were indifferent or hostile to its values and norms, it also became "expensive" in terms of lowered morale and the effort expended on coercion.

Work that fundamentally re-assesses Republican-era government has only just begun, but some possible avenues for future research may be put forward. This article has suggested that in the Republican period the critical problem for government was the issue of institutional capacity and that all Republican governments looked for ways to generate institutional breakthroughs. However, many more empirical studies of particular central government organizations are needed to reveal what the mix of Weberian/technocratic and normative/heroic orientations in fact was, and whether the predominance of one strategy over the other can be linked to a consistent set of conditions and constraints (such as the degree of the organization's technical orientation, its ties to political leadership, its importance to the rest of the government and basic agreement about the organization's goals within the top political leadership).

Secondly, the degree to which these processes were in evidence at lower levels of governments should be investigated: did, for example, provincial and county governments attempt their own versions of creating institutional breakthroughs on a smaller scale? Recent work on Guangxi and Guangdong suggests that provincial leaders in these provinces were at least as influenced by the military, obsessed with increased administrative efficiency, effectiveness and control over subordinate levels of government, and drawn to strategies of mobilization and normative commitment generation from below as was the central government.[46] But the provincial leadership of Guangdong and Guangxi was intimately connected to the KMT Party. Little is known of the possible variations in other, less KMT-dominated provinces of China, and still less about the details of local government strategies of institutionalization.

Thirdly, there is at present no work concerning two issues of fundamental importance. Nothing has been published that describes the policy-making process in a systematic fashion, nor are there any studies that lay out the linkages and information flows between central, provincial and local levels of government. In the Nanjing Decade "Shanghai mayors were no more than higher civil servants of the state," and presided over administrations run primarily on patronage, yet the Shanghai municipal government successfully resisted KMT Party pressure and achieved substantial results.[47] The large and populous province of Sichuan resisted the central government for so long that National Government administrators were only allowed into the province at all in 1936. But resistance to party indoctrination or central government expansion reveals little about communication, integration, local autonomy, and how policy was made and transmitted thoughout the layers of Republican-era government, and research in this area is much needed.

Finally, re-assessment of Republican China also demands re-consideration of fundamental issues of continuity and change in China's 20th-century revolution. As more empirical work is done on Republican-era government the implications of the findings for the post-1949 governments in both the People's Republic and in Taiwan must be considered. Even this preliminary assessment of Republican government suggests that there were continuities in substantial parts of the pre and post-1949 government agenda. Further, in the Republican period one can see in outline many of the trends and processes that would become immeasurably sharpened in the post-1949 People's Republic. Certainly, tensions between party indoctrination/normative generation of commitments and Weberian/technocratic approaches to state-building were in evidence in

46. See Eugene Levich, *The Kwangsi Way in Kuomintang China, 1931–39* (Armonk: M.E. Sharpe, 1993), and John Fitzgerald, *Awakening China: Politics, Culture and Class in the Nationalist Revolution* (Stanford: Stanford University Press, 1997).

47. Christian Henriot, *Shanghai, 1927–37: Municipal Power, Locality, and Modernization* (Berkeley: University of California Press, 1993), pp. 232–38.

Chinese government well before the articulation of the ideal of "Red and Expert" in the People's Republic of China of the 1950s.[48] If "Red and Expert," so long considered an essential of the ethos and problems of government in the revolutionary People's Republic, can be shown to have at least parallel institutional origins in the "non-revolutionary" KMT Republic of China, perhaps other aspects of state and society will be revealed to have significant continuities across the divide of 1949 as well.

48. For the original, and still extremely important Western analysis of the "Red and Expert" dichotomy in the People's Republic, see Franz Schurmann, *Ideology and Organization in Communist China*, 2nd ed. (Berkeley: University of California Press, 1966, 1968), pp. 162–172 and 75–76.

# The Military in the Republic

Hans van de Ven

In England in the late 1920s, authors like Siegfried Sassoon, Robert Graves and Edmund Blunden began to write about their experiences at the front of the Great War. They did not settle simply for a pacifist condemnation, but said goodbye to an old world of faith in progress and optimism about the future. A general questioning of the nature of the individual, the possibility of the good and the value of civilization followed in literature and elsewhere. A new sensibility especially of the individual but also of modernity and the nation was then formulated.[1] Part of the new understanding was that an army could only serve to overcome the forces of militaristic and perverted societies. Military conflict was at best a temporarily inevitable aberration.

In China the perspective on war has been strikingly different. Following the First World War pacifist voices speaking of harmonious Eastern cultures could be heard, but they did not last nor were they dominant. As in the West before the First World War, many saw the military as a symbol of modern values, advanced organizational practices and a patriotism that in society at large remained largely latent. The war itself and the rise of the warlords did counter the naive militarism of this period, but Nationalists and Communists alike believed not only in the inevitability of war but also in its positive potential. Armies were not merely the necessary instruments to overcome opposition and secure the new order, though even as such their armies, because of their size, needs in terms of human and material resources, and warfare, had very important implications for Chinese society, state structures and politics. But part of the revolutionary perception was also the belief in a violent catharsis as a positive process in which old, backward and inequitable practices would be eradicated. For both the Nationalists and the Communists their armies and military ways of operating served as models for imitation and sources of values and practices. During the War of Resistance against Japan warfare was easily embraced as simply a duty to China as a nation and civilization. Patriotic themes, heroism and sacrifice for the nation were the dominant themes in popular culture, drama and literature.[2]

In 20th-century Chinese literature the depiction of war is not simplistically positive. In Mao Dun's *Midnight*, Lu Xun's short stories and Ba Jin's *Family*, warfare and soldiers are pictured as products of the old

1. Paul Fussell, *The Great War and Modern Memory* (Oxford: Oxford University Press, 1975).

2. Hung Chang-tai, *War and Popular Culture* (Berkeley: University of California Press, 1994) and "The politics of songs," in *Modern Asian Studies*, Vol. 30, No. 4 (1996), pp. 901–930. There were of course significant dissenting voices, such as those of Zhou Zuoren in literature.

© The China Quarterly, 1997

Chinese culture and society. The implicit message is that in the future war and the military will not be necessary. The incidence of warfare is treated as an indication of the barbarity and backwardness of contemporary society. In these works, and especially so in the writings of Lao She and Qian Zhongshu, warfare is an alienating agent, severing a natural intimacy between the protagonists and their world, and implicitly between the author, who knows of a better future, and his society.[3] Thus the purpose of this article is certainly not to argue that China was militaristic in the same way as Prussian or Nazi Germany.[4] Foreign pressures forced a militarization upon China which in the case of Germany resulted from expansionist tendencies. And the worst features of Chinese militarism were unleashed within China in periods of civil war, rather than elsewhere outside China. But in the late Qing and again after the rise of the Nationalists and Communists, dominant perceptions of how to construct a state or conduct revolution did view the military as the midwife of a modern and cohesive China.

Besides drawing attention to this faith in the military as an instrument and model, this article also seeks to indicate the significance of the military in shaping the Republic institutionally, economically and politically. It drove state-building, altered modes of political organization and action, affected school curricula, moulded managerial habits, and propelled economic development. The impact of both militarism – respect for martial values and attitudes promoted in the military – and the militarization of Chinese society – the spread of organizational techniques, routines and attitudes characteristic of the military to other realms – have been profound. The command economy, work units, commune cafeterias and production campaigns illustrate the influence of military models during the 1950s. In the 1960s many genuinely wanted to imitate Lei Feng, and the Cultural Revolution relied heavily on the People's Liberation Army's (PLA) past for its models. It was also during the Cultural Revolution that the PLA stepped in and actually ran most of the major work units in Chinese cities, thus stopping the slide into destructive chaos. Fashions too derived from the military. Even if the PLA is now less genuinely popular, the rhetoric of many newspapers, the continued supply of rationed commodities through the work unit, the organization of production and the military past of such a company as Panda Electronics, which previously built communications equipment for the army,

3. On Lao She, see David Der Wei Wang, *Fictional Realism in Twentieth-Century China: Mao Dun, Lau She, Shen Congwen* (New York: Columbia University Press, 1992). I am indebted to Susan Daruvala for pointing out this work and for help with this paragraph.

4. The term militarism is difficult to define. In European history and in political science, where of course Prussian and Nazi militarism have been the focus of attention, it is often used to refer to the domination of the political by the military. A good discussion of the term and of German militarism can be found in Volker Berghahn, *Militarism* (New York: St Martin's Press, 1982). Militarism has also been interpreted as the political domination of the military. Here I use militarism more broadly, to refer to the appreciation of qualities normally associated with the military. By militarization I mean the imitation of organizational and attitudinal principles outside the military. For classic study of the influence of managerial habits of the modern military in other spheres of life, see William McNeil, *The Pursuit of Power* (Oxford: Blackwell, 1982).

continue to inscribe a recent past heavily shaped by the military in the daily life of China today.

*The Modern Military*

During and after the Taiping Rebellion of 1852–64 the first efforts were undertaken to create modern army units and a modern navy. Western models of training were adopted by some units, the Jiangnan and Fuzhou arsenals produced Western-type armaments, and defensive installations along the coast and along the Chang River (easily navigable by the ever more powerful foreign navies) were updated. But it was only after the modern navy that Li Hungzhang had carefully built up was sunk and its forces on land defeated during the first Sino-Japanese War of 1894–95 that military modernization and expansion became accepted as an absolute urgency.[5] The cessation of Taiwan as well as the loss of effective control over Korea and important parts of Manchuria meant that China had lost control of the Yellow Sea and that Beijing could be easily attacked by a naval expeditionary force. The Allied occupation of Beijing during the Boxer Rebellion illustrated the point. The scramble for concessions that followed the first Sino-Japanese War illustrated not only that the capital was far from safe but that fiscally and strategically important areas along the coast and along China's rivers too could not be defended. The disorder and rebellion of the Boxer Uprising also made clear that the Qing was in danger once more of losing control of local society, this time close to the capital. This context justified the adoption, finally, of radically new approaches, not just in the military but in other areas as well. The New Policies envisaged profound changes to China's constitution, including the creation of a national military, constitutional government and a new, Western-style educational system. By the time of the 1911 Revolution, the fate of the revolution was decided by the new military men in Beijing and in the provinces.[6]

The build-up of the modern military after 1895 is usually described from the perspective of the rise of the warlords.[7] As Arthur Waldron and

5. On the war, see Allen Fung, "Testing the self-strengthening: the Chinese Army in the Sino-Japanese War of 1894–95," in *Modern Asian Studies*, Vol. 30, No. 4 (1996), pp. 1007–32.

6. Ralph Powell, *The Rise of Chinese Military Power, 1895–1912* (Princeton: Princeton University Press, 1955); Stephen McKinnon, *Power and Politics in Late Imperial China: Yuan Shih-k'ai in Beijing and Tienjin* (Berkeley: University of California Press, 1980); Edmund Fung, *The Military Dimension of the Chinese Revolution* (Vancouver: University of British Columbia, 1980); Republican History Section, Modern History Institute of the Chinese Academy of Social Sciences, *Zhonghua minguo shi ziliao conggao, zhuanti ziliao xuanji, qingmo xinjun bianlian yange* (*A Draft Collection of Sources for the History of the Chinese Republic: Collections of Sources on Specialized Topics: History of the Establishment and Training of the New Army during the Late Qing and Early Republic*) (Beijing: Zhonghua shuju, 1978). See also the works mentioned in n. 7.

7. Wen Gongzhi, "Zuijin sanshinian Zhongguo junshi shi" ("The history of the Chinese military in the previous 30 years"), republished in Zhong Bofeng and Li Zongyi (eds.), *Beiyang junfa* (Wuhan: Wuhan Press, 1989), Vol. 1, pp. 1–18; Jerome Chen, *The Military–Gentry Coalition* (Toronto: University of Toronto and York University, 1979); Jiang Kefu, *Minguo junshishi luegao* (Beijing: Zhonghua shuju, 1987); Lai Xinxia, *Beiyang junfa*

Edward McCord have pointed out, the term was always political.[8] In the 1920s the Nationalists and the Communists applied the derogatory label "warlord" (*junfa*) to the power-holders of the time. The label suggested that they were in power only because they controlled military force, that their rule was corrupt and exploitative, and that they did nothing to foster progress or protect the nation from outside threats. From this perspective, armies recruited to fight the warlords were easily justified as combating warlord brutality and fighting for national rejuvenation, modernity and justice. The new armies were of course not seen in the same way in the late Qing and early Republic itself.

It is worth nothing that the image of a Qing China always vulnerable to foreign attack and a West inevitably victorious against any Chinese army needs to be re-examined on the basis of precise analyses of the causes of China's defeats. Clearly, by the end of the 19th century, industrialization, increased managerial efficiency, strengthened state capacity and developments in medicine to protect soldiers against disease did make European armies superior to many non-Western ones and able to invade other countries at will.[9] But China was capable even in the post-Taiping period of defending its interests in Xinjiang. If China's coastal vulnerability to the attack by a modern navy was demonstrated during the Opium War, this was possible only because of the very recent invention of the steam-driven gun-boat,[10] and this threat was confined to areas with navigable rivers. If not insignificant, only the first Sino-Japanese War made clear to both Chinese and foreigners that the occupation of substantial parts of China was possible.

Li Hungzhang's combination of naval development, strengthening of coastal fortifications and limited adoption of Western infantry training methods may well have been adequate to the actual threat and the nature of war in the 1870s and 1880s. It was also politically and fiscally feasible. The Qing court was afraid of the devolution of military power. Because of the constraints of central fiscal resources, the only way that China could build up its forces was to rely on regional financial resources. Demobilization of the existing Green Standard and Banner forces to finance military modernization was difficult. Although their ineffectiveness was widely recognized, it also was clear that their dispersal would merely swell the ranks of bandit gangs. The strategy did fail dramatically during the 1894–95 Sino-Japanese War. Why is not yet entirely clear.

---

*footnote continued*

*shigao* (*Draft History of the Northern Warlords*) (Beijing, 1983); Li Xin, "Beiyang junfa de xingwang" ("The rise and fall of the northern warlords)", in Li Xin and Li Zongyi (eds.), *Zhonghua minguoshi dierbian: beiyang zhengfu tongzhi shiqi* (*The History of the Republic of China, Part 2: The Period of the Regime of the Northern Government*) (Beijing: Zhonghua shuju, 1987), Vol. 1, pp. 1–18.

8. Arthur Waldron, "The warlord: twentieth century Chinese understandings of violence, militarism, and imperialism," *The American Historical Review*, Vol. 96 (October 1991), pp. 1073–1100; and Edward McCord, "Warlords against warlords," in van de Ven, *Modern Asian Studies*, special issue on war in modern China.

9. Daniel Headrick, *Tools of Empire: Technology and European Imperialism* (New York: Oxford University Press, 1981).

10. *Ibid.*; McNeil, *Pursuit of Power*, pp. 223–261.

Failure to keep its navy technologically up-to-date was very important to China's defeat in 1895, especially because naval capabilities advanced dramatically in the decade preceding the war. Problems in the training of naval officers, cowardice and difficulties in co-ordinating different naval forces and China's forces on land may have played a role as well.[11] In any case, a re-evaluation of the military strategy and policies pursued by the self-strengtheners in the context of the real nature of the threats that China faced seems necessary.

One consequence of the defeat and the Boxer Uprising was the rise of a group of modernizing officials including Yuan Shikai, Xu Shichang, Xiong Xiling and many others. These were the men who took charge of remoulding the institutions of the empire in the hope of securing it once more on firm if drastically altered foundations. Military academies were established, the military re-organized along Western lines, and Western training manuals translated and distributed.[12] Arms were purchased abroad or manufactured in China.[13] As mentioned, the traditional examination system was abolished and efforts made to broaden education and introduce a Western curriculum. Financial reform aimed at increasing central revenue and reducing corruption. Elites were drawn into the political system. They were permitted to tax local society and manage it, partly because Western countries and Japan suggested that this increased national strength.[14] It also was a way to reduce the financial burdens on the central state and shift them to provincial ones.[15]

A recent M.Phil. dissertation by Fang Kuo'an showed that in the last decade of the Qing the reappraisal of martial values became a preoccupation of leading intellectuals. Reformist thinkers such as the influential Kang Youwei and Liang Qichao, as well as Zhang Zhidong, one of the most powerful officials at the time, all believed that for China to become strong, it was necessary for the martial element of Chinese culture to be reinvigorated. Zhang wrote an influential essay making this point and took in hand the creation of a modern army with a supporting industry in central China. Schools established at this time included classes for physical and military exercises. Live ammunition was used in some. New textbooks promoted such martial qualities as discipline, aggression, sacrifice and daring. Japanese militarism impressed Chinese students studying in Japan, and they organized a student army at the time of the

11. Fung, "Testing the self-strengthening"; Qi Qizhang, *Jiawu zhanzheng shi* (Beijing, 1990).

12. Military manuals of the late Qing are reproduced in *Zhongguo bingshu jicheng* (*Collection of Chinese Military Writings*) (Beijing: PLA Press, 1991 and after), Vol. 50.

13. Udo Ratenhof, *Die Chinapolitik des Deutschen Reiches, 1887–1945* (Boppard am Rhein: Boldt, 1987)

14. Douglas Reynoulds, *China, 1898–1912; The Xinzheng Revolution and Japan* (Cambridge, MA: Harvard University Press, 1993); Philip Kuhn, "Local self-government under the Republic," in Frederic Wakeman and Carolyn Grant (eds.), *Conflict and Control in Late Imperial China* (Berkeley: University of California Press, 1975), pp. 257–298; Chang P'eng-yuan, *Lixianpai yu xinhai geming* (*The Constitutionalists and the 1911 Revolution*) (Taipei: Foundation for the Promotion of Chinese Scholarship, 1969).

15. Hans van de Ven, "Public finance and the rise of warlordism," *Minguo yanjiu*, Vol. 1 (1994), pp. 89–137 and Vol. 4 (forthcoming).

Russo-Japanese War fought in Manchuria. Student journals and even national and provincial publications frequently sounded militarist themes. Phrases such as national militarism (*minguojun zhuyi*) and nationalist military education (*junguomin jiaoyu*) became common.[16]

The linkage of respect for martial qualities with reform and revolution was an important characteristic of the new thinking. In *The Renewal of the People* Liang Qichao treated modern education, the fostering of a spirit of nationalism, political reform and the revival of martial attitudes as part of the same package.[17] Cai E was a disciple of Liang who led the powerful Yunnan Army in rebellion against Yuan Shikai and helped bring about his downfall in 1916. Writing in Liang's journal in 1902, Cai argued that militarist education would nurture the forces of revolution: "to train a good soldier is actually to train a good citizen."[18] To many, the military was a model for a modern, cohesive and orderly China.

Self-strengtheners like Li Hongzhang believed that a modern, industrial and prosperous China would come about in a process of gradual construction. This view continued to shape the minds of late Qing and early Republican leaders like Kang Youwei and Yuan Shikai. But at the same time, Benjamin Schwartz has pointed out, as repeated defeats lent a sense of urgency to the strengthening of China, strengthened by the social-Darwinism of this time with its notions of the survival of the fittest, a militarist view of how to achieve a modern and strong China emerged.[19] The future became imagined as one in which military conflict and armies played an important role. Like Lenin in Russia, revolutionaries like Sun Yat-sen, members of the Tongmenghui and others became convinced that an oppressive political order prevented the realization in China of the forces of progress. Only a violent uprising by a secretive but cohesive force could remove the blockage. Assassinations of high officials followed and revolutionary parties were established.[20]

### *The Warlords*

The naive faith in the military as a positive institution was brought into disrepute by the First World War and by warlordism. While some would argue that the warlord era began properly only in 1916 following the death of Yuan Shikai, it is clear that military leaders increased their

16. Fang Guo'an, "Qingmo minchu Zhongguo junguomin jiaoyu zhi yanjiu" ("An investigation of the Chinese militarist education in the Late Qing and Early Republic"), M.Phil. dissertation, Chinese Culture College, 1976.

17. Liang Qichao, "Shangwulun" ("On appreciating martial qualities") in *Yingbingshi congshu* (*Collected Works from the Ice-Cream Parlour*) (Shanghai: Commercial Press, 1916), Vol. 1.

18. Tien Chen-ya, *Chinese Military Theory: Ancient and Modern* (Stevenage: SPA Books, 1992), p. 132.

19. Benjamin Schwartz, "Themes in intellectual history: May Fourth and after," in John Fairbank (ed.), *The Cambridge History of China* (Cambridge: Cambridge University Press, 1983), pp. 408–418.

20. For the rise of China's revolutionary tradition, see Michael Gasster, "The Republican revolutionary movement," in John Fairbank (ed.), *The Cambridge History of China*, Vol. 11 (Cambridge: Cambridge University Press, 1980), pp. 463–534.)

authority significantly during the 1911 Revolution in many provinces.[21] If following Yuan's death there were more wars, men with military backgrounds dominated from the 1911 Revolution until Chiang Kai-shek's military unification of China in 1926–28. The period continues to be thought of in starkly negative terms. Many Chinese histories write about the warlord period as the time when the worst aspects of China were brought out: lack of concern for the nation, lawlessness, social disorder, corruption, factionalism and lack of any moral concerns. Images of gross brutality, arbitrariness, intrigue and assassination continue to come to mind.[22] Recent scholarship has begun to explain the origins of warlordism in other terms than moral perversity, sees connections with earlier and later periods, and assesses its impact more evenly. While there are good reasons to avoid the term warlord, this article continues to use it, as it has become a household term and no alternative has yet been established.

An important new trend in warlord scholarship, exemplified by the Nanjing historian Cai Shaoqing and Philip Billingsley, is the study of its links with banditry.[23] The last decade of the Qing and the early Republic saw the rapid expansion of banditry and social disorder. The broad causes were population growth, governmental breakdown, tax increases and perhaps changes in trading patterns, but the build-up of modern infantry armies, warfare and revolution also contributed. Soldiers turned deserter before battle and had to make a living as bandits. Even those who did remain with their units often ended up as bandits because demobilization was rarely managed well. If war fed banditry, banditry fuelled militarization because local elites with the support of government resorted to the old practice of setting up militias to protect local society. The strong point of this approach is that while the warlord period continues to be portrayed as morally bankrupt, the causes of chaos are not reduced simplistically to the moral failings of warlords.

Two issues that will repay further study are the financial background to warlordism and regional politics. In explaining the breakdown of the

21. For a review of the debate on the significance of the 1911 Revolution in the rise of warlordism, see Lai Xinxia, *Beiyang junfa shigao*, pp. 3–14.

22. See n. 7 for the most influential writings on warlordism in Chinese. See also the biographies of individual warlords, for instance in the series edited by Zhang Xianwen and Huang Meizhen, *Zhonghua minguoshi congshu* (*Collection of Writings on the History of the Republic of China*), such as Jiang Shunxing *et al.*, *Shanxi wang Yan Xishan* (*Yan Xishan: the King of Shanxi*) (Zhengzhou: Henan People's Press, 1990); Lu Weijun and Wang Degang, *Feng Guozhang he Zhixi junfa* (*Feng Gouzhang and Zhixi Warlords*) (Zhengzhou: Henan People's Press, 1993). The best works in English are Donald Gillin, *Warlord: Yen Hsi-shan in Shansi Province, 1991–1949* (Princeton: Princeton University Press, 1976); Gavan McCormack, *Chang Tso-lin in Northeast China, 1911–1928* (Folkestone: Dawson and Sons, 1977); James Sheridan, *Chinese Warlord: The Career of Feng Yu-hsiang* (Stanford: Stanford University Press, 1966); Donald Sutton, *Provincial Militarism and the Chinese Republic: The Yunnan Army* (Ann Arbor: University of Michigan Press, 1980); Odoric Y. K. Wou, *Militarism in Modern China: The Career of Wu P'ei-fu* (Folkestone: Dawson and Sons, 1978); Diana Lary, *Region and Nation: the Kwangsi Clique in Chinese Politics, 1925–1937* (Cambridge: Cambridge University Press, 1974); Ch'i Hsi-sheng, *Warlord Politics in China, 1916–28* (Stanford: Stanford University Press, 1976).

23. Cai Shaoqing, *Minguo shiqi de tufei* (*Local Bandits during the Republican Period*) (Beijing: The People's University of China Press, 1993); Phil Billingsley, *Bandits in Republican China* (Stanford: Stanford University Press, 1988), esp. pp. 15–40 and 193–226.

central government after the 1911 Revolution, too little attention has been paid to the enormous fiscal crisis that Beijing faced at the time. China had virtually no foreign debt before the Sino-Japanese War, but afterwards it escalated as a result of the imposition of indemnities (the Boxer indemnities were especially heavy) and borrowing during the crisis of the 1911 Revolution. One consequence was that provincial governments, which controlled large financial resources themselves because of the devolved nature of China's traditional taxation system, became involved in the build-up of new forces. Late Qing and early Republican budgets reveal that the central government controlled only one-third of all military finances. Large portions of China's modern army were financed by and therefore closely associated with regional powerholders. A further consequence was that severe financial shortages forced the late Qing authorities and the Yuan Shikai government to seek radical changes in taxation. Yuan even attempted a cadastral survey with the aim of eradicating local profiteering from the land tax and increasing land tax revenues. No government had even contemplated so difficult an action since a similar attempt had to be abandoned in the early Qing.[24] Such efforts placed the relation between the centre and the provinces under great stress. These relations had already become strained because of Yuan Shikai's attempt to remove the military figures that had collaborated with revolutionary and constitutionalist groups during the 1911 Revolution from their provincial posts and his closure of provincial and local assemblies.

In contrast to the national and local level, good studies of the provincial level of Chinese politics are rare.[25] The question of why militarists came to dominate at this level is important especially because historians of, for instance, South America have suggested that nationalism developed first at that level and not at the local or central one.[26] That in China this was a possibility is suggested by the emergence at this time of provincial assemblies and provincial hierarchies that administered education, promoted provincial economies and sought to ensure local order through the modern police and the militia. Newspapers and periodicals too were often regional in focus. The fiscal crisis and the competition for revenue between regions and the centre possibly stimulated regional cohesion. The New Policies also had the effect of strengthening provinces, as they assigned important administrative tasks to the provincial administrative hierarchies, including in such areas as local security, education and taxation. The relation of the military with provincial centres of political and economic power remains to be studied, but it is possible that in some places the provincial military helped protect regional and local interests against the escalating demands of the centre. An

24. Hans van de Ven, "Public finance," *Minguo yanjiu*, Vol. 1 (1994), pp. 116–128.

25. But see John Fincher, *Chinese Democracy: The Self-Government Movement in Local, Provincial, and National Politics* (London: Croom Helm, 1981) and Roger Thompson, *China's Local Councils in the Age of Constitutional Reform* (Cambridge, MA: Harvard University Press, 1995).

26. David Brading, *The First America: The Spanish Monarchy, Creole Patriots, and the Liberal State* (Cambridge: Cambridge University Press, 1992).

important question is why this may have been the case to a greater degree in places like Manchuria, Yunnan, Sichuan, Shanxi, Guangdong and Guangxi, and not for instance in Jiangsu.

Exciting new trends in warlord studies are the examination of the actual wars and their effects on China economically and ideologically. In a groundbreaking study of warfare in 1924 between two warlord factions, the Fengtian and Zhili factions of Zhang Zuolin and Wu Peifu, Arthur Waldron argued that the arms race between warlords contributed to industrialization. Modern industries were first established in China after the Taiping Rebellion, but in the 1920s an arms race developed in China as armies expanded and new weapons were introduced. In the early 1920s, warlord wars began to involve increasing numbers of soldiers. The Zhili and Fengtian factions both mobilized several hundred thousand soldiers. They used machine guns, mortars, rifles, trains, armoured trucks and aeroplanes. They were supplied in part by arms imported from abroad – Western arms manufactureres found China an attractive area for arms sales and breaking the embargo was easy – but also by large arsenals in Shenyang, Wuhan and Shanghai, and minor ones in other places. Iron and coal mining flourished as their products were consumed in large quantities by these arsenals. Because primary resources had to be transported over large areas, warlordism might in fact have contributed to China's commercialization.[27] More research will need to be done before there can be a reasonable estimate of the contribution to China's GNP of arms industries in the 1920s. But as elsewhere the needs of the modern army helped drive China's industrialization.[28]

According to Waldron, the increased size and destructiveness of warfare in the 1920s, when Chinese wars began to follow the First World War patterns, helped create an environment in which especially China's urbanites rejected the power-holders of the day and condemned them as warlords. Thus the May Thirtieth movement of 1925 brought students, professionals, entrepreneurs and workers together in massive strikes aimed against foreigners and warlords. The language of those that spoke of warlords now began to make sense to many. The Nationalist government would not have been established without this decisive change in public mood, or at least not have been founded so quickly. Nor could the Communists have begun to build a mass following.[29] Other factors were important, such as the lack of a clear legitimating device for the authorities of the time, a history of mutual conflict and economic downturn. The growth of the press, the spread of modern schools and the establishment of universities provided an infrastructure for the fashioning of "public opinion" and made it politically relevant. But Waldron surely is right that increasingly destructive war caused widespread dissatisfaction and made many willing to consider radical alternatives.

27. Arthur Waldron, *China's Turning Point* (Cambridge: Cambridge University Press, 1995), ch. 3.

28. For the British case, see McNeil, *The Pursuit of Power*.

29. Waldron, *China's Turning Point*, pp. 241–280. On the use by the Chinese Communists of the movement, see Hans van de Ven, *From Friend to Comrade* (Berkeley: University of California Press, 1991), ch. 4.

Anti-warlordism, as Edward McCord pointed out, became an important ingredient of the ideologies of both the Kuomintang (KMT) and the Chinese Communist Party (CCP) in the 1920s. One of the lasting consequences of warlord warfare was that the innocent militarism of the reformers and revolutionaries of the late Qing and early Republic was rejected. Militarist values remained important, but a purely militarist solution to China's problems became impossible. The overcoming of the warlord period remains an important idea in the commonly asserted conceptualizations of China.

### *The Militarization of Revolution*

It was on 7 August 1927 that Mao Zedong famously declared that "power comes out of the barrel of the gun."[30] He made this statement at an emergency CCP meeting following the KMT's decision to end the united front and attempt the CCP's extermination. Until 1927 the strategy of the Chinese Communists had anticipated that they would seize power in the same way as the Bolsheviks in Russia in a moment of mass unrest in urban centres. Mao's statement illustrated the growing awareness in the CCP that in China by that time mass movements alone could not deliver power. Only a party in control of its own armies, as the KMT was, could succeed. This realization was just as important as the discovery of the peasantry as a base for the making of revolution.

If 1927 was important as the year in which the CCP began to construct its own armed forces, as it did during the 1 August uprising at Nanchang in Jiangxi province, it would be wrong to believe that the year marked the beginning of the CCP's militarization. As mentioned, already in the late Qing revolutionaries had begun to conceive of the transition towards a new future in violent terms. Furthermore, when Chinese Communists began to organize their party – and the same is true for the KMT – they set up an institution that was modelled after the modern military. When Lenin wrote *What is to be Done?* in 1902, the party that he depicted borrowed heavily from the model of the Prussian army. The party was to have a clear chain of command. Discipline was crucial and was to be maintained rigorously. A small group of seasoned Communists – later institutionalized as the Politburo – was to oversee the current historical situation much as a general staff might assess the strengths and weaknesses of its side and the enemy, and then lay down a strategy to be implemented by all party units. The party was to relate to society in the same way as the modern army. It was to be an institution separate from society with its own culture and rules; yet for its success it depended on mobilizing society. Party members were to be like soldiers: the proud

30. "Mao Zedong guanyu gongchan guoji daibiao baogao de fayan" ("Mao Zedong's remarks concerning the report of the representative of the Communist International"), in Committee for the Compilation of Sources for Party History, CCP Central Committee (eds.), *Baqi huiyi* (*The August Seven Conference*) (Beijing: Sources for Party History Press, 1986), p. 58.

representatives of a modern, rational and energetic new world, and at the same time faceless cogs-in-the-wheel in the party machinery. Conceptualizations of violence too were militaristic, as mentioned. Revolution became an act of violence and struggle in which the new would conquer the old because it was more vigorous, aggressive, fair and suited to the modern, while the old was decadent, cowardly and exploitative. For revolutionaries the violence of revolution was an opportunity for self-realization and self-validation.

Initial CCP strategy aimed at recreating the model of the October Revolution. That is, it was to achieve political power in a wave of urban uproar, and then establish a military to consolidate its regime. The idea that the CCP was to have its own army was promoted partly by the Comintern itself. In August 1925 it sent instructions to the CCP to take the organization of its own military force in hand.[31] Students at Sun Yat-sen University in Moscow, who received military instruction, probably strengthened the tendency as well. The example of Sun Yat-sen and the KMT may also have been on the minds of Chinese Communists, especially those who worked in Guangdong in the 1925–27 period. Sun Yat-sen had learned from the KMT's failure to capture power during the 1911 Revolution that it needed its own military force. While first seeking to turn a warlord army into a KMT army, with Russian help he began to train his own army in Guangdong in the 1920s. The Whampoa Academy was to provide the officer corps.

The context of the late 1920s and 1930s was crucial to the entrenchment of militarized notions of revolution and of giving these a base in reality. The following paragraphs focus on a broad outline of the 1927 to 1935 period when there was a build-up of bases in central and south China.[32] This will make clear that the much better-known social and economic policies of the Yan'an period,[33] CCP policies and practices in

31. "Gongchan guoji zhixing weiyuanhui dongfangbu guanyu Zhongguo gongchandang junshi gongzuo de zhishi caoan" ("Draft instruction of the eastern department of the Executive Committee of the Comintern regarding the military work of the Chinese Communist Party"). I am grateful to Li Yuzhen, the Chinese translator of this instruction, which will shortly be published together with other Comintern sources, for making this text available.

32. Important new sources for the study of the Central Soviet include Central Committee Archives (eds.), *Zhonggong zhongyang wenjian xuanji* (*Selected CCP Central Committee Documents*) (Beijing: Central Party School Press, 18 vols, 1989–92), Vols.4–10 (*ZZWX*). A good introduction to the history of the PLA is Mo Yang *et al.* (eds.), *Zhongguo renmin jiefangjun zhanshi* (*The Battle History of the PLA*) (Beijing: Military Sciences Press, 3 vols, foreword 1987); Jiangxi Provincial Archives (eds.), *Zhongyang geming genjudi shiliao xuanbian* (Nanchang: Jiangxi People's Press, 1986, 3 vols.); History Department of Xiamen University and Fujian Provincial Archives (eds.), *Zhongguo suweiai gongheguo fahui wenjian xuanbian* (Nanhang: Jiangxi People's Press, 1984); and Women's Association of Jiangxi (eds.), *Jiangxi suqu funü yundong shiliao xuanbian* (*Selected Historical Sources for the Women's Movement in Jiangxi Soviets*) (Nanchang: Jiangxi People's Press, 1982).

33. For Yan'an, see Mark Selden, *The Yenan Way in Revolutionary China* (Cambridge, MA: Harvard University Press, 1971); David Apter and Tony Saich, *Revolutionary Discourse in Mao's Republic* (Cambridge, MA: Harvard University Press, 1994); Ch'en Yung-fa, *Yan'an de yinxiang* (*Yan'an's Shadows*) (Taipei: Institute of Modern History, Academia Sinica, 1990): Joseph Esherick, "Deconstructing the construction of the party state," *The China Quarterly*, No. 140 (December 1994), pp. 1025–52. For a general overview of the period, see Lyman Van Slyke, "The Chinese Communist Movement during the Sino-Japanese

the early decades of the PRC, and the Cultural Revolution have a long history of militarization behind them. The excesses of the "southern phase" of the Communist revolution did constitute a lesson and policies were changed. But nevertheless some basic patterns proved enduring.

After 1927 the KMT haunted Chinese Communists out of the cities. Small and scattered Communist forces fought for survival in central China. They had to withstand attacks not only by the KMT and provincial military units, but also by local militia and bandit gangs. Nationalist attacks became ever larger and involved new ways of waging war, including the use of propaganda and economic blockade.

The proper role of the military in the making of revolution nevertheless remained a topic of debate at first. Some, like He Mengxiong, argued that revolution could only be based on the urban proletariat. Mao Zedong's famous 1930 letter to Lin Biao, usually referred to as "A Single Spark Can Light a Prairie Fire" upbraided Lin, a brilliant Communist military commander, for pessimism. Lin believed that a Communist army could not emerge before revolution had begun. To build up bases, construct armies and fight in relatively large units seemed to Lin and his supporters unwise.[34] But for Mao the creation of a strong military was an immediate necessity. The issue was at the heart of the famous Gutian Conference of the Fourth Red Army where Mao won the debate and where the Red Army was defined as "the revolutionary army of the workers and peasants," "an army of the soldiers themselves," and the "armed collective for the implementation of the political tasks of its class."[35]

Initially the Red Army, as the PLA was called at the time, consisted of remnants of forces that had participated in the Nanchang Uprising, including former KMT units that had sided with the CCP, as well as peasant militia from Hunan and bandit forces that found it opportune to make common cause with the Communists. Some of the institutional means by which discipline was imposed on these heterogeneous, not necessarily very revolutionary forces are clear. Political education, the inculcation of easily memorized codes of conduct such as The Three Great Disciplines (*San Da Jilü*), and the fostering of a spirit of commit-

---

*footnote continued*
War, 1937–45," in John Fairbank, *et al.* (eds.), *The Cambridge History of China*, Vol. 13 (Cambridge: Cambridge University Press, 1986), pp. 609–722. An important new collection of primary sources is Shaanxi Provincial Archives and Shaanxi Academy of Social Sciences (eds.), *Shaan-Gan-Ning Bianqu zhengfu wenjian xuanbian* (*Selected Documents of the Government of the Shaan-Gan-Ning Border Region*) (Beijing: Archives Press, 13 vols, 1986–1990).

34. "Mao Zedong gei Lin Biao de xin," ("Letter from Mao Zedong to Lin Biao"), *ZZWX*, Vol. 6, pp. 553–563. Dated 5 January 1930.

35. Relevant documents can be found in Party History Institute of the Party School, Fujian Provincial CCP Committee (eds.) *Hongsijun rumin he gutian huiyi wenxian ziliao* (*Documents of and Sources for the Entrance of the Fourth Red Army into Fujian Province and the Gutian Conference*) (Fujian: People's Press, 1979). The first two quotations are from "Zhongguo hongjun disijun (Zhu Mao jun) gao Guomindang jundui shibing shu" ("Letter from the Fourth Red Army (The Zhu [De] and Mao [Zedong] Army) to the officers and soldiers of the KMT armies"), pp. 213–14, dated January 1930. The third quotation is from "Resolutions of the Ninth Party Congress of the Fourth Red Army," *ZZWX*, Vol. 5, pp. 800–835.

ment through drill and joint study formed one element. The construction of a commissar system that required all military orders to be countersigned by a representative of the party also ensured CCP control. This system went down to the company level. Campaigns to weed out "class enemies" from the army were conducted and recruitment orders insisted that new recruits be vetted on their class background. The available data suggest that the efforts to create a class army subservient to political leadership were very serious indeed. This allowed Chinese Communists to think of their army not simply as a mercenary warlord force but as a mass army fighting for a just cause. To underline the difference between the warlord armies and the Red Army, corporal punishment was considered inappropriate and abolished.[36]

Once the initial hesitation was overcome and a vision of a proper Communist army was formulated, the military became regarded as a model. Calls were made for the militarization of the party. Militarization was seen as something progressive and modern which would extinguish laziness, undisciplined behaviour and parochial attachments.[37] Perhaps swept up by the mood of the times but nevertheless not extraordinary was a document of a year later that demanded that all party members undergo military training and that "the party should become a military camp."[38] The ideal Communist was recreated in the image of the soldier. Communists were no longer the thinking, writing intellectuals of the 1920s who organized labour unions and urban strikes, or the rural activist like Peng Pai, but dedicated, optimistic, energetic and orderly soldiers. And those who did not behave in such a way might well be punished by the Red Army's internal police, as documents issued at the eve of the Long March warned.[39]

It was not only the party that was militarized. Both the positive view of militarization and the concrete needs of the Red Army made the militarization of the areas under Communist control nearly inevitable. The CCP quickly drew much of the population into its military machinery. In the early 1930s military service became a legal obligation for all males between the ages of 18 and 45 who were not class enemies.[40] Three

36. A detailed discussion of the early Red Army that is frank about problems of discipline is Chen Yi's 1929 "Guanyu Zhu Mao hongjun de dangwu gaikuang baogao," ("Report on Party affairs in the Red Army of Zhu [De] and Mao [Zedong]"), *ZZWX*, Vol. 5, pp. 749–790. The report was in two parts and dated 1 September 1929. The documents of the Gutian Conference are also useful. For the abolition of corporal punishment, see "Resolutions of the Ninth Party Congress of the Fourth Red Army," *ZZWX*, Vol. 5, pp. 828–831.

37. "Central Committee Announcement Number 29," *ZZWX*, Vol. 5, p. 40. Dated 7 February 1929.

38. "The current political situation and the organizational tasks of the Party," *ZZWX*, Vol. 6, p. 206. Dated 22 July 1930

39. "Political order by the General Political Department regarding preparations for the Long March and struggles," *ZZWX* , Vol. 10, pp. 399; "Instruction regarding political work by the General Political Department for the current attack," ZZWX, Vol. 10, pp. 402–08. Dated 11 October 1934. Signed by Li Fuchun.

40. "The Central Politburo's plan for current work in soviet areas," *ZZWX*, Vol. 6, p. 457. Dated 24 October 1930. On the legal obligation, see "General principles of the Constitution of the Chinese Soviet Republic," *ZZWX*, Vol. 7, p. 774. Dated 7 November 1931. The obligation was expressed as a right.

levels existed: the Red Army was a standing force; at the local level, peasants were organized in militias and were responsible for local security and assistance with transport and reconnaissance when necessary; and between these levels were guerrilla detachments which might leave their home territories and campaign for some time at a distance. If it is unlikely that before 1933 the system's coverage was complete, it no doubt soon became so, as the Fourth Encirclement campaign brought the CCP's bases under such pressure that at least in the Jiangxi Soviet monthly recruitment drives were conducted to supply the front. Numerical targets were set and local party officers were criticized if they did not meet their quota.

Military considerations shaped CCP policies in many areas, including an issue clearly at the heart of the revolution, that of land redistribution. The redistribution of land and the confiscation of landlord property was regarded as a potent way of motivating Red Army soldiers. By securing victory for the CCP they were also securing economic security for themselves and their families. In November 1933, as KMT attacks strengthened, the CCP intensified land confiscation and the extermination of landlords as a way of increasing the population's commitment to the party. In Western scholarship a radical land policy is held partly responsible for the defeat of the Communists in the 1930s. The CCP itself believed that the intensification of revolution would strengthen them.[41] The seizure of landlord property and its redistribution, as well as the assignment of confiscated land to Red Army families, gave soldiers very concrete reasons to see the army as the protector of its own interests.

War was a major reason for a higher level of government control over the economy. No attempt was made to eliminate markets and experiments with the idea were criticized as more damaging than helpful to the Communist economy. But in 1933 Zhang Wentian (Luo Fu), officially the highest ranking CCP member in China, wrote an article that justified bureaucratic management of the economy. Only a few industries, such as the arsenals, a mint and printing plants, were to be owned and managed by the soviet government directly. But the Communist economy would be steered by the CCP. Consumer co-operatives would ensure that surplus production in one area would be transported to deficit areas. Communist administrative organs would provide peasants with seeds, fertilizer, draught animals and tools when necessary. The work of handicraft workers would be directed so as to be of benefit to the front. Ploughing and harvesting campaigns were to be organized at the appropriate time of the year. A Trade Bureau was to take control of trade with non-Communist areas and Grain Adjustment Bureaus would ration grain fairly.[42]

41. See for instance "Letter of instruction by the CCP Central Bureau to all party branches in the soviet areas about the consolidation and development of new areas and border areas," *ZZWX*, Vol. 9, pp. 373–75. Dated 13 November 1933. "Resolution of the Central Bureau of the soviet areas regarding the campaign to investigate land-holding," *ZZWX*, Vol. 9, pp. 206–210. Dated 2 June 1933.

42. Luo Fu (Zhang Wentian), "Lun suweiai jingji fazhan de qiantu" ("On the future development of the soviet economy"), *ZZWX*, Vol. 9, pp. 483–87. Dated 22 April 1933. On a looming economic disaster, problems in feeding the Red Army, and the decision to use campaigns to extract more resources, see "Resolution by the Presidium of the Second Soviet Congress and the CCP Central Committee regarding the assault campaign to secure the

In the areas under CCP control in the early 1930s, bureaucratic networks multiplied, bureaucratic jurisdictions were carefully defined and the compiling of reports according to regular standards was enforced. Routine and regularity were carefully institutionalized. A wonderful example is the Communist officialese of a long document that sets out standards for the classification of the peasantry into classes. Sample cases for the instruction of local party officials were included. The recruitment, training, discipline, equipment and co-ordination of the 100,000 soldiers that set out on the Long March is testimony to the bureaucratic capabilities that the CCP had built up over the preceding years. The adoption of the marriage law, labour laws, setting of rents and so on illustrate how the CCP attempted to create a disciplined population. It is suggested that this bureaucratization of revolution was not necessarily seen as undermining the energy, individuality and independence of revolutionaries. Rather, discipline and order may well have been considered to provide an antidote to a scramble for individual advantage, disorder and corruption that dominated the times. They provided the tough structures, the skeletons, that made it possible for individuals to bring their best into play.

States tend to develop covert institutions and intelligence-gathering networks. These are not peculiar to Communist parties, nor can they be seen as the product of the modern military. At the same time, the violent conception of historical change and the belief in the existence of two antagonistic forces which will deploy any means at their disposal have led Leninist parties to concentrate a great deal of energy on the creation of secret institutions. The violent context of the early 1930s, in which enemies indeed were everywhere, only served to strengthen this tendency. In the 1920s the CCP had already developed secret communications, and violations of party discipline were regarded as extremely serious matters. In the 1930s, as the CCP faced KMT attacks externally and had to guard against many local enemies, the creation of secret party and state organizations came naturally. A secret shadow party existed so that in case of defeat it could continue to work. CCP Protection Bureaus were set up with the power of arrest and interrogation. These units made up an independent internal spy network to be used to combat "counter-revolutionaries."[43] By 1934 Kang Sheng was in charge of a network of Investigation Committees made up of the most reliable CCP members. It reported on all local activities and was responsible for ferreting out internal traitors. These secret services, it must be emphasized, were not in the hands of the military, but of the CCP. A remarkable aspect of the soviet areas of the early 1930s was an intense paranoia that led to witch-hunts. Most famously, several hundred local CCP members during

---

*footnote continued*
provision of the Red Army by completing the sale of public bonds, collecting the land tax, and collection of cereals," *ZZWX*, Vol. 10, pp. 82–86. Dated 23 January 1934.

43. See e.g. "Central Politburo's plan for current work in soviet areas," *ZZWX*, Vol. 6, pp. 440–43. Dated 24 October 1930; "Resolution by the Central Bureau in the soviet area regarding emergency work prior to the decisive battle to smash the fourth encirclement campaign," *ZZWX*, Vol. 9, pp. 64–69. Dated 8 February 1933.

the Futian Incident were murdered. CCP documents insisted again and again that one had to guard against "counter-revolutionaries" in soviet organizations and the CCP itself. A fear of KMT infiltrators, treason by local elites or bandit forces, and mutiny naturally fuelled the CCP's paranoia.[44]

The 1930s provided important lessons. The inability of the Jiangxi hill country, with at most two to three million residents, to support a large army capable of fighting positional warfare made sure that in future army construction the economic capacity of an area was taken into account. Land policies too were moderated, and attempts were made to dampen factional conflict and to limit the killing in dealing with internal problems. Important weight was also given to securing the base of the PLA in local society. But many basic patterns continued and were even intensified.

When the Communists faced a crisis of survival in the north because of Japanese attack and KMT blockade, all of society was drawn into one structure of authority; propaganda, criticism and self-criticism, and drama were used to establish a uniform set of values and norms. The economy was steered centrally so as to maximize the productivity of the area and make it contribute to the war effort. Kang Sheng again oversaw a covert system designed to deal with "counter-revolutionaries." After the CCP's conquest of power in 1949, the techniques that had produced victory were employed in the hope of establishing a revolutionary order in China. The creation of work units, production brigades, production campaigns, and purges of counter-revolutionaries all illustrate the continuing influence of war socialism after 1949. The individual, the private and the market were distrusted, while discipline, the state and the collective were promoted. During periods of crises, the CCP has tended to intensify revolution, as it did during the 1950s when of course it faced real threats, domestically, in Korea and from Taiwan. Only since the death of Mao, the easing of international tensions and especially the wreckage of the Cultural Revolution has the situation changed.

### *The Military and Nationalist China*

In mainland China a more inclusive view of the War of Resistance against Japan has emerged. Rituals commemorate famous generals of the Nationalist army killed in action,[45] source compilations and studies are published about various aspects of the war, and at the same time that the stock of Chiang Kai-shek has declined in Taiwan, it has risen considerably in China itself.[46] The War of Resistance is portrayed as the moment

44. Liu Bingrong, *Zuoqing tongshi* (*The Painful History of Leftist Deviation*) (Shijiazhuang: Huashan Literature and Art Press, 1993, 2 vols.) uses the "narrative literature" genre to portray the various campaigns to eliminate counter-revolutionaries in the Central Soviet.

45. Arthur Waldron, "Zhang Zizhong," in Van de Ven, *Modern Asian Studies*, special issue on war in modern China.

46. The study of the war of resistance has been a major focus of recent Chinese scholarship. Only a few examples can be mentioned here: the Number Two Archives of China (ed.), *KangRi kangzhan zhengmian zhanchang* (*Frontal Battlefields of the War of Resistance*) (Jiangsu guji Press, 1987). This is an important collection of primary sources. The Modern

when China finally pulled itself together after a period of internal feuding, selfishness and wilful destruction; China then earned its right to survive as a nation and a culture. It is now possible to begin to acknowledge the contributions made by all quarters. This reappraisal, the opening of important archives such as the Number Two Archives in Nanjing and the publication of memoirs have led to a revival of war studies in China and the Republican period generally.

That the history of Chiang Kai-shek's Republic was bound up with the military is of course generally recognized. In the West, Lloyd Eastman has made clear that Chiang Kai-shek depended on his control over the Nationalist military. Believing that the Republic could only have prospered if some sort of land redistribution had taken place and proper civil rule established, Eastman faults Chiang for militarizing the government and the party.[47] Ch'i Hsi-sheng showed how Chiang built up large modern forces only to see them destroyed in Shanghai in 1937 and in 1944. The result was, according to Ch'i, a demoralized government that could not combat corruption and was unable to take positive and firm action.

If the importance of the military is no news, the centrality of affairs to the Nationalist government still needs to be studied in detail and analysed in terms of its corrosive effects not just on the KMT or politics generally but also on culture, taxation, commerce, industry, communications, mentalities and so on. The importance of the army is suggested by its sheer

---

History Institute of the Chinese Academy of Social Sciences has compiled collections of source materials on most of the major campaigns that include numerous Japanese documents. For an example see Editorial Group for "Selected Sources for the Taierzhuang Campaign" and the Number Two Archives of China (eds.), *Taierzhuang zhanyi ziliao* (Beijing: Zhuanghua shuju, 1989). The series is part of the Institute's *Zhonghua minguo shi ziliao congshu* (*A Collection of Sources for the History of the Chinese Republic*); an example of a narrative account is Zhang Xianwen *et al.*, *KangRi zhanzheng de zhengmian zhanchang* (*The Frontal Battlefields of the War of Resistance Against Japan*) (Zhengzhou: Henan People's Press, 1987); Department for Military History Research, Academy of Military Science, *Zhongguo KangRi zhanzheng shi* (*The History of China's War of Resistance Against Japan*) (Beijing: PLA Press, 1991); The Society of the Historical Study of the War of Resistance Against Japan and the Museum for the Chinese People's Resistance of the War of Resistance Against Japan (ed.), *Kangzhan shiqi de wenhua jiaoyu* (*Cultural Education during the War of Resistance*) (Beijing: Peking Press, 1995). Geng Chengkuan, *KangRi zhanzheng shiqi de qin Hua ri jun* (*The Japanese Army of Invasion during the War of Resistance Against Japan*) (Beijing: Chunqiu Press, 1987). For an example from Taiwan, see Jiang Yongjin, *Kangzhanshi lun* (*On the War of Resistance*) (Taipei: Datong Dushu Co., 1995). Attention has also been paid to the "puppet" governments. See for instance Huang Meizhen, *Wang Jingwei hanjian zhengquan de xingwang* (*The Rise and Fall of the Regime of the Traitor Wang Jingwei*) (Shanghai: Fudan University Press, 1987). For recent mainland biographies of Chiang Kai-shek, see Number Two Historical Archives of China and Archives Press, *Jiang Jieshi nianpu chugao* (*First Draft of a Chronological Biography of Chiang Kai-shek*) (Beijing: Archives Press, 1992); Song Ping, *Jiang Jieshi zhuan* (*A Biography of Chiang Kai-shek*) (Changchun: Jilin People's Press, 1987); Yang Shubiao, *Jiang Jieshi zhuan* (*A Biography of Chiang Kai-shek*) (Beijing: Unity Press, 1989), and Zhang Xianwen and Fang Qingqiu, *Jiang Jieshi quanzhuan* (*A Complete Biography of Chiang Kai-shek*) (Zhengzhou: Henan People's Press, 1996). *KangRi zhanzheng yanjiu* (*Research on the War of Resistance against Japan*) is an important journal edited at the Modern History Institute of the Chinese Academy of Social Sciences.

47. Lloyd Eastman, *The Abortive Revolution* (Cambridge, MA: Harvard University Press, 1974) and *Seeds of Destruction* (Stanford: Stanford University Press, 1984).

size. In 1928, Chiang Kai-shek commanded an army of 240,000 men, out of a total of two million men under arms in China at this time. Just before war began with Japan, Chiang's forces had reached 450,000. By the end of the war China had some 3.5 million men under arms. This figure included regional armies, many of which continued to be coloured by warlordism. The Central Army itself had 650,000 troops in 1945.[48] Perhaps even more telling is the fact that in 1928, the revenues of the central government were well short of covering army expenditures that year. During the next ten years, 85 per cent of all revenue went to the army. While the financial background of the War of Resistance has not been studied, that the government was bankrupt will be clear from the fact that the loss of Shanghai meant that Chiang lost 85 per cent of his revenues.

Even before the Japanese invasion of China proper, war was nearly constant. Nanjing went to war in 1929 with the Guangxi Clique of Pai Chongxi and Li Zongren who commanded 230,000 troops. Fighting lasted for two months. Two months later Chiang defeated Feng Yuxiang's army of 220,000 troops, in part by securing the defection of nearly half of them. In 1930, war raged for four months between Chiang and a Northern Coalition that had established an alternative government in Beijing. If the Japanese invasion of Manchuria in September 1931 brought about at least a cessation of hostilities between Nanjing and regional forces, the Communists had by this time secured bases in several provinces in central and south China. It took Chiang five campaigns and much hard fighting before in 1934 a force of many hundreds of thousands of troops finally succeeded in closing down most of the bases and forcing the Communists to leave for the north in what has since become known as the Long March. The Japanese invaded China south of the Great Wall only two years later.

What the effects of all this warfare has been remains largely open to question. Even if Prasenjit Duara's work has alerted us to the possibility that more bureaucracy is not necessarily stronger bureaucracy,[49] a perusal of the catalogues of the Number Two Archives suggests that state-building actually did happen during the Nationalist period. The bureaucracy added new areas and new issues to its jurisdiction and range of concerns as Nanjing extended its reach and brought regional oppositions to heel. State expansion possibly happened "in waves," with each wave of warfare and mobilization precipitating bureaucratization and penetration of new regions. Of course war also meant that the regime had to shift its base: until 1937 it was the lower Changjiang area, then the Free China that had its capital in Chongqing in the inland province of Sichuan, and finally back again. The peripatetic nature of the Nationalist government may

48. Eastman, "Nationalist China during the Nanjing decade," in Fairbank, *et al.*, *Cambridge History*, Vol. 13, p. 125 and Eastman, "Nationalist China during the Sino-Japanese War," in *ibid.* p. 552. See also F. F. Liu, *A Military History of Modern China* (Princeton: Princeton University Press, 1956).

49. Prasenjit Duara, *Culture, Power, and the State: Rural North China, 1900–1942* (Stanford: Stanford University Press, 1988).

help to explain why it was not able to consolidate its bureaucratic structures.

War not only had bureaucratic and geographic implications. In the period between the beginning of the Northern Expedition in June 1926, leading to the creation of a new Nationalist government in Nanjing in 1928, and 1933, Chiang Kai-shek fought wars of national unification. It is not likely that this was simply because of his militarist orientation. He continued a trend that had already become entrenched.[50] If Chiang was to conquer the resources to build a strong China, he had to establish his dominance over China's provinces as much of China's fiscal resources were in their control.[51] Chiang was largely successful in that he did emerge from the period as China's strongest military figure. But the expansion of CCP bases in central China, internal KMT dissatisfaction, famine and economic crises all made clear that the defeat of the warlords would not automatically produce a vigorous and modern nation.[52] The Japanese seizure of Manchuria and its attack on Shanghai also pushed Chiang to attempt to develop a more truly nationalistic government.

Chiang Kai-shek's response was multi-faceted and partly modelled on the German example. Hans von Seeckt, who had rebuilt Germany's military after the First World War, visited China in 1934 and presented Chiang with a wide-ranging plan for military reconstruction. Seeckt's plan called for the recruitment of a new elite force of 100,000 men. This army was to be armed by Germany with supplies paid for by the export to Germany of raw materials such as tungsten. China would be helped with the creation of an industrial base, including an iron-and-steel complex, ore-processing facilities, and arsenals for the supply of the army, air-force and navy.[53] Chiang was also a great admirer of Zeng Guofan, the Confucian-minded general who had led the famous Hunan Braves to defeat the Taiping rebels in the middle of the 19th century. Chiang's advocacy of *li*, *yi*, *lian*, *chi* (propriety, justness, honesty and shame) as a core set of Confucian values to guide one's behaviour, the reintroduction of the traditional mutual policing and responsibility system called the *baojia*, and his belief that the spiritual strength and determination of a population unified in ambition and commitment were just as crucial as a well-equipped army, illustrated that background.

The New Life Movement had elements of both the German and Chinese approaches. Its aim was the creation of a population that was disciplined, patriotic and vigorous. The movement hoped first to foster a sense of common destiny and joint purpose between the population and its government and leader. It was to give the regime the mass base that

50. Both Eastman, "Nationalist China during the Nanjing Decade" and Ch'i Hsi-sheng, *Nationalist China at War*, pp. 5–39 stress Chiang's militarizing instincts.

51. See Waldron, *China's Turning Point*, pp. 119–140. Real fiscal shortages probably forced Chiang to demand donations and extort money from the Shanghai bourgeoisie. For Chiang's treatment of the Shanghai bourgeoisie, see Parks Coble, *The Shanghai Capitalists and the Nationalist Government* (Cambridge, MA: Harvard University Press, 1980).

52. William Kirby, *Germany and Republican China* (Stanford: Stanford University Press, 1984), pp. 85–90, 148–166, 176–185.

53. *Ibid.* pp. 122–25.

it lacked, and it was no coincidence that it was inaugurated in the city of Nanchang in Jiangxi province where the CCP had its strongest base. As noted before, the rhetoric of the movement was highly militaristic. Chiang himself declared once that "in the home, the factory, and the government office, everyone's activities must be the same as in the army ... there must be obedience, sacrifice, strictness, cleanliness, accuracy, diligence, secrecy."[54] The disciplining of local society itself was fostered by bureaucratizing local government. Local self-government in which local elites had again involved themselves became a branch of the local government and brought under its control. The sub-county ward (*qu*) became a public security unit that was to maintain order partly through the *baojia*.[55] The Confucian values mentioned above were also promoted. The intrusion of the bureaucracy and the attempt to regulate society occurred in other areas as well. In Shanghai and elsewhere, prostitution was licensed. Universities were brought under state supervision, national universities were established in various provinces, and regulations were issued for curricula. Student political activity was proscribed.[56]

Governmental control over the economy too was strengthened. The army construction programme that was begun with German help in 1934 led in 1935 to the creation of a National Resources Commission. It drafted a five-year plan which focused on the creation of heavy industry especially in inland provinces. Steel, heavy equipment, electricity and mining were emphasized, and a number of important private enterprises were taken over.[57] During and also after the Sino-Japanese War, the National Resources Commission expanded enormously in size until by 1944 it controlled directly 103 manufacturing, mining and electrical enterprises. State production accounted for 35 per cent of all heavy industrial production. War led to the creation of a military-industrial complex and direct state management of important elements of the economy, setting patterns that have continued to mould the economies of mainland China and Taiwan.[58]

As in Communist areas, the secret state too advanced tremendously in the 1930s and subsequently. In the case of the KMT the influence of the military was probably greater in these than in the CCP's case. The Blue Shirts were a secretive organization of young military officers. They controlled political training in the army, but were also involved in the police, schools and the Boy Scouts. The Bureau of Investigation and Statistics, headed by Dai Li, was a secret police dominated by the Blue Shirts. Blue Shirts members believed that the bureaucracy, the KMT and society at large were threatened by internal traitors and weakened by selfish and corrupt people. It was their duty to save China by enforcing

54. Eastman, "Nationalist China during the Nanjing Decade," p. 146.

55. Philip Kuhn, "The development of local government," in Fairbank *et al.*, *Cambridge History*, Vol. 13, pp. 348–350.

56. E-tu Zen Sun, "The growth of the academic community, 1912–49," in *ibid.* pp. 388–396.

57. Kirby, *Germany and Republican China*, pp. 206–223.

58. Kirby, "The Chinese war economy," in James Hsiung and Steven Levine, *China's Bitter Victory* (Armonk: M. E. Sharpe, 1992), pp. 192–98.

discipline, patriotism and frugality, even if this required assassination.[59] Despite the radical measures that they frequently took, they never succeeded.

Without a close study of the military conflict of the Civil War period,[60] no conclusions can be drawn about the causes of the demise of the Nationalist government. It is possible that bad strategy or tactics, logistical breakdown, ineffective command, or lack of co-ordination meant the difference between victory and defeat at some crucial moment. This should be a warning to judge what went before in the light of what happened after. At the same time, there are some good long-term factors that suggest that the KMT's defeat was not the result of a mere accident of history. Mainland historians suggest that whereas the CCP and the PLA had a true mass base, the KMT was never able to secure enduring popular support. The CCP's effective propaganda too was, it is suggested, important, as was the fact that the PLA under Mao Zedong was effectively organized and cohesive, especially during the Civil War period, whereas the Nationalist armies remained heterogeneous.

The KMT furthermore had to face the problems of having to fight a long war against a modern army, whereas the CCP did not bear the brunt of the fighting against the Japanese. The Japanese invasion meant that the Nationalist regime lost control over the area that had been its major source of revenue. The sale of bonds and foreign exchange reserves helped the government for some time, but by 1940 the Nationalist government was desperate for new sources of revenue. The income tax was extended, a new transit tax was implemented, and monopolies were established on salt, sugar, matches and tobacco. Nevertheless central revenue covered only 11 per cent of wartime cash expenditures. How desperate the government truly was is suggested by the fact that in July 1941 it took over control of land tax collection and reverted to payment of this tax in kind. At least this ensured the supply of food to the army and the bureaucracy. As in the past, the collection became an immediate source of exploitation, social strife and corruption. The cost of war also led to severe inflation. After 1940 the financial resources of the state declined, money was printed, and the purchasing power for instance of government officials rapidly declined. Shortages fed corruption and factionalism. Inflation reduced the income derived from the overseas sale ofmorale, bureaucratic capacity and governmental prestige. With victory against Japan only in part attributable to the Nationalists,[61] with large

59. Frederic Wakeman, *Policing Shanghai, 1927–37* (Berkeley: University of California Press, 1995); Kirby, *Germany and Republican China*, pp. 158–162.

60. An important beginning is made in Stephen Levine, *Anvil of Victory* (New York: Columbia University Press).

61. The issue is whether the KMT could have defeated the Japanese even if the USA had not dropped a nuclear bomb. In mainland China, the discussion has taken the form of a debate about whether the KMT had begun a serious and effective counter-offensive after the Japanese Ichigo offensive. Some argue for its existence, while others believe that the armies of the Nationalists were doing no more than advancing where the Japanese withdrew. That withdrawal was not the result of Nationalist pressure, according to them, but of the Japanese decision to narrow its defensive perimeter. See for instance Ma Zhendu, *Cansheng* (*Bitter Victory*) (Guilin: Guanxi Normal University Press, 1993) pp. 2–8.

Communist forces fighting in north China and Manchuria, and with a demoralized army and bureaucracy, it was unsurprising that the first major defeats in Manchuria precipitated a rapid and total collapse of the Nationalist government in the rest of China.

## *Conclusion*

This article has attempted to suggest that the drive for military efficiency begun in the late Qing profoundly affected the Republic and that its effects continue to be felt today. The first Sino-Japanese War, the warlord wars of the 1920s and the War of Resistance against Japan all had long-lasting effects. Political change was often a product of war. The regimes that ruled China during the Republican period were also shaped profoundly by military necessity and ambition. But more than that, leading conceptions about China's future and how to reach that future were influenced by the military and military ways of thinking. Organizational characteristics of the military were influential in many other areas as well. The use of bureaucratic means to redistribute resources, plan for growth and manage large economic entities would be influential beyond 1949 in Taiwan and on the mainland.

One of the challenges is to avoid an easy condemnation of the military and militarization. This article has suggested that militaristic conceptions of society and change led to paranoia and murderous purges in the case of both the CCP and the KMT. But that should not lead one to ignore the profound effects that militarization has had in all kinds of areas. To the extent that the CCP did bring greater equity to China, it could not have done so without building up its military forces. National resistance too would not have succeeded without it. Militarization stimulated industrialization and social discipline, both necessary for the creation of a modern society. The military's effect cannot be reduced to a merely destructive one on true revolutionary purpose or the expression of conflict between regional military interests.

This article has pointed to some of the obvious themes for analysis once one includes the military as a factor in the making of modern China. However there are many areas about which little is known. Popular perceptions of and attitudes towards the military are important examples. In local society, perhaps especially in areas with a considerable degree of social dislocation, the military may have been seen as an escape from routine, oppressive social control, or as offering a path toward the fulfilment of ambition or adventure. At the same time, the CCP for instance was well aware of the dangers of incorporating bandit forces andmade sure to subordinate them to its will by the strict maintenance of a system of political control.

Further issues are the impact of China's own military traditions and elite perceptions of the military. Differences in terrain, culture, technical ability, social practices and education meant that war in modern China did have its own characteristics, even if foreign models, material and practices were also influential. One example is that political and military leadership have been combined in one person in this century. The strict separation of the military and the civilian did not apply. Yuan Shikai, Mao Zedong and Chiang Kai-shek each became leaders of China to a considerable degree because they constructed an army and were acknowledged as its leader. Yet they also remained concerned to strive toward civilian rule. It is striking that most of the PRC's ten Great Marshals had lost much of their power by the time of the Cultural Revolution.

Another example is that the PLA was an army of peasants with low educational levels even at the time of the Korean War, let alone before. This meant that a command system based on the written word or class-room instruction with written materials were not possible. Mao Zedong could rely on radio communications to direct the movements of large army units during the Civil War period, but communications were nevertheless backward. Soldiers had to carry their own food and ammunition, or "borrow" from local areas. Except when transport by rail was possible, logistics probably continued to use the practices of the past. The effect on the CCP leadership of what was considered a victory of a peasant army against a modernized one in the Korean War can only be guessed. The great number of casualties may have caused Peng Dehuai to seek to step up the pace of modernization. It also may have strengthened Mao Zedong's faith in mass energy and voluntarism.

These examples are raised merely to suggest that how China's armies worked, or how armies and warfare figured in the Chinese world, have only just begun to be explored. Much basic work will need to be done before the effects of the military in this century can be properly assessed. Yet, I hope that it is nevertheless clear that China has become what it is today, a proud country with a successful economy, and one that remains deeply divided in itself, in the context of war and militarization.

# Shanghai Modernity: Commerce and Culture in a Republican City

Wen-hsin Yeh

One of the most active areas of research in recent years concerns the urban history of Shanghai in the Republican period. Beginning in the 1980s, scholars have gone beyond an overview of Shanghai's rise as China's leading metropolis in the hundred years after the Opium War (1839–42), and produced richly contextualized analyses on the various aspects of the city's history and society.[1]

Roughly speaking, two lines of questioning have been developed concerning Shanghai's urban history. One, inspired largely by Max Weber's writings on the city, focuses attention on guilds and native-place associations and asks questions about the relationship between state and society. This line of inquiry owes a fair share of intellectual debt to the ground-breaking research done by an earlier generation of scholars, notably by G. William Skinner and Ping-ti Ho, on urban hierarchies and merchant organizations in late imperial Chinese society.[2] The new research has been carried out mainly by social historians and political scientists interested in the social basis of urban politics. Their findings, along with works done on other major Chinese cities – Hankou prior to the rise of the Taipings (1850–64), Beijing under the rule of the northern militarists (1911–27) and Tianjin during the Republican period (1911–49), for example – constitute parts of a larger scholarly construction of the nature of late imperial and modern Chinese urban society.[3]

A second line of inquiry, drawing inspiration not from sociology but from economic history, focuses attention on the various businesses that developed in Shanghai in the Republican period. The shipping, silk, cotton and cigarette industries each received its due share of attention.[4]

1. Two outstanding examples are Frederic Wakeman, Jr., *Policing Shanghai* (Berkeley: University of California Press, 1995), and Christian Henriot, *Shanghai, 1927–1937: Municipal Power, Locality, and Modernization* (trans. Noel Castelino) (Berkeley: University of California Press, 1993). A significant amount of research has been done on Shanghai in recent years. See discussion below for other works.

2. G. William Skinner, "Cities and the regional hierarchy of local systems," "Regional urbanization in nineteenth-century China," "Introduction: urban and rural in Chinese society," "Introduction: urban development in Imperial China," all in Skinner (ed.), *The City in Late Imperial China* (Stanford: Stanford University Press, 1977). Ping-ti Ho. "The geographic distribution of Hui-kuan (*Landsmannschaften*) in Central and Upper Yangtze Provinces," *Tsinghua Journal of Chinese Studies*, No. 5 (December 1966), pp. 120–152, and *Zhongguo huiguan shilun* (*On the History of Landsmannschaften in China*) (Taipei, 1966).

3. William T. Rowe, *Commerce and Society in a Chinese City, 1796–1889* (Stanford: Stanford University Press, 1984), and *Hankow: Conflict and Community in a Chinese City, 1796–1895* (Stanford: Stanford University Press, 1989). David Strand, *Rickshaw Beijing: City People and Politics in the 1920s* (Berkeley: University of California Press, 1989). Gail Hershatter, *The Workers of Tianjin, 1900–1949* (Stanford: Stanford University Press, 1986).

4. See for instance Lillian M. Li, *China's Silk Trade: Traditional Industry in the Modern World, 1842–1937* (Cambridge, MA: Harvard University Press, 1981); Robert Eng,

© The China Quarterly, 1997

The continuing growth of *qianzhuang* (native banks) after the rise of Western-inspired modern-style banking institutions has further sparked a fair degree of scholarly interest.[5] Much has been done to shed light on the commercial networks and the business practices that linked an elaborate system of domestic trade to an international market.[6] By and large, scholars see the rise of a new form of urban economy as a concrete expression of relationships between China and the West, and seek to determine the nature of this interaction – whether imperialist and exploitative or mutually beneficial – by examining the economic dynamics of the connection.[7]

It was not until recently that historians turned their attention to the institutional aspects of cultural industries such as printing, publishing and advertising in Shanghai.[8] In the field of literary studies, scholars have gone beyond discretely defined projects that examined the life and work of individual writers, and have begun to focus attention on aesthetic modernism as a broadly contextualized literary phenomenon.[9] In the field of art history, similarly, scholars have rejected conventional approaches to the works of leading painters, and begun serious examination of the new urban visual culture and its material foundation. The convergence of these research interests in issues of culture and commerce has led to a new appreciation of Republican Shanghai in light of the phenomenon of modernity, both as a set of new institutional arrangements and as an emerging cultural ideology.

The multitude of projects that deal with Shanghai commerce and culture treat a broad range of issues from the mundane to the sublime, from the nuts and bolts of business dealings to the most abstract and rarefied of humanistic aspirations. No single interpretive position informs

---

*footnote continued*

"Imperialism and the Chinese economy: the Canton and Shanghai silk industry, 1861–1932," University of California, Ph.D. dissertation, 1978; Hou Chi-ming, *Foreign Investment and Economic Development in China, 1840–1937* (Cambridge, MA: Harvard University Press, 1965); Albert Feuerwerker, "Handicraft and manufactured cotton textiles in China, 1871–1910," *Journal of Economic History*, Vol. 30, No. 2 (1970); Richard Bush, *The Politics of Cotton Textiles in Kuomintang China, 1927–1937* (New York: Garland Publishers, 1982); Sherman Cochran, *Big Business in China: Sino-Foreign Rivalry in the Cigarette Industry, 1890–1930* (Cambridge, MA: Harvard University Press, 1980).

5. Andrea McElderry, *Shanghai Old-Style Banks (Ch'ien-chuang), 1800–1935: A Traditional Institution in a Changing Society* (Ann Arbor: University of Michigan, 1976); Susan Mann. "The Ningpo Pang and financial power at Shanghai," in G. William Skinner and Mark Elvin (eds.), *The Chinese City Between Two Worlds* (Stanford: Stanford University Press, 1974); Marie-Claire Bergère, "The Chinese bourgeoisie, 1911–1937," in John K. Fairbank (ed.), *Cambridge History of China*, Vol. 12 (Cambridge: Cambridge University Press, 1983), pp. 721–825; Parks Coble, *The Shanghai Capitalists and the Nationalist Government, 1927–1937* (Cambridge, MA: Harvard University Press, 1980).

6. Hao Yen-p'ing, *The Commercial Revolution in Nineteenth-Century China: The Rise of Sino-Western Mercantile Capitalism* (Berkeley: University of California Press, 1986).

7. Albert Feuerwerker, "Economic trends, 1912–49," "The foreign presence in China," in Fairbank, *Cambridge History of China*, Vol. 12, pp. 28–127, 128–207.

8. Leo Lee and Andrew Nathan, "The beginning of mass culture: journalism and fiction in the Late Ch'ing and beyond," in David Johnson, Andrew Nathan, Evelyn Rawski (eds.), *Popular Culture in Late Imperial China* (Berkeley: University of California Press, 1985); Wen-hsin Yeh, "Progressive journalism and Shanghai's petty urbanites: Zou Taofen and the *Shenghuo* enterprise," in Frederic Wakeman and Wen-hsin Yeh (eds.), *Shanghai Sojourners* (Berkeley: Center for Chinese Studies Monograph Series, 1992), pp. 186–238.

9. Perry Link, *Mandarin Ducks and Butterflies: Popular Fiction in Early Twentieth-*

the research designs of these various projects. Not much has been done, furthermore, to integrate the findings of the socio-economic historians on the one hand and the humanistic scholars on the other.

Implicit in this second line of inquiry, however, is nevertheless a focused concern with Shanghai as the birthplace of a new kind of urban culture in the context of a new pattern of economy, enabled in part by the introduction of new technology. This culture and economy were seen not only as the product of Sino-Western contacts, but also, in the particular forms that they took, unique to Shanghai society. Shanghai, in other words, was not simply yet another Chinese city, but the seat of an emerging form of Chinese modernity.[10] Research on Shanghai thus sheds light not so much on the nature of modern Chinese politics centred around the political dynamics between the rural and the urban as on the very question of Chinese identity evolving against the backdrop of cultural interactions between China and the West.

The two lines of inquiry sketched above rarely mix in the designs of contemporary research projects on China. This absence of internal dialogue points to major differences in both intellectual concerns and analytical problems central to the study of Republican China. This article does not attempt to mount an effort to integrate the two, but to draw attention, instead, to this fundamental divergence in basic conceptual assumptions. Issues of state and society, of course, were closely connected to those of culture and commerce in Shanghai in the early 20th century. But the fact remains that the history of modern Shanghai is still a tale of two cities. By drawing attention to the differences in scholarly concerns that led to the construction of two such different entities, it may be possible to gain a more sophisticated appreciation of the historical Shanghai that continues to elude everyone.

*Republican Shanghai*

In Weberian sociology, the bourgeois transformation of the European political system has often been traced to the unique qualities of medieval cities and their tradition of civic autonomy.[11] Within this framework, Weber saw traditional Chinese cities primarily as military and administrative centres dependent upon the state for their importance. He drew sharp contrasts between Chinese cities and their European counterparts, and suggested that the former, unlike the latter, had never been able to function as a new source of dynamics that eventually transformed the rest of society.

---

*footnote continued*

*Century Chinese Cities* (Berkeley: University of California Press, 1981); Leo Lee, *The Romantic Generation of Modern Chinese Writers* (Cambridge, MA: Harvard University Press, 1973), and "Literary trends 1: the quest for modernity, 1895–1927," in Fairbank, *Cambridge History of Modern China*, Vol. 12, pp. 451–504. See also Edward Gunn, *Unwelcome Muse: Chinese Literature in Shanghai and Beijing, 1937–1945* (New York: Columbia University Press, 1980), and Po-shek Fu, *Passivity, Resistance, and Collaboration: Intellectual Choices in Occupied Shanghai, 1937–1945* (Stanford: Stanford University Press, 1993).

10. The most important statement on this subject is perhaps Leo Lee's forthcoming book. *Shanghai Modern* (tentative title).

11. Max Weber, *The City* (trans. and ed. Don Martindale and Gertrud Neuwirth) (Glencoe, IL: Free Press, 1958).

Modern Shanghai, however, was no replica of a traditional Chinese city. A treaty port administered simultaneously by three separate municipal regimes, Shanghai in the first half of the 20th century emerged to become China's largest metropolis for trade, finance, manufacturing, publishing, higher education, journalism and many other important functions, performed by a growing population increasingly diversified into multiple classes of different incomes and interests. The city, because of the creation of the foreign concessions, contained enclaves beyond the immediate reach of the Chinese state, which permitted sections of it to become havens of dissent.[12] In much of the recent scholarship on Shanghai, therefore, one of the leading questions has evolved around whether the city, as a bastion of Western influence, bourgeois wealth and working class activism, was capable of transforming a largely traditional Chinese political system long under the dominance of the inland capital to the north.

Was Republican Shanghai a powerhouse sufficiently charged to change China? Did the trade and diplomacy that flourished on the China coast in the century after the Opium War prepare the ground for the rise of a new political system, such as Western-style democracy? With Mao's persistent declaration that his revolution amounted to a rural Chinese conquest of the Westernized city, many had come to see Shanghai in terms of its political failure rather than success. In case after case, researchers conceptualized their projects as an examination of what the city lacked rather than what it possessed, drawing attention to key political arenas in which the city appeared to have shown weakness rather than strength.

On the important question of why the Shanghai bourgeoisie, despite its wealth and political activism, failed to launch Republican China on a course of democratic transformation, Marie-Claire Bergère has drawn attention to the weakness of the Chinese state, and argued persuasively that it was this frailty that accounted for the corresponding weakness of the Chinese bourgeoisie.[13] In the context of a global capitalist system, according to Bergère, the nascent Chinese bourgeoisie needed a powerful national government to make decisions on important matters such as tariffs, labour laws, currency regulation, raw material acquisitions and trade agreements to help protect its interest against foreign rivals. The rise of the Shanghai bourgeoisie was thus hindered rather than aided by the absence of an effective Chinese state in the 1920s.

Bergère goes on to note that democracy in the domestic context did not simply result from a mere lifting of the state's coercive presence. In an admirable exercise of conceptual rigour, she draws clear distinctions between democratic institutions built on bourgeois values of individualism, and gentry-merchant self-governing bodies that had arisen in the

12. On student protest, see Jeffrey Wasserstrom, *Student Protests in Twentieth-Century China, The View from Shanghai* (Stanford: Stanford University Press, 1991). On organized crime and "compradore of violence," see Brian Martin, *The Shanghai Green Gang: Politics and Organized Crime, 1919–1937* (Berkeley: University of California Press, 1996). On the pleasure quarters of the city that thrived under a divided municipality, see Gail Hershatter, *Dangerous Pleasure* (Berkeley: University of California Press, 1997).

13. Marie-Claire Bergère, *The Golden Age of the Chinese Bourgeoisie, 1911–1937* (trans. Janet Lloyd) (Cambridge: Cambridge University Press, 1989).

early 20th century to assert their communal rights to local autonomy. Although Shanghai's bankers formed voluntary associations to take action on matters of common concern, Bergère shows that the Shanghai bourgeoisie, despite the wealth it had enjoyed in the economic boom during the aftermath of the First World War, was unable either to sustain itself economically or to articulate a viable political vision for the nation as a whole. The golden age of the Chinese bourgeoisie thus closed without an enduring legacy, whether in the form of political institutions or political culture, that might otherwise have contributed to the democratic transformation of China.

On the question of workers and the Chinese revolution, official Chinese Marxist historiography had conventionally depicted the party's early attempts to unite the workers and the intellectuals in the 1920s as efforts that ended in betrayal and tragedy. This urban strategy of revolution, which consisted mainly of strikes and mass organization, differed significantly from the party's subsequent road to success via peasant mobilization and guerrilla warfare. Although many urban workers later joined the New Fourth Army, they occupied a much less prominent place than the peasant soldiers and the Eighth Route Army in accounts of Mao's revolution.[14]

Recent scholarly research, inspired in part by E. P. Thompson's work on the making of the English working class, endeavours to show that it would indeed be difficult to point to the emergence of a working class with its own consciousness among Shanghai's factory workers.[15] Shanghai's labour force was divided, according to Emily Honig and Elizabeth Perry, along particularistic lines of native-place origin.[16] Honig shows that these divisions led to the development on the peripheries of the city of working-class neighbourhoods that resembled the inhabitants' native villages. Such residential patterns in turn contributed to the articulation of sub-ethnic divisions among Shanghai's immigrant population.[17] Perry draws attention to the high level of strikes and militancy among Shanghai workers, and suggests that it stemmed from communal tension as well as solidarity. The strikes, which were mobilized on the basis of social networks instead of communities of belief, bore no definite relationship to the articulation of new political demands.[18] Labour and politics, in other words, stood in an uncertain relationship to each other, because the workers, despite their capacity for militancy, lacked a clear sense of larger political purpose and were consequently susceptible to ready manipulation by dominant political parties.

14. Gregor Benton, *Mountain Fires* (Berkeley: University of California Press, 1994).

15. These works take as their point of departure the earlier contribution by Jean Chesneaux, *The Chinese Labor Movement, 1919–1927* (trans. H. M. Wright) (Stanford: Stanford University Press, 1968).

16. Emily Honig, *Sisters and Strangers: Women in the Shanghai Cotton Mills, 1919–1949* (Stanford: Stanford University Press, 1986); Elizabeth Perry, *Shanghai on Strike: The Politics of Chinese Labor* (Stanford: Stanford University Press, 1993).

17. Emily Honig, *Creating Chinese Ethnicity: Subei People in Shanghai, 1885–1980* (New Haven: Yale University Press, 1992).

18. Perry, *Shanghai on Strike*.

Honig and Perry, by putting emphasis on native-place ties, presented the picture of a traditional society fragmented by rural or provincial identities, which remained strong even as the villagers found themselves in an urban setting. The "deparochialization" of sojourning merchants that William Rowe described for 19th-century Hankou thus hardly ever took place among the migrant labourers of Republican Shanghai.[19] Nor did these men – unlike the middle-class bankers and merchants studied by Bryna Goodman – ever lend their native place associations to the mobilization for modern nationalism.[20] Despite their Shanghai residence and occupations, migrant workers, according to Honig and Perry, remained encapsulated in their provincial cultural milieus. Their politics, if they had any, was derivative of their ethnicity. Some, such as the migrant workers of northern Jiangsu origin, came to be regarded, indeed, as the tradition-bound "Subei" people in the new surroundings of modern Shanghai. This Subei identity, despite its constructed nature in such a semi-foreign urban context, was ascribed rather than acquired, hence expressing parochialism rather than attributes of an opposite sort. Few rural provincials, by Honig and Perry's reckoning, were able to disengage themselves from the norms and ties into which they had been born.

This picture of village-style localism among Shanghai's metropolitan labour force was further employed by David Strand, who extended it to include other sectors of Shanghai society, to explain the absence of democracy.[21] Strand turns his attention first to the political history of the city. He suggests that in Republican Shanghai there were political movements as well as leadership networks that harboured democratic aspirations, despite the presence of older Chinese cultural elements. Democracy, however, ultimately failed as a new form of institutionalized political order – not because endeavours for its realization were lacking, but because the process was frustrated by the absence of a strong and oppressive state.

Pursuing a counter-intuitive line of argument, Strand treats the state's capacity for violence as functionally useful, for it would have imposed uniformity through oppression on a social landscape fragmented by traditional ties. Where Ernest Gellner sees the forces of industrialization as liberating European peasantry from the insularity of their village lives, Strand sees the modernizing state performing a comparable function in breaking down social barriers erected by traditional ties in an urban setting.[22] The modern state, in attempting to gain greater control over society, Strand reasons, would surely spur the various segments of society

19. On deparochialization, see Rowe, *Hankow: Commerce and Society in a Chinese City.*

20. Bryna Goodman, *Native Place, City, and Nation: Regional Networks and Identities in Shanghai, 1853–1937* (Berkeley: University of California Press, 1995).

21. The following discussion is based on David Strand, "Conclusion: historical perspectives," in Deborah S. Davis *et al.* (eds.), *Urban Spaces in Contemporary China: The Potential for Autonomy and Community in Post-Mao China* (Cambridge: Cambridge University Press, 1995), pp. 394–426.

22. See Ernest Gellner, *Nations and Nationalism* (Cornell: Cornell University Press, 1983).

to unite in oppositional politics, thus transcending their parochialism. In this view, the modernizing state, despite its hegemonic intention, could paradoxically assert a democratizing effect by levelling embedded social differences. Strand, like Bergère, thus rests his explanation of the failure of Shanghai democracy on an analysis of the weakness of the state.

### *"Modern" versus "Traditional"*

Much of the scholarship described above can be characterized as attempts to gauge whether a new type of urban economy had laid the foundation for the emergence of a new form of Chinese polity. Reflecting an ultimate concern with the relationship between state and society, scholarly debates along these lines have evolved around the issue of whether there emerged, in Shanghai, socio-political features that could be seen as comparable to the rise of civil society and a public sphere in the West.[23]

It is certainly a question of major importance as to whether or not Shanghai ever functioned in ways that served to democratize China. Those who pursue these projects, to the extent that they focus their attention on the dynamics between a modernizing Shanghai and a less forward-looking China, have by and large framed the interactions as a national question within the Chinese domestic context. Implicit in this line of inquiry, in other words, is an identification of Shanghai as a *Chinese* city analysed against processes and values that are presumed to be of universal validity. Shanghai parochialism and the weakness of its bourgeois institutions were seen, by implication, as indicative of an overall *Chinese* inability to achieve democratic transformation.

But Republican Shanghai, by virtue of its commerce and culture and with its foreign concessions, was as much a product of global forces as of national politics. The "national" approach, with its focused attention on politics and institutions, risks overlooking not only the transformation of the material foundation of urban life that was brought about by the forces of commerce, but also the very phenomenon of Shanghai modernity, which developed in the foreign concessions under the authorities of the British, the Americans and the French, and, in the words of Leo Lee, was tangible in the surface glamour of a commodified popular culture and its hybrid images that mixed the East and the West.[24]

Much as Republican Shanghai was a part of China, it was, at the same time, a city shaped and defined by global forces that linked developments across national boundaries. For its Chinese contemporaries, early 20th-century Shanghai was indeed a setting where many could not but find their inherited and established Chinese way of life problematic. There

23. See the essays by Frederic Wakeman, William Rowe and Mary Rankin in Philip C. C. Huang (ed.), " 'Public sphere'/'civil society' in China? Paradigmatic issues in Chinese Studies, III," *Modern China*, Vol. 19, No. 2 (April 1993).

24. Leo Lee, "The cultural construction of modernity in Early Republican China: some research notes on urban Shanghai," paper presented at the conference "Becoming Chinese: Passages to Modernity and Beyond," University of California, Berkeley, 2–4 June 1995, pp. 28–29.

was no "normalcy" sanctioned either by tradition or consensus. What used to be seen as a "natural" way of life came under scrupulous scrutiny and required entirely new justifications. The valorization of the "modern," meanwhile, forced urbanites to set aside the familiar and to try on new styles brought in as the latest fashion from the outside.[25] Urban existence involved not only a totally changed sense of time, but also an expanded imaginary space that reached foreign shores. Such fundamentally different experiences entailed new social practices and redefined boundaries of community identities in a way that ultimately led to the very reconstitution of Chineseness itself. How these forces manifested themselves is vividly captured in the following episode from a turn-of-the-century piece of popular fiction.

In chapter 16 of the novel *Wenming xiaoshi* (*A Short History of Civilization*), Master Yao, a provincial degree-holder, takes his son and three disciples, all of old-fashioned landed gentry background, to Shanghai for a visit.[26] The goal was to broaden the intellectual horizon of the young men by showing them first-hand signs of Western civilization, which they had come to admire earlier upon acquiring paraffin lamps and other foreign gadgets in their country homes. Over a breakfast of dumplings and *shaomai* in a teahouse near their inn in the International Settlement, therefore, Master Yao announced the curriculum that he had planned for his disciples. Each day they were to spend their morning and afternoon seeking out friends, and visiting bookshops, publishing houses and at least two new-style schools to familiarize themselves with the course offerings. In the evenings they were to attend a variety of theatres to savour the latest in story-telling and theatrical presentations. They would end the day by eating late meals in selected restaurants, where connoisseurs enjoyed regional cuisine and "Western food." At weekends they were to ride in horse-drawn carriages to view the sights and hear the sounds of the city. They were also to attend the gatherings at Zhang Garden (Zhangyuan), where speeches were delivered amidst political rallies.[27]

But the teahouse, as a micro-organism of the city, turned into a classroom even as Master Yao spoke. A newspaper hawker, loaded with the day's *Shenbao*, *Xinwenbao* and *Hubao*, approached their table no sooner had they finished eating. As the five pored over the papers, a fight broke out at the next table following a tense session over tea – an instance of *jiangcha* ("talk tea," or informal mediation of disputes) that had apparently ended in failure. The country gentlemen looked up from their newspapers to find a young woman in her 20s in the company of three

25. Leo Lee suggested that this constant effort to keep up with time was one of the key characteristics of modernity. See Leo Lee, "In search of modernity: some reflections on a new mode of consciousness in twentieth-century Chinese history and literature," in Paul A. Cohen and Merle Goldman (eds.), *Ideas Across Cultures: Essays on Chinese Thought in Honor of Benjamin I. Schwartz* (Cambridge, MA: Council on East Asian Studies. Harvard University Press, 1990), pp. 109–136.

26. Li Boyuan, *Wenming xiaoshi* (*A Short History of Civilization*) (Reprinted Beijing: Tongsu wenyi chubanshe, 1955), pp. 99–105.

27. *Ibid.* p. 100.

men, who – against all Confucian expectations about proper decorum – "not only shared the same pot of tea but were also busily engaged in an excited discussion."[28] The woman, whose casual style of clothing, gaudy display of jewellery and immodest manner of speech frustrated the provincial gentrymen's attempts to speculate on her identity, turned out to be a former new-style school student and a mistress to the man sitting across the table, who was employed as a clerk in a Western trading firm. The other two were the couple's original introducer, a coach-driver who made money by facilitating such illicit liaisons, and a runner in the detective's office of the Shanghai Municipal Police, who presided as the figure of authority. The young woman did not simply dominate the presentation; she underscored her points by pounding on the table, causing her many gold bangles to clash against each other. Presently, she leapt out of her seat to grab her estranged lover by his vest. The detective rose swiftly to his feet. Unable to separate the couple, who by then were entangled in a fight, he dragged them both down to the street, where two waiting policemen, "one Chinese and the other a foreigner with red turban and dark face,"[29] stepped forward and took the couple away to appear before the foreign judges of the municipal court.

This entire scene, with sexual relationships undefinable in conventional terms and a cast of unfamiliar characters staged in a new setting following a novel script, intrigued the young provincial disciples who were eager to find a plausible account of it. Master Yao, baffled by the immorality of the intrigue and fearful of its corrosive influence on young minds, however, refused to answer questions about what had happened. But "from other tables" in the teahouse there arose various voices – fragmentary comments delivered in a desultory fashion, offering reactions to what they had just witnessed. The disciples, aided by these voices, were thus able to weave an account about occupations and relationships beyond their provincial experience. Gradually they recalled ideas such as "free marriage" and "anti-foot-binding associations" that they had read about in newspapers in the past. They were also left to ponder the significance of what they had heard and seen without the mediating voice of their teacher.

The teacher, repelled by the incident, motioned the waiter to bring the bill. Just as he tried to rush the group out of the teahouse, however, a tall man of darkened complexion appeared at the entrance, clad in a Western-style suit, a straw hat and a pair of brown leather shoes, and carrying a walking stick. The newcomer was instantly hailed by an acquaintance seated in a corner wearing an old cotton gown with patched-up holes, who was later identified as Huang Guomin, literally "yellow-skinned countryman." When the Western-suited man removed his hat, he revealed a "full head of hair tied into a bun, rather different from the short hair of the foreigners,"[30] thus showing his true identity as "a transformed Chinese" to all observers in the teahouse.[31]

28. *Ibid.* p. 101.
29. *Ibid.* p. 102.
30. *Ibid.* p. 103.
31. *Ibid.*

Huang Guomin proceeded to strike up a conversation with the Western-suited Chinese and the two shared thoughts on clothing, hairstyles and daily lives. The newcomer reported that "ever since I adopted Western-style clothing, I have changed all my habits of eating, drinking, sleeping and walking" in order to become thoroughly Westernized.[32] He now ate two meals a day and resisted the temptation of snacks in between. He had had a disastrous experience trying to take a cold shower in the Western style and now made serious though futile efforts to take a bath every day. And he made a point of reminding himself, whenever he was to decide on whether to have a haircut, of what the foreigners had to teach about physical health.

Although chapter 16 ends without drama or tension, the episodes described above are parts of a much larger account that skilfully depicts China's early encounter with the West as seen through the eyes of provincial gentrymen from Shanghai's hinterland. Earlier in the novel, in their large mansions in the countryside, the youths are shown leading secluded lives behind high walls, catching glimpses of the West via paraffin lamps and treaty-port newspapers. Although paraffin lamps were ten times brighter than the oil lamps used by the majority of their fellow townsmen, these youths learned that the foreigners in Shanghai used electric lights that were ten times brighter still. And though they had access to Shanghai periodicals, they knew that their newspapers, by the time they reached them via the local county seat, had spent at least a week travelling by cart and boat, while Shanghai residents routinely read papers no older than overnight.

The trip to Shanghai, then, was a journey to a place with a different kind of time. As they sat in the teahouse, these youths watched the scenes depicted in the newspapers firsthand. This immediacy rendered the provincial teacher, who had wished to fashion a curriculum, utterly ineffectual. His pupils were brought face to face not only with the appearance of new social roles and the rise of unimagined public authorities, but also – as in the case of the "transformed Chinese" – with the very transmogrification of the Chinese appearance from head to toe, in basic patterns of everyday activities.

These changes, induced by the import of Western goods and propelled by the creation of Western-inspired institutions such as newspapers and new-style schools, were subversive to the old ways in norms as well as in styles. The *Wenming xiaoshi* chapter thus vividly captured the deeply diffused sense of shock in the early stage of China's encounter with the West in Shanghai. Apart from the wonders of electric lights and the novelty of horse-drawn carriages, there were, in full view in the public places of the city, happenings that could only be understood as open violations of moral norms, blatant transgressions of gendered roles and foreign assertions of political authority, along with the absurd sight of a

32. *Ibid.*

Chinese imposing Western discipline upon his resisting body. What happened around the provincial gentrymen called into question virtually all of the familiar aspects in their everyday existence, both as a result of changing social conditions and of these strikingly new cultural encounters.

As is suggested by the actual physical movements of the provincial youth in the story, Shanghai emerged in the eyes of contemporaries both as a new centre of gravity pulling the country into its orbit and as a source of change projecting its influence outward towards the surrounding countryside. The flow of ideas and goods went in both directions. Provincial youths travelled to the centre in search of a Westernizing education, a broadened intellectual horizon and a better view of the West's material splendour. Many others meanwhile travelled in the opposite direction, working busily to distribute Shanghai newspapers and imported goods throughout the hinterland.

Cultural encounters between China and the West have often been seen as clashes between cultural systems that were utterly incompatible.[33] Joseph Levenson, in his seminal work on Confucian China and its modern fate, argued compellingly that there were inherent contradictions between "being modern" and "being Chinese."[34] In light of recent scholarship, however, this viewpoint does not take into sufficient account the cultural effects of trade and the mediating role played by commercial interests. The case of Shanghai shows, in fact, that there was more to the relationship between China and the West than mere clash and contest. Much of Shanghai's urban culture in the Republican years, from the elite to popular levels, was the result of incessant attempts to bring about the indigenization of the foreign and the domestication of the novel. These processes were visible, for example, both in the cultural packaging of material goods, such as the advertising of foreign goods by Chinese merchants in the domestic market, and in the normative refashioning of critical social institutions such as the family, which were placed on a new ideological foundation. These newly shaped phenomena reflected the working not so much of national factors such as politics and institutions as of global forces of commerce and finance, which resulted not only in the commodification of culture but also in the rise of new social interests and occupational classes that radically redefined what it meant to be "Chinese." It was inevitable, then, for the "national" to acquire a new set of meanings within the context of a dialectical relationship with the "global" – meanings that exceeded a simple stark contradiction between identities and values.

33. For a recent formulation of this position, see Samuel P. Huntington, *The Clash of Civilizations and the Remaking of World Order* (New York: Simon & Schuster, 1996).

34. Joseph Levenson, *Confucian China and Its Modern Fate: A Trilogy* (Berkeley: University of California Press, 1958), Vol. 1. See also Levenson, *Liang Ch'i-ch'ao and the Mind of Modern China* (Cambridge, MA: Harvard University Press, 1965).

*Advertising*

In a fascinating paper on the rise of advertising for Chinese-manufactured goods in Shanghai in the 1920s and 1930s, Xu Dingxin, a senior researcher with the Shanghai Academy of Social Sciences, showed how these advertising practices contributed to the appearance of a "Nanjing Road Phenomenon" on the busiest street in the International Settlement during the Republican period.[35] Nanjing Road was the birthplace, according to Xu, of a novel commercial culture that combined new styles of product display, new standards of quality control and new attitudes in customer service. These changes turned shopping into such a pleasant experience that Shanghai residents subsequently viewed a shopping trip not as a chore but as a diversion, not as an economic transaction but as a cultural consumption. As bargaining and window shopping became leisure-time activities, the entire commercial district of Shanghai also developed into a lavish entertainment complex of restaurants, theatres, cinemas and amusement halls. Nanjing Road thereby acquired natural fame as the leading shopping district in the country. Commerce and consumption also acquired a certain glamour that was closely associated with a modern way of life.

The pull of Nanjing Road began much earlier, when country folk, for example, were told about it and came to the foreign concessions to see the electric lights, the horse-drawn carriages and the high-class courtesans who set the latest trends in clothing and hair styles. Already by the turn of the century, the fame of Nanjing Road stemmed not only from the concentration of large numbers of jewellers and silk merchants, but also from the availability of novel imports procured from far-away places. Competition was keen, and next-door neighbours were also business rivals. A variety of means were devised as shop owners vied for the attention of prospective patrons. In addition to smiling clerks and attractive merchandise, banners were flown and signs were put up on the streets in front of the shops to announce special discounts and to affirm the quality and durability of the products. Even before the rise of modern advertising, in short, Nanjing Road was already the hub of a thriving commercial culture. But the "Nanjing Road Phenomenon" of the 1920s – and here I differ with Xu – was no mere intensification of traditional forms of commercial activities. Something qualitatively different intervened, and the phenomenon, on closer analysis, was not just about the promotion of goods, but also about the production and consumption of images.

Modern advertising played a crucial role in this juncture. Thanks to the use of the mechanical printing press and the rise of a new printing industry that originated in the West, Shanghai merchants and manufacturers availed themselves of such unconventional media as mass-produced

35. Xu Dingxin, "Ershi sanshi niandai Shanghai guohuo guanggao cuxiao ji qi wenhua tece" ("National goods advertising in Shanghai and its distinguishing features, 1920s and 1930s"), paper presented at the seminar on "Consumer Culture in Shanghai," Cornell University, July 1995.

posters, calendars, pictorial and textual advertisements in newspapers and journals, and the radio to propagate their messages.[36] The result was that the "Nanjing Road Phenomenon" was far more than a simple aggregation of all the shops. It was, instead, a collage of images and signs about these sources of modern merchandise. As representations, these images were disengaged from immediate physical association with the goods they represented. They could be seen in the countryside as well as in cities throughout the lower Changjiang valley. Shanghai, viewed at a distance, thus emerged as the very centre of glamour, luxury, comfort and modernity. A whole industry of guidebooks and tour maps about it arose in conjunction with the circulation of these images, enticing an growing number of provincials to come to the city and see these urban wonders for themselves.

Advertising via cheaply reproducible modern media, in this sense, was not only the principal means with which the commerce on Nanjing Road was transformed into a modern phenomenon; the images and signs thus produced were the staple of a commodified popular culture that helped to define the nature of Shanghai modernity. The "modern" here, however, pertained not quite so much to the substantive aspects of the symbols – to the origins and the meanings of the specific signs – as to the means of their reproduction and consumption in a chain of economic transactions. Media advertising engendered a system of signs and images in which the latter were dislodged from their social context. This altered, but did not obliterate, the substantive significance of the symbols themselves. Shanghai advertising, as the following examples show, involved in practice both the mobilization of established genres of communication towards the production of new meanings, and the adoption of new-style media to circulate age-old ideas. Although the means were markedly modern, the cultural components that supplied the content were of mixed temporal and spatial origins.

Carlton Benson's study of the transformation of popular story-telling (*tanci*) in Shanghai focuses in part upon the commercial advertising of Laojiuhe, one of the city's largest fabric shops that specialized in silks and furs for an affluent clientele. The firm not only hired a professional story-teller to broadcast its advertisements on radio, but also sponsored the publication of a collection of popular songs that promoted the apparel as an essential part of the good life.[37] This one-man performing operation, which went on the air almost as soon as commercial radio became available in Shanghai in the late 1920s, was among the city's very first private advertising agencies. The advertisers selected the genre of story-

36. On the use of posters and calendars for advertising, see Sherman Cochran. "Marketing medicine and advertising dreams in China, 1900–1950," paper prepared for the conference on "Becoming Chinese: Passages to Modernity and Beyond, 1900–1950" at the University of California, Berkeley, 2–4 June 1995.

37. Carlton Benson, "Story-telling and Radio Shanghai," *Republican China* (April 1995); also Xu Dingxin, "National goods advertising," p. 10. For an original and full treatment of the subject, see Benson, "From teahouse to radio: storytelling and the commercialization of culture in 1930s Shanghai," Ph.D. dissertation, University of California at Berkeley, 1996.

telling precisely because it was a well established form of popular entertainment that had been an integral part of urban life for decades. The form itself, however, was inevitably transformed as a result of this manipulation. Benson shows that while story-telling began at the turn of the century as an interactive performance presented in teahouses by travelling female entertainers and attended by a predominantly male audience from the immediate neighbourhood, it changed into a different kind of genre altogether after its migration to radio. Story-telling on the radio facilitated the rise to stardom of a dozen or so male performers who, as disembodied voices, now reached tens of thousands of female listeners in the privacy of their homes. These women, previously isolated in the boredom of their sheltered lives, thus became part of a network of consumption via story-telling on "broadcast radio." A new social space was opened up and a new "listening public" (*tingzhong*) was constituted into an implied subject as a result of this new medium of intimate anonymity.

Although Laojiuhe, a well-established shop that operated initially out of the old Chinese part of the Shanghai municipality, was selling familiar lines of products, the advertisements that it sponsored nevertheless sought to make the use of silk gowns and fur coats into an indispensable part of modern life. In the printed song collections, the pictorial images that accompanied the verses often featured fashionable young women with bobbed hair and high-heeled shoes, clad in silk or fur, walking light-heartedly down a street lined by Shanghai's multi-storeyed buildings. These women typically carried home bags of new purchases; the visual images were in themselves celebrations of this moment of consumer triumph. The radio advertisements of the store, similarly, sang the delight of sisterhood when modern women shopped together with discriminating taste at Laojiuhe's attractively furnished emporium. Modern women found a new arena of relative autonomy when going on shopping excursions, the songs suggested. Such acts of shopping were integral to a newly found modern sense of female identity.

When the products to be promoted were new or unfamiliar to the prospective customers, by comparison, advertisers did not simply broadcast the pleasure of shopping. They presented, instead, a picture of a "modern Shanghai" in which their products occupied a prominent place. This new style of life was often promoted in terms of progress and advancement.

Susan Glosser's research on You Huaigao's attempts to sell dairy products, especially milk, is a case in point.[38] You, the son of Jiangsu gentry, returned to Shanghai in the mid-1930s after a stint at Cornell's school of agriculture to open a dairy farm in the city's suburbs. Milk, however, was neither tea nor ice cream, and You appeared to have trouble getting the beverage accepted either for regular drinking or as a special treat. To promote his product, You became the one-man author, editor

38. Susan Glosser, "The business of family: You Huaigao and the commercialization of a May Fourth ideal," *Republican China* (April 1995).

and publisher of a weekly pamphlet which he distributed free of charge to his paid and prospective customers. In this weekly, *Jiating xingqi* (*Family Weekly*), You idealized the image of happy, prosperous urban nuclear families (*xiao jiating*), ably managed by women no less fashionably dressed than the customers of Laojiuhe. These women, however, now appeared not as care-free shoppers but as wives and mothers shouldering familial responsibilities; the drawings placed them in the interior of their homes rather than in the city's streets. Regular consumption of milk, You wrote, meant health not only for babies but for all members of the family. Yet milk-drinking was a habit still to be acquired by most Chinese. A decision to include milk as part of the dietary routine of the family thus required knowledge and innovation on the part of the lady of the house. Only a modern woman, You suggested, would be sufficiently enlightened and thoughtful to see in the unfamiliar project a major opportunity to benefit her family.

As might be expected, images of chubby babies and overflowing milk bottles adorned the pages of You's journal. In addition, it dispensed advice to housewives on matters such as how to open a family savings account and other suggestions related to "scientific" child-care and home economics. Those who bought his bottles of pasteurized milk, then, were also delivered a variety of pragmatic suggestions about what to do with the rest of their lives. You's advice was presumably intended for the all-round health, physical as well as financial, of every member of the family.

While the owners of Laojiuhe fashioned traditional luxury items such as silk and fur into images of modernity, You Huaigao promoted milk by prescribing an entirely new system of home management – so much so that it became virtually impossible to tell whether You was primarily a family reformer or a dairy farmer. Those who sold known products and those who promoted new items therefore faced different kinds of advertising challenge. If an entrepreneur happened to be dealing with something quite new, he was obliged to explain the product's use and justify its proper place in a desired way of life.

Goods in themselves, of course, did not drive cultural changes. They changed the way people led their lives only insofar as uses were found for them. For this very reason, imported gadgets, to the extent that they remained foreign, odd and exotic, continued to occupy only a marginal place in Chinese lives. Goods that played a large role in changing a whole way of life, on the other hand, were necessarily those that had become domesticated. Those of foreign origin engendered changes built around their usages in the process of indigenization. That process was often characterized by "push-and-pull" between the foreign attributes of the thing in itself and the domesticating practices that had been mobilized to acclimatize them. This tension between the foreign and the domestic was prominent in the material transformation of Chinese lives in Shanghai during the Republican period. A closer examination of the city's recurrent advertising campaigns to promote "national goods," much lauded by contemporaries as spontaneous urban expressions of anti-foreign sentiments, helps further to illuminate this critical paradox.

The "national goods" (*guohuo*) campaigns of the 1920s and 1930s had their origin in the popular boycotts against foreign goods. The most notable of the latter included, for example, the late 19th-century anti-American boycotts organized in Guangdong in protest against American exclusionary acts against the Chinese, the nation-wide anti-Japanese boycotts in the aftermath of the May Fourth Movement in 1919, and the massive anti-British boycotts of 1925 as a popular reaction against the killing of Chinese workers by the Shanghai Municipal Council police force during the May 30th Incident. The national goods campaign, which gathered momentum in the years after 1925, turned a negative campaign to boycott the foreign into a positive campaign to promote Chinese products.[39] Riding on the high tide of popular anger against the British in 1925, for instance, the Nanyang Tobacco Company sought to undercut the business of its arch rival, the British American Tobacco Company, by running advertisements that appealed to the patriotic sentiments of fellow Chinese. These urged Chinese consumers to support fellow Chinese producers and to buy "national goods." Choice and consciousness on the part of the consumers were lauded as patriotic deeds.[40]

The national goods movement, as the case of the Nanyang Tobacco Company suggests, was launched by Shanghai's new-style manufacturers and supported by the city's leading financiers. It used the language of nationalism to promote Chinese-manufactured goods, propagated, among other media, in the pages of Chinese-owned newspapers that sought to fuse mass anti-foreign campaigns with a buy-Chinese merchandising push. Whatever the effects of such efforts, their high visibility and multiple recurrences drew attention to the critical role played by Shanghai's modern business interests in the construction of a nationalist discourse.

But the nationalist language and avowed patriotism of the commercial campaigns were quite misleading at times. Sherman Cochran has shown that in a global capitalist economic system, it was difficult to determine the exact "national" content of any manufacturing process or product.[41] The Jian brothers, owners of the Nanyang Tobacco Company, in fact held Japanese passports and had developed very close business connections with Japanese suppliers in their South-East Asian operations. The company's use of patriotism in its advertising campaigns, furthermore, produced at best mixed results in various sectors of the domestic market. This was because as normative categories, the "nation" and the shared sentiments of "citizenship" were largely urban constructions that were yet

39. A Society for the Use of National Goods (Quanyong guohuo hui) was formed by Chinese leaders of Shanghai's 20 major guilds on 23 March 1915, less than two months after the Twenty-One Demands presented by Japan to China were made public. Cochran, "Marketing medicine and advertising dreams," p. 14.

40. On the boycotts, see Cochran, *Sino-Foreign Rivalry*, and Parks M. Coble, *Facing Japan: Chinese Politics and Japanese Imperialism, 1931–1937* (Cambridge, MA: Council on East Asian Studies, Harvard University, 1991).

41. Cochran, *Sino-Foreign Rivalry*.

to take hold in the country as a whole. Provincial consumers, Cochran shows, did not always make the connection between their choice of cigarettes and their allegiance to the country. Nationalism, like modernity, was itself a new idea born in the city.

The patriotism of the national goods movement was also misleading in another sense. There were, generally speaking, at least four sets of dichotomies commonly used by contemporaries as they tried to determine the national content of any given set of goods. A product could be either "domestic" or "imported," "native" or "foreign," when classified spatially with a line drawn along China's national borders. A product could also be either "Chinese" or "Western," "traditional" or "modern," when classified temporally with an eye on the differences between China's past and present. Thus oriented, "national goods" such as tobacco, matches or bedroom linen were "national" only in the sense that they were domestically produced and not imports. To the conservatives they could readily represent a foreign rather than a native line of products in a not so distant past. In other words, though safely "Chinese" as a result of associations with their Chinese owners and promoters, these goods were nevertheless "modern" as opposed to "traditional" in Chinese terms. They challenged rather than maintained established ways. Consequently, each one of the national goods, insofar as it entailed a criss-crossing of attributes along these spatial and temporal divisions, was a product of an active process of indigenization. Indeed, the indigenization of these goods was vigorously pursued by a new generation of Chinese entrepreneurs who did not mind mixing the foreign and modern with the Chinese and domestic. In the process of doing so, they succeeded in constructing a new material culture which they labelled "national."

Because national goods were not traditional, Chinese manufacturers of Western-style products thus became active promoters of a new style of life that often combined both Chinese and Western elements. To sell bath robes and cotton facial towels, for example, the Sanyou Company ran advertisements that directed attention to new rhythms in everyday life. One series of such advertisements, constructed around the theme of "rising early in the morning," featured images of birds and blossoms under a clear sky. These pictures were accompanied by texts that urged viewers to be sure to exercise their body, and thereafter to protect themselves from the chills of the morning dew by putting on the manufacturer's recommended brand of bath robe.[42]

Similarly, to sell bedroom linen, mosquito nets, pillow cases, window curtains and other items of interior decoration, the Sanyou company created an entire display room on Nanjing Road that was furnished like a private urban home. Calling the place "Peach Blossom Stream," the manufacturer used it both to showcase home furnishing products and to suggest new ways to arrange the interior at one's dwelling. "Peach Blossom Stream" contained multiple rooms with clearly differentiated functions. To suggest how such homes must have accommodated happy,

42. Xu Dingxin, "National goods advertising," p. 14.

Westernized families, there was even on display a doll in the form of a child in bed, peacefully asleep in a pair of pyjamas of the company's own brand.[43] The model home, with its various areas furnished as living room, dining room, bedroom, study, kitchen and so forth, and predicated upon the needs of an urban nuclear family, followed a pattern of spatial arrangement that was distinctively different from traditional Chinese gentry compounds. In its attempts to sell a full line of Western-inspired products that were promoted as "national goods," the company ended up merchandizing images of an utterly unconventional new-style home.

It is notable that the company named its display room after a sixth-century Daoist wonderland.[44] It was characteristic of national goods advertisements to mix the visually new with the textually conventional, and the foreign with the traditional, so that companies like Sanyou were among the major sponsors behind the production of a whole new genre of commercialized art for advertisements that mixed cultural elements of diverse origins.[45] Artists on the payroll of the company worked in teams and produced commercials following a variety of formulas. Advertisements in the *meiren* (beauty) genre, for instance, featured young Chinese women in *qipao* as well as in Western-style clothing. These figures were placed in landscapes punctuated by Suzhou-style moon gates as well as Italianate marble benches. They promoted a whole range of goods from electric space heaters to powders and pills. They appeared on calendar posters, cigarette cards and in magazines that contained, sometimes right on the next page, yet another advertisement featuring, for example, a photographed segment of a Han stele that helped to announce the imminent publication of a new book.[46] As the result of the mass production and the proliferation of these images, Shanghai urbanites took part in a visual culture that was a virtual emporium of cultural motifs with diverse styles juxtaposed in close proximity.

The advertisements for national goods were not only part of a larger effort to change the old ways of life and to indigenize the foreign. Commercial advertising, by dislodging cultural motifs and styles from their original contexts, emptied them of their embedded social meanings and thereby turned them, for purposes of commercial packaging, into dislocated signs and symbols of exchange. The national goods movement, by this measure, was not only instrumental in the indigenization of a foreign line of goods, but also played a key role in the commercial production of a new urban consumer culture that was both modern and Chinese. The process of this production followed no fixed formula; it was responsive to local initiatives as well as to global

43. *Ibid.* pp. 14–15.
44. *Ibid.* p. 14.
45. Kuiyi Shen, "Comic, illustrations, and the cartoonist in Republican Shanghai," paper presented in the Annual Meeting of the Association for Asian Studies, Chicago, 13–16 March 1997.
46. Ellen Johnston Laing, "Commodification of art through exhibition and advertisement," paper presented in the Annual Meeting of the Association for Asian Studies, Chicago. 13–16 March 1997.

imperatives. Eventually, with the forces of commerce working incessantly towards that end, the "transformed Chinese," who in the eyes of turn-of-the-century observers had seemed so blatantly absurd with his plans for daily showers and Western-style clothing, was by the early 1930s naturalized into an ordinary urban consumer of perfectly respectable national goods.

## *Conclusion*

Shanghai modernity, as the above discussion suggests, owed much of its emergence to the workings of commercial interest through the city's cultural industries. The images and texts produced by printing, publishing and advertising targeted women as well as men as the implied subjects of this popular culture of consumption. The use of female images, meanwhile, constituted in itself a sub-genre in the production of commercial art. A key feature of Shanghai modernity in the Republican years was precisely this commodification of a new image about women and the feminine.[47]

One may very well ask, in this connection, what was the relationship between this new form of commodity culture and a new urban society? What, in other words, was the social foundation of Shanghai modernity? Recent research has shown that together with the rise of a new pattern of economic life and the creation of new cultural institutions, there arose in Shanghai during the Republican period a new class of white-collar professionals who held jobs in the city's modern sectors and who formed nuclear households. The idealization of the *xiao jiating* (nuclear family) versus the *da jiazu* (extended lineage) in the pages of *Shenghuo Weekly*, one of the best-selling popular journals of the early 1930s, corresponded to the popularity of this new form of family organization in the urban setting, which was evidenced elsewhere in the law codes, court papers, state practices, social science surveys and newspaper reports of this time.[48] In addition, white-collar employees such as those who worked for the Bank of China formed residential corporate communities that paced themselves to the ticking of the mechanical clock. The creation of such corporate compounds with modern conveniences helped to enhance the bank's image as one of the most enlightened and progressive institutions in the city.[49]

47. For treatment of the issue of gender in the context of Shanghai, see Rey Chow, *Woman and Chinese Modernity: The Politics of Reading Between West and East* (Minneapolis: University of Minnesota Press, 1991); and Yingjin Zhang, *The City in Modern Chinese Literature and Film: Configurations of Space, Time, and Gender* (Stanford: Stanford University Press, 1996).

48. Wen-hsin Yeh, "Progressive journalism and Shanghai's petty urbanites." For a full treatment of the subject of "small family," see Susan Glosser, "A contest for family and nation in Republican and Early Communist China, 1919–1952," Ph.D. dissertation, University of California at Berkeley, 1995. See also Kathryn Bernhardt, "Women and the law: divorce in the Republican Period," in Bernhardt and Philip C. C. Huang (eds.), *Civil Law in Qing and Republican China* (Stanford: Stanford University Press, 1994).

49. Wen-hsin Yeh, "Corporate space, communal time: everyday life in Shanghai's Bank of China," *American Historical Review*, Vol. 100, No. 1 (February 1995), pp. 97–122.

Within the modern sector of the city's economy, the ideal of the small family took its proper place as a building block within corporate compounds such as those constructed by the Bank of China, thereby laying the foundation for a new urban middle-class society. New ideas about home were bound up with new ideas about work. While urban men were fashioned into office workers and business employees, urban women were transformed into household managers and keepers of domestic bliss. The culture of consumption that emerged in Republican Shanghai was predicated, in this sense, upon a general acceptance of this new order, which entailed both a new articulation of the gendered differences between men and women, and a modern conception of the spatial demarcation between the public and the private, between work and home.

Thanks to the packaging and distribution of these images and ideals by the forces of commerce and cultural industry, the appeal of an idealized *xiao jiating* and a white-collar position went far beyond the small number of people who were actually able to lead this kind of life. "Modernity," as it captured the imagination of an emerging urban constituency in the Republican period, touched upon the norms and practices of everyday existence in a widening circle of Chinese society.

These developments, as they altered the basic structure of urban life, changed the way a growing number of women and men spent their time, allocated their private resources, arranged their personal lives, and gained access to the public domain of information, ideas and goods. It is beyond the scope of this article to address the social and political consequences of these changes. But although Shanghai might not have been the birthplace of Chinese democracy, Shanghai modernity certainly entailed major changes in the way public power and authority intersected with private lives. Urban culture and society in Shanghai may well have fallen short by the yardsticks of contemporary Parisian cosmopolitanism. It is just as misleading, on the other hand, to characterize the city's social milieu mainly in terms of native-place parochialism.

The full ramifications of the emergence of modern Shanghai, of course, await further study. To the extent that it is recognized how the global forces of commerce and culture dislodged Republican Shanghai from its age-old Chinese context, it would be well to expand study of the city's politics and institutions beyond the framework of a simple Weberian dichotomy between tradition and modernity. There are certainly more ways than one to reconceptualize descriptive categories of such fundamental analytical importance. Whatever the agenda and assumptions, the task should be approached with a heightened sensitivity about culture not just as objectified sets of fixed traits, norms and characteristics but as evolving practices in a living context centred upon historical subjects.

# A Revisionist View of the Nanjing Decade: Confucian Fascism

Frederic Wakeman, Jr.

*This essay is dedicated to the memory of Lloyd Eastman*

The foundation of this association has now been laid. People call us Blue Shirts or terrorists. That is nothing. The important problem to be solved is how to create a new revolutionary atmosphere so as to lead the revolutionary masses.... In China today definite action must be taken for temporary relief as well as for fundamental cure. However, what we need now is a fundamental cure. Our present problem is not the Japanese. Our problem is not the invasion of our north-eastern provinces and Jehol. If we can maintain the status quo, it will be enough for the present time. As a revolutionary government, the loss of a little territory does not mean much. A revolutionary movement has both to advance and retreat. When our strength is not enough, it is natural to retreat. We have lost territory today, but we will take it back the next day when we have strength. History tells us that those who have lost territory must work hard to recover it. The important problem is that of national existence. To save China from destruction we must revive our national spirit. Though we should have only one *xian* of territory, we can recover the lost territory if we can revive the Chinese national spirit. Our organization should take the responsibility for this fundamental cure – revival of our national spirit.... *Zhong* [loyalty], *xiaoshun* [filial piety], *dexing* [virtue], *ai* [love], *he* [harmony] and *ping* [peace] should be our central guiding principles for the achievement of *li* [propriety], *yi* [righteousness], *lian* [purity] and *chi* [sense of shame] – which comprise the national spirit of China. The success of the Japanese fascists and the Italian fascists is due to this. If we want our revolution [to be] a success, we must create a party dictatorship.

*Secret speech attributed to Chiang Kai-shek spring, 1932*[1]

The Master said: "To be fond of learning is to be near to knowledge. To practice with vigour (*lixing*) is to be near to magnanimity (*ren*). To possess the feeling of shame is to be near to energy (*yong*)."

*The Doctrine of the Mean*, ch. 20, part 10[2]

Two of the most important debates among Western scholars over the political formations of the Nanjing decade (1927–37) took place between the late Lloyd Eastman and his fellow scholars 16 and 11 years ago respectively. The first was a dispute with Maria Hsia Chang and, less directly, James A. Gregor, about "fascism and modern China."[3] The

1. Quoted in Wilbur Burton, "Chiang's secret blood brothers," *Asia*, May 1936, p. 309.
2. James Legge, *The Chinese Classics with a Translation, Critical and Exegetical Notes, Prologomena, and Copious Indexes* (Taipei: Wenxing shudian, 1966), Vol. 1, p. 407.
3. Maria Hsia Chang, " 'Fascism' and Modern China," *The China Quarterly*, No. 79 (September 1979), pp. 553–567; Lloyd E. Eastman, "Fascism and Modern China: a rejoinder," *The China Quarterly*, No. 80 (December 1979), pp. 838–842.

© The China Quarterly, 1997

second was a debate with Joseph Fewsmith and Bradley Geisert about "the nature of the Nationalist regime."[4] In each instance, the controversy occurred just before the appearance of a critical new piece of evidence in the form of a memoir (Gan Guoxun's 1979 recollection of the activities of the Fuxingshe) or book (Deng Yuanzhong's 1984 recapitulation of his father Deng Wenyi's memories of the founding of the Lixingshe) that later forced a reconsideration of the question of Chinese fascism and a revision of the understanding of the nature of Chiang Kai-shek's regime.[5] This article primarily addresses the former issue, but it will invariably entail the latter.

Was China's Nationalist government, especially during the Nanjing decade when Chiang Kai-shek attempted to extend his control over the country's central and eastern provinces, a fascist regime? If fascism is defined by Friedrich's classic criteria, then the question is patently misguided.[6] Chiang Kai-shek's China simply lacked the totalitarian means of control that Italy or Germany possessed during those same years. For that very reason, however, Mussolini and Hitler's regimes held great appeal for Chiang Kai-shek, who privately spoke to his followers of the need to "*nacuihua*" (Nazify) China and who accepted personal adulation as the "Führer" (*lingxiu*) of a movement that secretly emulated the Black Shirts and Brown Shirts of Europe.

Although Chiang Kai-shek's Blue Shirts (*lanyi*) were far from identical copies of either Italian Fascisti or German Nazis, heated debates among Western historians about the presence of a fascist movement in Nationalist China have treated them as such. The title of this article deliberately (and perhaps too provocatively) uses the term "Confucian fascism" to invoke the remarkable blend of Chinese and Western components that went into the founding of the Blue Shirts and that made this movement something other than either traditional personalism or modern fascism. In describing the formation of the Blue Shirts' core group, the Lixingshe or "Society for Vigorous Practice," it is hoped

4. Lloyd E. Eastman, "New insights into the nature of the Nationalist regime," *Republican China*, Vol. 9, No. 2 (1984), pp. 8–18; Joseph Fewsmith, "Response to Eastman," *Republican China*, Vol. 9, No. 2 (1984), pp. 19–27; and Bradley Geisert, "Probing KMT rule: reflections on Eastman's 'new insights'," *Republican China*, Vol. 9, No. 2 (1984), pp. 28–39.

5. Gan Guoxun, "Guanyu suowei 'Fuxingshe' de zhenqing shikuang," ("The true conditions and actual circumstances of the so-called Fuxingshe"), *Zhuanji wenxue* (*Biographies*), *shang*, Vol. 35, No. 3 (1979), pp. 32–38; *zhong*, Vol. 35, No. 4 (1979), pp. 68–73; *xia*, Vol. 35, No. 5 (1979), pp. 81–86; and Deng Yuanzhong, *Sanminzhuyi lixingshe shi* (*A History of the Sanminzhuyi Lixingshe*) (Taipei: Shixian chubanshe, 1984). See also Deng Yuanzhong, "Sanminzhuyi lixingshe shi chugao" ("Preliminary draft history of the Sanminzhuyi lixingshe"), *Zhuanji wenxue*, Vol. 39, No. 4 (1983), pp. 65–69; and Xiao Zuolin, "Fuxingshe shulüe" ("A brief account of the Revival Society") in Chinese People's Political Consultative Conference National Committee, Wenshi ziliao yanjiu weiyuanhui (eds.), *Wenshi ziliao xuanji* (*Selections of Historical Materials*) (Beijing: Zhonghua shuju, 1960), fascicle 11, pp. 21–71.

6. Carl J. Friedrich (ed.), *Totalitarianism; Proceedings of a Conference Held at the American Academy of Arts and Sciences, March 1953* (Cambridge, MA: Harvard University Press, 1954); Carl J. Friedrich and Zbigniew K. Brzezinski, *Totalitarian Dictatorship and Autocracy* (Cambridge, MA: Harvard University Press, 1956); Carl J. Friedrich, *Totalitarianism in Perspective: Three Views* (New York: Praeger, 1969).

to adumbrate several of the symbols of post-imperial power in China that dominated the Nationalist period and that also, implicitly, may have continued to hold sway after 1949.

### *The Society for Vigorous Practice*

The Lixingshe was so secret that hardly any outsider knew of its existence between 1932 and 1937. It was perpetually confused with its front groups, whose members were thought by the public to be Blue Shirts, and its activities were often inextricably connected with covert propaganda and intelligence work conducted by Chiang Kai-shek's special services. Yet the Lixingshe was the single most important political formation within what the public called the "Whampoa clique," and its members constituted a military freemasonry that admired fascism and pledged itself to carry out Sun Yat-sen's Three People's Principles under the guidance of its supreme leader, Chiang Kai-shek.

Although its presence was concealed for more than 40 years, during the society's heyday it controlled an elaborate organizational structure of more than 500,000 members, and it clandestinely orchestrated public mobilizations involving millions more, ranging from the New Life Movement and the Chinese Boy Scouts to university military training programmes and high school summer camps. Now, thanks mainly to memoirs published on Taiwan during the last decade, the importance of the Lixingshe can be openly recognized and its political role in the years of conflict between the Manchurian and Marco Polo Bridge incidents fully acknowledged.

The Lixingshe was created as a direct result of the political crisis that erupted during the summer and autumn of 1931 and that eventually forced Chiang Kai-shek to surrender his government posts and go into temporary retirement in Zhejiang. After the collapse of Feng Yuxiang, Wang Jingwei, and Yan Xishan's "enlarged conference movement" in 1930, the National Government decided to meet some of the defeated rebels' demands by convoking a national assembly to adopt a provisional constitution. Hu Hanmin – adhering stubbornly to Sun Yat-sen's notion that a single-party dictatorship was an essential part of the process of political tutelage – refused, as president of the Legislative Yuan, to support this proposal, which had the backing of the newly elected *zongtong*, Chiang Kai-shek. Announcing his opposition, Hu resigned his presidency on 28 February 1931. Chiang promptly ordered him placed under house arrest, and shortly after this had him taken to Tangshan near Nanjing.

The elders of the Kuomintang (KMT) were outraged by Chiang's illegal action.[7] On 30 April four senior members of the Central Supervisory Committee of the KMT, Lin Sen, Gu Yingfen, Xiao Focheng and Deng Zeru, impeached the new president of the National Government.

7. William Wei, *Counterrevolution in China: The Nationalists in Jiangxi During the Soviet Period* (Ann Arbor: University of Michigan Press, 1985), p. 45.

Four weeks later, these and other opponents of Chiang's arbitrary authoritarianism – eminences such as Wang Jingwei, Sun Fo, Tang Shaoyi, Eugene Chen and Li Zongren – met in Guangzhou under the protection of the "king of the south," Chen Jitang, and there, on 28 May 1931, announced the formation of a national government of their own.[8] During the next three months, when the Changjiang valley was devastated by severe floods, the country was politically cut in two and civil war between north and south seemed imminent.[9] Chiang Kai-shek himself believed that he and his cause were in grave jeopardy. His closest followers, such as Teng Jie and He Zhonghan, could not but agree.[10]

Teng Jie, who was eventually to become the first secretary-general of the Lixingshe, was an experienced student agitator. He was the son of a landlord from Funing in Jiangsu and had been the student president at an American Protestant vocational school in Nantong when the May 30th Movement broke out in 1925. Many students at missionary schools were among the most strongly opposed to Western cultural imperialism, and when a delegation of students from other schools arrived to *chuanlian* (establish ties), Teng Jie found his leadership being challenged by radicals. He eventually decided that the American institution had to be dissolved and chaired the meeting that summer which led to the students' unanimous withdrawal from the school. At the age of 18 he joined the Sociology Department at Shanghai University.[11]

In the autumn of 1925 Shanghai University was the main recruiting centre in the lower Changjiang region for the Whampoa Military Academy. The Communists were quite influential, with Liu Shaoqi acting as a student leader and Shi Cuntong serving as the chairman of the Sociology Department. Teng Jie was already a keen admirer of Sun Yat-sen, whose Three People's Principles he had studied in Nantong, and he joined the Nationalist Party shortly after his arrival in Shanghai. Disgusted by what he took to be the cowardice and insincerity of the Communist students, who appeared to him only to pretend to be co-operative members of the United Front, Teng Jie was convinced that the less clandestine Nationalists were at a disadvantage when it came to organizing students. He was secretly recruited for the Whampoa Academy and left Shanghai for military training in the south.

After studying in Guangdong at the Whampoa Academy and a military stint in Central China during the Northern Expedition, Teng Jie went to Japan to study. This was part of a plan developed by Chiang Kai-shek in 1928, after his first retirement from office, systematically to send Whampoa graduates to Japan for further training. Five students were hand-

8. Howard L. Boorman, *Biographical Dictionary of Republican China* (New York: Columbia University Press, 1967–1971, 1979), Vol. 2, pp. 164–65; Zhang Weihan, "Dai Li yu 'Juntong ju'" ("Dai Li and the Military Statistics Bureau") in Wenshi ziliao yanjiu weiyuanhui (eds.), *Zhejiang wenshi ziliao xuanji*, No. 23 (Zhejiang: Renmin chubanshe, 1982), p. 83.

9. Christian Henriot, "Le gouvernement municipal de Shanghai, 1927–1937," Ph.D. dissertation, Université de la Sorbonne Nouvelle, 1983, p. 102.

10. Deng Yuanzhong, *Sanminzhuyi lixingshe shi*, pp. 33–34, 104.

11. *Ibid.* pp. 64–65.

picked by Chiang himself from each of the first six Whampoa classes. By the summer of 1931, there were more than 60 former Whampoa pupils in Japan enrolled in the Imperial Army College or other schools including the Shikan Gakko (Japan's elite military academy), Waseda, the Artillery School and the Cavalry School. Teng Jie was sent to Meiji University, where the school authorities had set up a Department of Political Economy exclusively for Chinese students. After two years of frugal study he returned to China in late July 1931, just at the time that tensions in Korea over the Wanbaoshan incident made an outright war between Japan and China seem very likely.[12]

Teng Jie had hoped that the prospect of war with Japan would unite the country. Instead, he found the nation fragmented and divided, and politics just as corrupt and self-interested as when he had left. If the people were to be mobilized, some new form of organization would have to be devised to create a genuinely strong political party. Remembering the success of the Communists in clandestinely dominating student groups during the May 30th Movement, Teng drafted a plan to use Whampoa graduates as backbone cadres to build up a top-secret organization which would unite elite military and civilian youth according to the principle of "democratic centralism (*minzhu jiquan*) [in order] to build up a strong organization with a united will, with iron discipline, with a clear division of responsibility, and with the ability to act with alacrity."[13]

Teng Jie put his idea to his friend Zeng Guoqing, who was assigned to the military division of the party centre in Nanjing. Zeng was enthusiastic and as a first step invited nine friends to dinner. All were graduates of Whampoa, including two Hunanese – Feng Ti and Deng Wenyi – who were members of the first class.[14] Whampoa cadets from Hunan, strongly conscious of the military tradition of their fellow provincials, including the great 19th-century regional viceroys Zeng Guofan and Zuo Zongtang, felt that they had special cause to take a leading role in the salvation of the nation. Feng Ti and Deng Wenyi thus helped secure unanimous approval for the proposal and they agreed to meet again, each bringing another person. When they met a third time there were more than 40 present, including He Zhonghan, the officer in charge of propaganda for the anti-Communist extermination campaign in Nanchang.[15]

He Zhonghan, the leader of the Hunanese clique within the inner Whampoa circle, was born in 1898 in Yueyang, near Changsha.[16] His family lived in "comfortable" (*xiaokang*) circumstances, and He was educated by a private tutor until, at the age of 13, he was raising questions that the tutor could not answer, and was enrolled in one of the new-style elementary schools in the district and began to study "modern learning" imported from the West.[17] In 1915 He transferred to a special secondary

12. Maria Hsia Chang, *The Chinese Blue Shirt Society*, pp. 55–56.
13. Deng Yuanzhong, *Sanminzhuyi lixingshe shi*, pp. 104, 105, 127.
14. Gan Guoxun, "Guanyu suowei 'Fuxingshe' de zhenqing shikuang," *zhong*, p. 71; Deng Yuanzhong, *Sanminzhuyi lixingshe shi*, p. 70.
15. Deng Yuanzhong, *Sanminzhuyi lixingshe shi*, pp. 63, 106–107.
16. *Ibid.* p. 322.
17. *Ibid.* p. 67.

school for Hunan provincials in Wuchang, where he was noted for his skill at composition. From 1917 to 1919 he worked as a student reporter for a news agency at Wuchang, and during the May Fourth Movement was elected a student leader. In the winter of 1920 Dong Biwu and Chen Tanqiu organized a Marxist study group in Wuhan, and He became a student member.[18] The following spring he went to Shanghai with fellow Hunanese Marxists to study Russian at the special school Chen Duxiu had established, and in September 1921 he was elected a delegate to the Congress of the Toilers of the East. Later that year he travelled to Moscow with Zhang Guotao to attend the Congress.[19] He remained in Russia for seven months, but did not join the Chinese Communist Party. He returned to China the following year impressed by the "progressive" (*jinbu*) quality of the Soviet political system but dismayed by the "harshness" (*ku*) of life in Russia on the eve of Lenin's NEP; and he concluded that the Communist strategy of revolution was not suitable for his own country.[20]

Shortly after his return He Zhonghan accepted a post in a Wuchang secondary school, and, like another fellow teacher from the same area – Mao Zedong – threw himself into the turmoil of Hunanese politics, becoming a reporter for the People's News Agency (Renmin tongxun she) in Wuhan. In 1923 the agency was closed down and He went to Changsha to establish the Commoner's News Agency (Pingmin tongxun she). This coincided with the ouster of the military governor Zhao Hengti from Changsha by Tan Yankai, and He Zhonghan was able to publish revolutionary propaganda in his bulletins. One of his tracts was about the murdered labour leaders Huang Ai and Pang Renquan, and was highly critical of Zhao Hengti.[21] After Zhao recovered control of Changsha, the warlord ordered He's arrest, and he nearly died in prison before two members of the Provincial Assembly mediated his release and he went back to Yueyang. His father asked him to stay at home and teach, but He felt that political obligations came first and left for Nanjing, planning to enrol at Southeastern University. Instead, in the spring of 1924, he learned that the revolutionaries in Guangzhou were recruiting students for the Whampoa Military Academy. He entered Whampoa in May 1924 as a member of its first class.[22]

At Whampoa it was He Zhonghan who first objected to comments directed against Sun Yat-sen that appeared in a publication of the Young Soldiers' Association, founded by Soviet adviser Borodin and the Communists; and who together with Miao Bin founded the Sun Yat-sen Study

18. Boorman, *Biographical Dictionary of Republican China*, Vol. 1, p. 239, and Vol. 3, p. 342.

19. Chang Kuo-t'ao, *The Rise of the Chinese Communist Party, 1921–1927* (Lawrence: The University Press of Kansas, 1971), Vol. 1, pp. 179–181.

20. Deng Yuanzhong, *Sanminzhuyi lixingshe shi*, p. 67; Boorman, *Biographical Dictionary of Republican China*, Vol. 2, p. 64.

21. The tract was called *Huang* [*Ai*] *Pang* [*Renguan*] *zhi zhenxiang* (The true facts about Huang Ai and Pang Renquan). For Huang and Pang see Boorman, *Biographical Dictionary of Republican China*, Vol. 2, p. 94.

22. Deng Yuanzhong, *Sanminzhuyi lixingshe shi*, pp. 67–68.

Society on 29 December 1925.[23] He Zhonghan had a second period of study in the Soviet Union early in 1926 when he went through the regular training course at the Frunze Military Academy in Moscow. His experiences in the Soviet Union, coming on top of his active leadership of the Sun Yat-sen Study Society, had confirmed his anti-Communist belief that socialism lacked "humaneness" (*rendao*). When he and Xiao Zanyu returned from Russia in January 1928, Chiang Kai-shek assigned him to command the cadets' unit at the military training centre at Hangzhou.[24] After a stint in KMT headquarters for Nanjing municipality, He and Xiao received permission from Chiang Kai-shek to go to Japan, where He became Teng Jie's room-mate for over a year in 1929 and 1930. During that period he published two books criticizing Wang Jingwei and the Reorganizationists. In February 1931 he was ordered back to China to take over the office in charge of political propaganda in military headquarters at Nanchang.[25]

His attendance at Teng Jie's third dinner meeting was fortuitous: he just happened to be in the area at that time, which was shortly after the Manchurian Railway Incident on 18 September 1931. Boycotts and demonstrations were taking place throughout the country as thousands of students descended on Nanjing to demand that the National Government and the separatists in Guangdong unite together to resist the aggressors. On 14 October Chiang Kai-shek released Hu Hanmin and agreed to hold peace talks in Shanghai to bring the two sides together. However, the student protests continued. By early December, Beijing's university classrooms would be empty, Nanjing under martial law, and 15,000 students demonstrating in the streets of Shanghai.[26]

Against this backdrop He Zhonghan was receptive to Teng Jie's appeal to support their effort to establish a "preparations department" (*choubei-chu*). He Zhonghan realized that his support would be vital to their success if they truly hoped to establish a clandestine network of "men of will" (*zhishi*) among the cadets. Nevertheless, He Zhonghan was cautious. He knew full well that Chiang Kai-shek had often voiced his disapproval of the Whampoa cadets forming political cliques, saying that "these Whampoa cadets lack political experience and cannot effectively engage in political activities."[27] He was also afraid that the *xiaozhang* might misinterpret activities taking place behind his back and without his knowledge were he to discover the plan, but Teng Jie assured him that he intended to report the entire matter to Chiang Kai-shek once the "preparatory work" was completed. Consequently, He gave his approval to

23. Boorman, *Biographical Dictionary of Republican China*, Vol. 3, pp. 36–37.
24. Deng Yuanzhong, *Sanminzhuyi lixingshe shi*, p. 73.
25. *Ibid.* p. 83; Huang Yong, "Huangpu xuesheng de zhengzhi zuzhi ji qi yanbian," ("Whampoa students' political organizations and their evolution") in Chinese People's Political Consultative Conference National Committee, *Wenshi ziliao xuanji*, fascicle 11, p. 14.
26. Boorman, *Biographical Dictionary of Republican China*, Vol. 1, p. 161; John Israel, *Student Nationalism in China, 1927–1937* (Stanford: Stanford University Press, 1966), pp. 59–63.
27. Deng Yuanzhong, *Sanminzhuyi lixingshe shi*, p. 108.

the scheme and suggested that Teng Jie be appointed secretary and his wife, Chen Qikun, assistant secretary. Deng Wenyi contributed 300 *yuan* from his bookshop for expenses, and three rooms were rented in Nanjing on the second floor of a wooden building on Erlengmiao Street near the Kangji Hospital. Kang Ze, a 28-year-old bachelor from a Sichuanese peasant family so poor that his fiancée's family cancelled their engagement, moved into a downstairs room to provide cover and the preparations department set to work.[28]

The *choubeichu* was established, then, as part of a broadly felt quest for an organizational solution to the nation's peril.[29] In a certain sense, the situation was similar to the May 30th Movement six years earlier. As the crisis with Japan deepened, the nation's students and intellectuals were gripped with patriotic fervour.[30] The mobilization of youth was also undeniably influenced by the contemporary rise of fascist movements in Italy and Germany. Liu Jianqun, who later took credit for recommending the formation of the Blue Shirt Society in a pamphlet distributed to a plenary session of the Central Executive Committee of the KMT in October 1931, wrote that: "The Kuomintang should follow the example of the organization of Mussolini's Black Shirts in Italy, completely obeying the orders of the leader and creating members who will use blue shirts as the symbol of their will."[31]

Even though outsiders, and especially the Japanese, were quick to cast this mobilizing effort in a foreign fascist light, it had strong nativist tones. In the eyes of Teng Jie and He Zhonghan it was probably most like the reformers' movement at the turn of the century insofar as it manifested the notion that patriotic leaders could arouse popular support by organizing leagues of youthful *zhishi* to succour the nation, whether they be the civilian students targeted by the CC clique or the military cadres led by former Whampoa Academy cadets.[32]

The latter already had an organizational focal point in the Whampoa Alumni Association (Huangpu tongxue hui), which carried on the anti-Communist tradition of the by-now disbanded Sun Yat-sen Study Society.[33] In addition to assigning jobs (*fenpei*) for its members, the association encouraged the formation of clubs like the Society to Establish the Will (Lizhishe), with its headquarters on Whampoa Road in Nanjing. Clubs like this, with names that instantly recalled the action-oriented teaching of the 16th-century philosopher Wang Yangming, were both modern and traditionalistic. They smacked vaguely of Western or

28. *Ibid.*.
29. Xiao Zuolin, "Fuxingshe shulüe," p. 73.
30. Parks M. Coble, "Super-patriots and secret agents: the Blue Shirts and Japanese secret services in North China," paper presented at the Center for Chinese Studies Regional Seminar, Berkeley, 21 March 1987, p. 13.
31. Cited in Hung-mao Tien, *Government and Politics in Kuomintang China, 1927–1937* (Stanford: Stanford University Press, 1972), pp. 55–56.
32. Yun Yiqun, *Sanshi nian jianwen zaji* (*Miscellaneous Jottings on 30 Years of What Was Seen and Heard*) (Zhenjiang: Jinling shuhuashe, 1983), p. 43.
33. Deng Yuanzhong, *Sanminzhuyi lixingshe shi*, p. 78.

Japanese ultra-nationalist youth groups while also drawing upon the late imperial tradition of scholar-gentry academies and associations.[34]

The traditionalistic tone of the *choubeichu* was manifested in the group's name, Lixingshe. The term *lixing* – literally "strength act" – was taken from the *Doctrine of the Mean*. As suggested by He Zhonghan, the full title was to be the Society for Vigorous Practice of the Three People's Principles (Sanminzhuyi Lixingshe). The "preparatory work" that its proposers carried on during the next five months consisted mainly of meeting in the offices of the *choubeichu* to write drafts of its rules and principles. All the members were Whampoa cadets of classes one to six in their 20s and 30s, born during the last years of the Qing and mainly educated in traditional classical learning before attending modern schools during the early years of the new Republic. According to Deng Wenyi's son, they came from all over China, but the majority were from the Changjiang region, and especially "from provincial grass roots and small towns," which "very much retained the qualities – the strengths and the weaknesses – of traditional Chinese society. These youths personally experienced that society, so they possessed the intention to conserve (*baocun*) its strength, but they also knew the weakness of the society as well and so were eager to reform (*gaige*) it."[35]

As Whampoa graduates, these cadets had been put through a military formation that trained them to be highly conscious of efficiency in action and personal discipline in daily life; they accepted the necessity of obedience and hierarchical order. They had also experienced education abroad: among the founders, all but Gui Yongqing, who was trained in Germany, were educated in Japan or the Soviet Union. There was a major influx of former Whampoa students from Japan after the Manchurian Incident, which they publicly protested against at the time, as a result of Japanese police persecution. Many of them joined the Anti-Japanese National Salvation Association of Returned Students from Japan (Liu-Ri xuesheng kang-Ri jiuguo hui), formed by Gong Debo and others under the leadership of He Zhonghan's classmate, Xiao Zanyu. Gong Debo's newspaper, *Jiuguo ribao* (*National Salvation Daily*), printed editorial after editorial calling for the Chinese to "resist the Japanese and root out traitors" (*Kang Ri chu jian*), and although Gong himself took no part in the activities of the Lixingshe, many members of it used the newspaper as a cover for their own work, pretending to be editors or reporters. A major impulse of these youthful disciples of Chiang Kai-shek was actively to pursue a militant defence against Japan – a policy which was at that period coming to be disavowed by Chiang, who was growing increasingly convinced of the importance of appeasing Japan in order to buy time to exterminate the Communists.[36]

Yet this policy was running directly counter to the mood of the country, and especially of students, who continued to agitate for resistance against the Japanese. In Shanghai, students from Fudan University

34. Xiao Zuolin, "Fuxingshe shulüe," p. 35.
35. Deng Yuanzhong, *Sanminzhuyi lixingshe shi*, p. 62, 109.
36. *Ibid.* pp. 79, 109, 110, 126–27.

called for a major demonstration on 8 December. On that day they held a general assembly, bringing together representatives from all the universities of Shanghai together with two delegates from Nanjing and Beijing. At the end of the meeting the two outside delegates were attacked by a gang of about a dozen local KMT members, while plainclothesmen from the Public Safety Bureau looked passively on. The Beijing delegate was abducted and taken off in a car. Recognizing some of the party toughs, the students reassembled in front of the city hall on 9 December to demand that their Beijing comrade be liberated and that the KMT attackers be punished. The municipal government tried to defend itself by declaring a curfew, but in the end it failed to calm the protesters, who gutted KMT headquarters; and Mayor Zhang Qun – a known Chiang Kai-shek partisan – had to resign.[37] Eight days later, partly as a result of this student pressure, Chiang Kai-shek resigned as Chairman of the National Government and returned to his home in Fenghua.[38]

Although Chiang may have spoken to his closest followers about the importance of devising a solution to the national crisis, he was still being kept in the dark about the plans being made to form the Lixingshe. The members of the *choubeichu* wanted to wait until they had completed their preparation work before seeking his permission actually to found the organization.[39] However, when Teng Jie learned that there was a danger of the news being leaked, he decided to send a personal message to Chiang's secretary, Deng Wenyi, who was with him at Fenghua, asking that he report the project instantly. The Generalissimo's response – conditioned by the conviction that he had to mobilize support for his policy of internal pacification – was quite positive. There were a number of proposals before him to form societies or associations to "save the country," and he evidently believed that the Lixingshe plan was the most promising "to cope with the domestic and international crisis."[40]

Meanwhile, Chiang Kai-shek was preparing to recover his official posts while he worked out a compromise with Wang Jingwei. On 17 January 1932 it was announced that Chiang was going to resume command of the government, and four days later he returned to Nanjing. On 6 February, the Military Affairs Commission (Junshi weiyuanhui) was formed, and a month afterwards, on 6 March, Chiang was appointed its chairman. During these critical two months the Lixingshe was transformed from a paper plan into a top secret organization of 300 devoted Chiang loyalists who would eventually constitute the nucleus of a new national political force of over half a million followers, identified in the public's eye as members of front groups like the Renaissance Society (Fuxingshe).[41]

37. Henriot, "Le gouvernement municipal de Shanghai, 1927–1937," pp. 105–106.
38. Israel, *Student Nationalism in China*, pp. 71–75; Boorman, *Biographical Dictionary of Republican China*, Vol. 1, pp. 328–29.
39. Zhang Weihan, "Dai Li yu 'Juntong ju,' " p. 84.
40. Deng Yuanzhong, *Sanminzhuyi lixingshe shi*, p. 111–13.
41. *Ibid.* pp. 25, 112.

*The Founding*

The process of the transformation of the putative Lixingshe into a major political force began with a summons to the three principal leaders of what was by now called the "preparations department for protecting the party and saving the nation" (*hudang jiuguo choubeichu*) to attend a meeting in Chiang Kai-shek's office on 22 January 1932, the day after he returned to Nanjing.[42] The three men – Kang Ze, Teng Jie and He Zhonghan – first met Secretary Deng Wenyi and the four of them decided that when they walked into Chiang's presence they would for the first time greet him not as "principal" but by an entirely new title, "leader" (*lingxiu*). Chiang Kai-shek made no comment at first about the new form of address but listened to a detailed report of their plan.[43] Then he said: "Why don't you continue addressing me as the *xiaozhang*? You understand what the current situation requires. This plan is very appropriate. However, you are all very young and inexperienced and I am afraid that you may fail. Let me lead (*lingdao*) you." He summoned all the members of the *choubeichu* to his official residence, the Lingyuan Villa (Lingyuan bieshu), in the grounds of the Sun Yat-sen Mausoleum in the hills outside the city, for a "discussion meeting" (*tanhuahui*) on an evening in the last week of February.[44] As for his title, Chiang was addressed as *lingxiu* by his closest followers ever after.[45]

At the first of the February *choubeichu* meetings 25 men were present. In addition to Teng Jie, they were: He Zhonghan, Pan Youqiang, Feng Ti, Sun Changjun, Du Xinru, Gui Yongqing, Deng Wenyi and Xiao Zanyu of the first class of Whampoa; Wan Wuqi and Cai Jinjun of the second class; Zhou Fu, Kang Ze, Han Wenhuan, Li Yimin, Huan Zhongxiang, Qiu Kaiji and Ruo Derong of the third class; Lou Shaokai of the fourth class; Gan Guoxun, Peng Mengji and Yi Deming of the fifth class; and Dai Li, Liu Chengzhi and Chen Xi of the sixth class. Three other members were absent: Hu Zongnan and Zeng Guoqing of the first class and Ye Wei of the fourth class.[46]

After Teng Jie presented a roster, including the three who were unable to attend, Chiang Kai-shek looked at each individual in turn. After a pause he said, "Our party and our nation are now in a situation of extraordinary disaster (*weinan*), so I have especially invited you to come and chat, in order to get your individual views. Therefore I deliberately will not adopt formal meeting procedures. My emphasis is on hearing each one of you express your own ideas. I put no limitations on the time you may take." They followed the usual practice of Whampoa alumni

42. Gan Guoxun, "Guanyu suowei 'Fuxingshe' de zhenqing shikuang," p. 35.

43. Interview with Deng Wenyi and Teng Jie, cited in Deng Yuanzhong, *Sanminzhuyi lixingshe shi*, p. 113.

44. Gan Guoxun, "Guanyu suowei 'Fuxingshe' de zhenqing shikuang," pp. 35–36; Deng Yuanzhong, *Sanminzhuyi lixingshe shi*, p. 114; Maria Hsia Chang, *The Chinese Blue Shirt Society*, p. 56.

45. Deng Yuanzhong, *Sanminzhuyi lixingshe shi*, p. 130.

46. Gan Guoxun, "Guanyu suowei 'Fuxingshe' de zhenqing shikuang," p. 35; Deng Yuanzhong, *Sanminzhuyi lixingshe shi*, p. 76.

gatherings to have those of the earliest class and highest seniority speak first, and each spoke for 20 to 30 minutes. During the discussion there were no guards posted outside, which was extremely unusual. Dai Li, who was armed, would occasionally check inside the room and move around the building. According to Gan Guoxun's recollection, Chiang Kai-shek sat quietly and listened attentively. He seemed calm and patient, which was totally different from his usual severe, stern and commanding attitude, and he appeared to want to invite comments, letting each presentation run its course.[47] Gui Yongqing took the longest; he had just returned from Germany by way of the USSR, through Kalgan (Zhangjiakou) and Beijing to Nanjing, and reported on the reactions in Europe and North China to the Manchurian and 28 January incidents. At 11.00 p.m. Chiang said that those who had not had a chance to speak could do so the next evening at the same time and place.

This continued for two more nights until finally, at the end of the third night, came the turn of the secretary of the *choubeichu*, Teng Jie. Teng should have spoken after Lou Shaokai, but as "the initiator and responsible party from beginning until end," he waited until the end in order to conclude Chiang's disciples' remarks.[48] He announced that, in his view, they must strengthen their organization, recover their revolutionary spirit under the guidance of the leader, internally eliminate dissidents and externally resist the Japanese, "striving for victory with all their strength" (*sili qiusheng*). He firmly believed that "if we manage to get a handle on the situation, we will survive." According to Teng Jie, history had already proved them invincible. In Guangdong with only a few thousand men they had been able to enlist allies and eliminate enemies more than ten times their size. They had felt no fear of the British imperialists in Hong Kong who supplied their enemies with enormous amounts of ammunition and money, nor of the Communists in their midst who were puppets of the Russians. Irregardless, they had unified Guangdong and completed the Northern Expedition. Now, with a military mass of 300,000 men occupying the core zone of several provinces, how could they not form alliances or activate friendly forces to exterminate the Communists and to resist the Japanese imperialists? Expressing the strongest confidence in their cause, Teng Jie declared that they would certainly be able to carry out the unfinished tasks of the Chairman (*Zongli*), Sun Yat-sen, by completing the revolution and building the nation, so that even the spirits of the mountains and rivers were aroused. This was the only way to comfort the souls of Sun Yat-sen and the revolutionary martyrs and meet the hopes of the people of the entire nation.[49]

Behind Teng Jie's bold and sweeping rhetoric lay a simple message: the Chinese, under the leadership of Chiang Kai-shek, could simultaneously crush their internal enemies, the Communists, and repel the

47. Gan Guoxun, "Guanyu suowei 'Fuxingshe' de zhenqing shikuang," p. 35.
48. *Ibid.*
49. *Ibid.* p. 36.

external aggressors, the Japanese. But this was not a message that Chiang Kai-shek was prepared to heed. Already the domestic political situation was changing in his favour, and he was about to become chairman of the Military Affairs Commission while Wang Jingwei was named head of the Executive Yuan. From that point of domination, Chiang thought that he would be able to turn all his resources upon exterminating the Communists, though this meant momentarily conceding to the Japanese. A slogan – *rangwai bi xian annei* (if you want to repel foreign aggression, then you must first pacify the interior) – was fast becoming a policy. And in Chiang's eyes, the success of counter-insurgency depended entirely upon securing the total consent of his closest followers to implement *annei*.[50]

In responding to Teng Jie's ebullient address, Chiang Kai-shek first chose to stress the overwhelming danger that the Japanese posed to their nation:

> The Japanese militarists have spent 50 years preparing for the invasion of China. Their army, air force and navy are all modernized. Once conflict broke out on the battlefield our officers and soldiers in the front lines were almost unable to raise their head to take aim and shoot. All they could do was to strike back and sacrifice themselves. After they had suffered enormous casualties, they retreated and pulled back. Once our back is against the wall and we can find no more soldiers for the battlefield, then all that we will be able to do is to sign an unconditional surrender. And once the surrender is signed, then the country is lost and the race is exterminated.[51]

He went on to say that during their 268 years of rule the Manchus had carried out the multiple massacres of Yangzhou and Jiading, conducted numerous literary inquisitions, and enacted all kinds of harsh laws to mistreat the Han people. But Japan's rule of Korea and Taiwan over the past 50 years had been even crueller than the Manchu reign. Unfortunately, since Sun Yat-sen's death: "The responsibility of revolution has fallen upon my shoulders. Given my knowledge of ourselves and of our enemies, I must not act irresponsibly to disappoint our Chairman and our martyrs, our country and our people."[52]

Chiang insisted that the Japanese with their modernized armies could do practically anything they wanted to, while the Chinese were utterly defenceless:

> Before we resist foreign enemies, we must pacify domestically, which means first of all that we must unite domestically. Then we can mobilize the entire country in material production and education, so as to acquire the capability to resist the Japanese in a protected way. Only after that can we engage in comprehensive resistance. Only at that point will we have the confidence that we can secure a final victory. We cannot afford to lose this war. Only after we have won the war will we have an opportunity to begin to construct our ideal nation based upon the Three Principles of the People.[53]

50. Zhang Weihan, "Dai Li yu 'Juntong ju', " p. 84; Xiao Zuolin, "Fuxingshe shulüe," p. 38.
51. Gan Guoxun, "Guanyu suowei 'Fuxingshe' de zhenqing shikuang," p. 36.
52. *Ibid.*
53. Deng Yuanzhong, *Sanminzhuyi lixingshe shi*, p. 117.

Meanwhile, Chiang said, the millions of Chinese who opposed his policy of withdrawal and praised the heroes of the Nineteenth Route Army for their suicidal defence of Shanghai were indulging themselves in individualistic heroic posturing. In reality there was not a single one of them volunteering to go to the front lines, whereas what China needed now were "anonymous heroes" (*wuming yingxiong*) to carry out "solid work, tough work, quick work, hard work" (*shigan, yinggan, kuaigan, kugan*).[54]

Chiang Kai-shek told his disciples that he did, indeed, have a 300,000-man army. If his only goal were to be a popular "national hero" (*minzu yingxiong*), without regard for the greater historical consequences of the crisis, then that ambition was surely not beyond his reach. But to sacrifice the nation to his personal reputation would betray the souls of the Chairman and the revolutionary martyrs, and pass disaster on to posterity. "All I can do is to sustain humiliation and carry the heavy burden [of public opprobrium]," Chiang declared.

> I will not lightly speak of laying down our lives before we have come to the last critical moment (*guantou*). We will never give up peace until we totally despair of continuing. We must gain time for preparation. And what I mean by the last critical moment, or a time when all hope for peace is completely gone, is the time when the enemy attacks without any consideration of consequences, intending to force us to sign an unconditional surrender and extinguish our country.[55]

With these words, Chiang Kai-shek appeared to have completely won over his audience. The Whampoa men all rose to their feet to show they accepted their lesson respectfully. By then it was 1.00 a.m. and Chiang told them to meet him again the following morning at 8.00 at the offices of the Lizhishe.

The following morning they were taken to a rectangular classroom with a portrait of Sun Yat-sen on the wall bracketed by a couplet: "Revolution has yet to succeed. Comrades must still exert themselves" (*Geming shang wei chenggong, tongzhi reng xu nuli*). Like pupils in class, the Whampoa alumni lined up and sat down in order of seniority. Then Chiang Kai-shek, wearing a blue scholar's gown and accompanied by Deng Wenyi, came in to greet them. Chiang wrote on the blackboard: "Knowing is hard and doing is easy; the philosophy of principle and nature" (*zhi nan xing yi, li xing zhexue*). Then he commenced to lecture. The lecture, which was on Sun Yat-sen's variant of Wang Yangming's "the unity of knowledge and action" (*zhi xing he yi*), went on for over an hour.

At the end Teng Jie passed around paper and each of the former cadets wrote down his choices for the leadership of the new organization. The ballots were sealed in an envelope by Teng and passed to Chiang. The *lingxiu* then assigned two examination themes: "A discussion of Bismarck's policy of iron and blood" (*Lun Bisemai tiexue de zhengce*) and "An essay on the significance of a co-operative society"

54. Gan Guoxun, "Guanyu suowei 'Fuxingshe' de zhenqing shikuang," p. 36; Deng Yuanzhong, *Sanminzhuyi lixingshe shi*, p. 117.
55. Gan Guoxun, "Guanyu suowei 'Fuxingshe' de zhenqing shikuang," p. 36.

(*Shishu hezuo she de yiyi*). He instructed each person to choose one of the two and compose an essay in classical or vernacular Chinese of whatever length he wished. The paper was due the next morning at 8.00.[56]

The following morning, 29 February, they returned to the classroom and turned in their essays to Teng Jie.[57] Chiang Kai-shek read the essays, writing comments and assigning grades. One paper, Yi Deming's, he found wanting. The rest he gave to Teng Jie to hand back. Chiang would use the students' essays, their verbal presentation in the evening meetings, their appearance, their Whampoa class, their past experience and the number of votes they had received in the election to assign each man a position in the new organization in ranked order.[58]

The *lingxiu* and his disciples then walked over to the Lizhishe auditorium, which was dominated by another large photograph of Sun Yat-sen. They formed a circle, holding hands. Chiang said: "This organization is going to be named the Sanminzhuyi Lixingshe." Then they stood at attention, facing the Chairman's portrait, and, raising their right hands, pledged:

> I swear in all my sincerity to practise the Three People's Principles with vigour, to recover revolutionary spirit, to revive the Chinese race, to sacrifice all personal interest, to obey orders, to adhere strictly to secrecy, and to complete the task of revolution and of building the country.[59] If I breach my oath, I am willing to accept the most severe punishment. I pledge this sincerely.[60]

Each stamped his right thumb print on the oath, which was chopped with Chiang Kai-shek's seal. The paper texts were then collected by Teng Jie and solemnly burned, just as one would burn paper money to the spirits. Holding hands again, they were addressed by Chiang Kai-shek. "I will do my best to lead you," he said. "From now on all of you must exert yourselves even harder than before to unite in society, to strive and to struggle. We will not stop until we achieve our goal. I wish you success." The Sanminzhuyi Lixingshe was thereby formally established.[61]

### *Core and Front Groups*

The existence of this small freemasonry of Chiang Kai-shek loyalists within the right-wing movements and secret service organizations of the Nationalists was from the start hopelessly confused with its front groups or "satellite" (*waiwei*) organizations: the Revolutionary Army Comrades Association (Geming junren tongzhi hui), the Revolutionary Youth Comrades Association (Geming qingnian tongzhi hui), the Renaissance Society (Fuxingshe), and the notorious Blue Shirts Society (Lanyishe),

56. *Ibid.*; Deng Yuanzhong, *Sanminzhuyi lixingshe shi*, pp. 118, 119.
57. Maria Hsia Chang, *The Chinese Blue Shirt Society*, p. 57.
58. Deng Yuanzhong, *Sanminzhuyi lixingshe shi*, p. 118–19; Gan Guoxun, "Guanyu suowei 'Fuxingshe' de zhenqing shikuang," p. 37.
59. Maria Hsia Chang, *The Chinese Blue Shirt Society*, p. 41.
60. Gan Guoxun, "Guanyu suowei 'Fuxingshe' de zhenqing shikuang," p. 37.
61. Deng Yuanzhong, *Sanminzhuyi lixingshe shi*, p. 119.

which never really existed as a formal Lixingshe instrument as such but which was identified with it in official documents, taking on an existence of its own.[62] This was partly because of the effort to keep the existence of the Lixingshe a secret known only to its members.

> The secretiveness of the Lixingshe can be viewed from three angles: in terms of personnel, in terms of organization, and in terms of activities. The secrecy in these three areas was closely interconnected. In terms of personnel, no one should disclose their identity in the organization to anyone else, not even to one's own family members, or else one would be disciplined. Comrades who are not involved in the same area of functional assignments should avoid contact, so as to avoid the chance of revealing one's identity. The names of high-level cadres within the organization may not be known to all comrades.[63]

Concealed within its front groups, the Lixingshe appeared to the public as Blue Shirts: fascist-seeming fanatics and terrorist thugs whose formal organization was the Renaissance Society. In truth, the Lixingshe retained a separate identity, acting through the more widely known Fuxingshe, just as it tried to operate secretly within the propaganda, police and special services to further the cause of Chiang Kai-shek and the Three People's Principles.[64]

On 1 March 1932, the day after they swore to form the Lixingshe, the founders held a "cadres meeting" (*ganbu huiyi*) in the offices on Whampoa Road.[65] The purpose of the gathering was to organize a directorate and form front groups. Deng Wenyi read out Chiang Kai-shek's list of the society's staff officers (*ganshi*). Their Commission (Ganshihui) would constitute the executive directorate of the organization. Its director during the first year of the society's existence was secretary-general Teng Jie. He was to be succeeded in the second year by He Zhonghan, and in the third by Liu Jianqun.[66] Alongside the secretariat were four departments: General Affairs, headed by Li Yimin; Organization, under Shao Zhangyu; Propaganda, directed by Kang Ze; and Special Services, commanded first by Gui Yongqing, and then by Dai Li.[67]

In January 1933, when the delegates to the Lixingshe from its various front groups grew too numerous, an additional Control Commission (Jianchahui) was created. It supervised the branch offices' performance, meted out discipline, scrutinized budgets and presided over the oathtaking of new members. Its inspectors answered to the Staff Officers Commission, but they were granted the authority to imprison and execute

62. Yun Yiqun, *Sanshi nian jianwen zaji*, p. 43; Hu Menghua, "CC waiwei zuzhi Chengshe shimo" ("The whole story of the CC front organization in the Sincerity Club"), in Chinese People's Political Consultative Conference National Committee, *Wenshi ziliao xuanji*, fascicle 14, p. 147.

63. Deng Yuanzhong, *Sanminzhuyi lixingshe shi*, p. 128.

64. *Ibid.* p. 129.

65. Gan Guoxun, "Guanyu suowei 'Fuxingshe' de zhenqing shikuang," p. 28.

66. *Ibid.*, *zhong*, p. 71.

67. Gan Guoxun, "Guanyu suowei 'Fuxingshe' de zhenqing shikuang," p. 37. See also Xiao Zuolin, "Fuxingshe shulüe," pp. 23–24.

malefactors within the organization, and their secret reports were forwarded directly to the Lixingshe secretariat.[68]

Following the principles of secrecy they had all pledged to uphold, the cadres decided to organize two front groups. The first was the Revolutionary Army Comrades Association (Geming junren tongzhi hui), with Pan Youqiang as the standing staff officer and secretary-general. It was relatively short-lived, largely because Chiang Kai-shek feared that it would disrupt the regular chain of command in the army. However, he did authorize the formation of a Military Affairs Department (Junshichu) within the headquarters of the Lixingshe and appointed Du Xinru its chief.[69]

The second front group lasted as long as the Lixingshe itself, constituting an "inner layer" (*neiceng*) called the Revolutionary Youth Comrades Association (Geming qingnian tongzhi hui) (RYCA).[70] Ge Wuqi was the standing staff officer and secretary-general, with Gan Guoxun in charge of organization, Kang Ze responsible for propaganda and Liu Chengzhi directing general affairs. The RYCA was the Lixingshe's primary cover group: its name was used to recruit followers, and it was under its aegis that many of the "special services" (*tewu*) activities were implemented in other organizations and offices. Most of the members were Whampoa graduates or medium-level cadres from other right-wing organizations. There was in addition a contingent of higher-level intellectuals, including university professors, and middle-level bureaucrats like party secretaries, section chiefs, department chiefs, bureau chiefs and provincial department chiefs. All the "backbone cadres" or secretaries of this "inner layer" organization were either Lixingshe members or, as the organization expanded through branch offices, central party cadres.[71] The headquarters of the RYCA was located in the Investigation Department (Diaochachu) of the Alumni Information Bureau in the Central Military School's Mingwalang compound in Nanjing.[72] The "democratic centralism" of the RYCA – which at one time had about 20,000 members – was reinforced by its budgetary practices.[73]

"Elder" and "younger," "core" and "inner layer," together quickly came to control several crucial indoctrination programmes for officers and officials going through the Nationalist military and civil training system. Members of the Lixingshe and the RYCA took part in the political training of cadres in the infantry, artillery, engineering and quartermaster corps; and they were deeply involved in seminars for district administration personnel run by the Ministry of the Interior, and in summer training programmes held at Lushan for higher-ranking party

68. Gan Guoxun, "Guanyu suowei 'Fuxingshe' de zhenqing shikuang," *zhong*, p. 72.
69. *Ibid.* p. 37.
70. Huang Yong, "Huangpu xuesheng," p. 13; Hung-mao Tien, *Government and Politics*, p. 56.
71. Xiao Zuolin, "Fuxingshe shulüe," pp. 23–24. See also Yun Yiqun, *Sanshi nian jianwen zaji*, p. 43.
72. Paul T. K. Sih (ed.), *The Strenuous Decade: China's Nation-Building Efforts, 1927–1937* (New York: St John's University Press, 1970), p. 50.
73. Xiao Zuolin, "Fuxingshe shulüe," pp. 24–27.

and political military personnel. Lixingshe members also commanded the Chief Brigade for the Higher Education of Army Officers (Junguan gaodeng jiaoyu zongdui), which conducted a six-month training course for 600 graduates of the first six classes of the Central Military Academy in 1932.[74]

Members of the Lixingshe and the RYCA furthermore dominated the leadership of the Training Class for Army Officers Attached to the Military Academy (Junxiao fushe junguan xunlianban). The four brigades of this training unit were put together in August 1932 with more than 1,700 officers between the ranks of lieutenant and colonel who were detached from their regular units for a year. The flavour of their allegiance was partly captured in their class anthem, "Song of the Leader" (*Lingxiu ge*):

China is indeed great!
Each generation has its worthy and able men.
Though there have always been disorder and upheaval
We've always been able to recover (*fuxing*).
Today Chiang Kai-shek is our saviour (*jiuxing*).
We march forward together with him.
*Fuxing! Fuxing!*[75]

The brigades' graduates, who had three German officers as their advisers, mostly returned to their original posts, though a small number were retained in the Military Academy as members of the Chief Brigade for Military Instruction (Jiaodao zongdui).

The most important additional group created by the Lixingshe was the Renaissance Society (Fuxingshe). This "third tier satellite organization" (*di sanji waiwei zuzhi*) was added to the structure in July 1932, when Ren Juewu was serving as the secretary-general of the RYCA. It was proposed by Ren to preserve secrecy and screen the character of applicants.[76]

### *The Renaissance Society*

The Fuxingshe became well known, according to Gan:

> Because it had no cadres, no organization, no offices, and no funding from the central level all the way down to branch and local organizations. All of its affairs, in fact, were taken care of by the Revolutionary Youth Comrades Association. Also, recruitment on this level was not very strict. So the Renaissance Society flourished. That is why this national revival movement (*minzu fuxing yundong*) acquired such fame.[77]

Membership in the satellite organizations was automatic for those who belonged to the Lixingshe. However, membership in the other direction was tightly controlled the closer one got to the core. The Fuxingshe was relatively easy to join, once one had been recommended by older or

74. Gan Guoxun, "Guanyu suowei 'Fuxingshe' de zhenqing shikuang," *zhong*, pp. 68, 70.
75. *Ibid.* p. 69.
76. *Ibid.* p. 37.
77. *Ibid.*

former members of the group. The application form was simple, and usually initiations were conducted in groups of ten before portraits of Chiang Kai-shek. On some occasions in Nanjing, where Chiang Kai-shek accepted the oaths in person, 300 to 600 people participated in the swearing-in ceremonies.[78]

If a Fuxingshe member was nominated for the RYCA, on the other hand, he had to be endorsed by a general meeting of that group, and then be screened by the Lixingshe before his name was passed on to the supreme leader for his approval. The same procedure worked for the next level up: "A member of the RYCA [wanting to join the Lixingshe] had to pass through a Lixingshe general meeting and then be presented to the leader for approval, and only after getting his approval would he take his oath and become a member of the Lixingshe."[79]

The Fuxingshe did not have the authority to make official appointments, but its higher-level cadres did use the cover of deputy in the Political Indoctrination Department (Zhengxunchu).[80] In its internal governance, the Fuxingshe was dominated by a Staff Officers Committee (Ganshihui).[81] But power was wielded by its secretary-general who was appointed directly by the chairman, Chiang Kai-shek.[82] Under the secretary-general, who was initially Teng Jie, there were groups (*zu*) or departments (*chu*) for organization, propaganda and training led respectively by Zhou Fu, Kang Ze and Gui Yongqing.[83] The Special Services Department, of course, was put in Dai Li's hands. This same structure was replicated at the provincial and municipal levels, with the fundamental grassroots unit being the small-group or cell (*xiaozu*), which usually held weekly meetings.[84]

General meetings were hardly ever held, except for those rare occasions when district (*qu*) and branch (*fen*) associations held convocations. All decisions came from the top down, and there was nothing resembling a congress or representative assembly.[85] The content of the weekly cell meeting was dictated by the higher-level organization's written instructions. Usually, the meetings were about internal and international political events, important propaganda points, activities of the local group and investigation activities towards suspected Communist elements and CC clique members. After each meeting, the head of the cell was supposed to write a report that was sent up to the next level. Intelligence reports went directly to the central organization, bypassing the branch committees.[86]

78. Huang Yong, "Huangpu xuesheng," p. 16.
79. Gan Guoxun, "Guanyu suowei 'Fuxingshe' de zhenqing shikuang," pp. 37, 38.
80. Xiao Zuolin, "Fuxingshe shulüe," p. 26.
81. Zhang Weihan, "Dai Li yu 'Juntong ju,' " p. 85.
82. Shen Zui, *Juntong neimu* (*The Inside Story of the Military Statistics (Bureau)*) (Beijing: Wenshi ziliao chubanshe, 1984), pp.i–ii; Huang Yong, "Huangpu xuesheng," p. 13.
83. Huang Yong, "Huangpu xuesheng," p. 14.
84. Xiao Zuolin, "Fuxingshe shulüe," p. 25.
85. Burton, "Chiang's secret blood brothers," p. 310.
86. Xiao Zuolin, "Fuxingshe shulüe," pp. 24–25.

Each level of the Fuxingshe, from central headquarters to branch offices, was supposedly attached to parallel organs at an identical level in the RYCA. The "responsible person" (*fuzeren*) in the RYCA was also the "responsible person" in the Fuxingshe. However, there were efforts to draw a visible distinction between membership in each group. RYCA members addressed each other as "best friends" (*zhiyou*), while Fuxingshe members were only supposed to exchange greetings as "good friends" (*haoyou*). Both Fuxingshe and RYCA members who received more than 200 *yuan* a month were supposed to tithe to the organization (a duty that was almost never carried out), but while the former could only be dismissed for a Fuxingshe infraction, RYCA members could be placed under house arrest and even in some cases executed for infringing the association's rules. In practice, membership often overlapped, and the distinction between cells in each group often became confused. "The Revolutionary Youth Comrades Association and the Renaissance Society, except for the distinction between inner and outer layers, actually was one single thing," explained one former provincial secretary of both groups. "Thus it is quite possible to use the term 'Fuxingshe' to represent these two organizations together."[87]

Altogether, then, there were three tiers, with the Lixingshe at the "core" (*hexin*), encircled by two front groups. All three constituted parallel hierarchies, extending downward from the capital to the provinces via bureaucratic offices and occupational associations.[88] At the peak of its activities, this entire three-ringed structure consisted of more than 500,000 members, with those in the outer circles supposedly not knowing about the existence of the inner ones until they were tapped for membership.[89] The innermost core always remained the Lixingshe, whose name was sometimes shortened to the Lishe or Power Society, and its 80 or 90 activists continued to be predominantly Whampoa graduates.[90] A few civilians were also invited to join, such as Counsellor Liu Wendao, who had served in the diplomatic corps in Italy and had good contacts with the Fascists there.[91]

If it was possible for members of the RYCA and the Fuxingshe to refer to their own separate "inner layer" and "satellite organization" together as the Fuxingshe, then it is little wonder that the public at large identified the entire structure collectively as the Renaissance Society. In addition, however, the Fuxingshe was lumped together indiscriminately with the ubiquitous and amorphous Blue Shirts. This confusion arose when one of the "outsiders" recommended to Chiang Kai-shek for membership in the

87. *Ibid.* pp. 24–26.
88. Deng Yuanzhong, *Sanminzhuyi lixingshe shi*, p. 129.
89. Xiao Zuolin, "Fuxingshe shulüe," p. 24. Informants in the PRC who have had access to detailed information on former Fuxingshe members report that they seldom knew the "inner" details of the entire organization's top tiers.
90. *Ibid.*; Huang Yong, "Huangpu xuesheng," pp. 12–13.
91. "Blueshirts – Fascisti Movement in China," Special Branch Secret Memorandum, 20 June 1933, in Shanghai Municipal Police (International Settlement) Files, No. D-4685, p. 4. The non-military members were especially important to Chiang Kai-shek. Hung-mao Tien, *Government and Politics*, p. 59.

original Lixingshe freemasonry tried to claim personal credit for the foundation of a separate Lanyishe or Blue Shirts Society.

During the second "preparations department" evening meeting held in late February 1932 at Chiang Kai-shek's bungalow, Gui Yongqing, who had spoken at such length the night before about his trip across Europe and Asia, surprised everyone by raising his hand. He said he wanted to recommend a "talent" (*rencai*) to the *lingxiu* in the presence of them all, and that person was He Yingqin's secretary-general Liu Jianqun, who – like General He, former Minister of War, member of the Special Affairs Committee of the Central Political Council and Chiang Kai-shek's closest military supporter – hailed from Guizhou.[92] To these former Whampoa cadets Liu Jianqun was an outsider.[93] Although many among them knew and respected him, he had never attended the academy, and as a civilian he only held a rank equivalent to major general. Nevertheless, Gui said, "he is a party loyalist and a patriot, and he has concrete proposals about protecting the party and saving the country. We must get him and make use of him." Chiang Kai-shek agreed.[94]

The introduction of Liu Jianqun into their proceedings completely entangled the founders of the Lixingshe with what became known to the public at large as the notorious Blue Shirt Society. This confusion has persisted to the present, largely due to the Japanese press, which for years referred indiscriminately to all the activities of the Lixingshe and its front organizations as the doings of the Blue Shirts, regardless of whether they were actual Special Services Department operations or spontaneous acts of patriotic resistance. However, the confusion was initially perpetrated by Liu Jianqun himself, who was eager to take credit for the formation of this paramilitary force in order to press his own claims for recognition within the ranks of Chiang Kai-shek's right-wing supporters.[95]

### *The Blue Shirts*

Liu Jianqun put forward these claims to reporters eleven months after the Lixingshe founding in a press conference that he convened in January 1933, when he was serving as commander of the North China Propaganda Brigade (Huabei xuanchuan dui) in Beijing. At that meeting he distributed three treatises of his creation, including one entitled "The Organization of the Blue Shirt Society of the Chinese Kuomintang." This was the proposal that he had circulated to the KMT Central Executive Committee meeting in Nanjing in October 1931, calling for the formation of a Blue Shirt Society "in an endeavour to strengthen the internal organization of the party" at a time when so many members of the KMT were said by him to be avaricious militarists, corrupt officials, local bullies and rotten gentry.[96]

92. Boorman, *Biographical Dictionary of Republican China*, Vol. 2, pp. 79–80. See also Wei, *Counterrevolution in China*, pp. 35–36.
93. Deng Yuanzhong, *Sanminzhuyi lixingshe shi*, p. 69.
94. Gan Guoxun, "Guanyu suowei 'Fuxingshe' de zhenqing shikuang," p. 35.
95. Deng Yuanzhong, *Sanminzhuyi lixingshe shi*, pp. 13–14, 16–17.
96. "The Blue Shirt Society," *Beiping chenbao*, date unknown. Translated in Special

Liu's tract went on to say that there had been dispute over the name of this proposed society, with some people favouring "Youth Corps" while others wanted to call it the "Cotton Cloth Corps."[97] Liu felt that both these were unsuitable "as the former might be misunderstood for the youth group of the Communist Party, while the second name is not complete as there are other native products such as silk." Since the KMT regarded blue-green (*qing*) and white as party colours, and since blue shirts were both stipulated formal attire for the Nationalists and the standard dress of the common people since ancient times, Liu proposed taking the name "Blue Shirt Society of the Chinese Kuomintang" for his new group. "Members of the society must use native goods everywhere, and those who attend a formal conference of the society must wear the Sun Yat-sen uniform."[98]

The briefing may have been held because Liu wanted to elevate his position among Chiang Kai-shek loyalists alongside as well as within the Lixingshe power structure. After he was recommended by Gui Yongqing, Liu was introduced by He Zhonghan and Teng Jie to the inner circle of the Lixingshe. Through their formal recommendation he was invited to join the second tier of the organization as a full-fledged member of the RYCA. Now, by claiming to have urged Chiang Kai-shek to set up a Blue Shirts Society 18 months earlier, Liu Jianqun was both seeking to create a power base of his own and establish a claim to higher office within the core and satellite organizations of the Lixingshe.[99]

His effort proved successful. More than a year later, in April 1934, he was transferred from the Beijing branch of the Department of Political Indoctrination (Zhengxunchu) to become secretary of the headquarters of the Renaissance Society in Nanjing. At the same time he was made standing staff officer of the Society for Vigorous Practice – an office he was reappointed to after Feng Ti's disgrace over the Wang Jingwei assassination attempt in November 1935. Although his Lixingshe post was kept secret, his position as secretary-general of the Renaissance Society must have strengthened the link in the public's mind between the Fuxingshe and the Lanyishe, which infuriated Lixingshe insiders who later claimed to have been dismayed by the connection that this appeared to forge between their movement and a fascist Blue Shirts movement. Gan Guoxun, who was the standing staff officer of the RYCA and a founding member of the Lixingshe, accused such latecomers as Liu Jianqun of belonging to satellite organizations that were deliberately excluded from the highest tier or innermost circle of the structure and prohibited from

---

*footnote continued*
Branch Report, 29 June 1933, in Shanghai Municipal Police (International Settlement) Files, No. D-4685, p. 2. See also Zeng Kuoqing, "He Mei xieding qian Fuxingshe zai Huabei de huodong," ("The activities of the Fuxingshe in north China before the He Mei Agreement") in Chinese People's Political Consultative Conference National Committee, *Wenshi ziliao xuanji*, fascicle 14, p. 131; Deng Yuanzhong, *Sanminzhuyi lixingshe shi*, pp. 16–17.

97. Maria Hsia Chang, " 'Fascism' and Modern China," pp. 564–65; Eastman, "Fascism and Modern China: a rejoinder," p. 842.

98. "The Blue Shirt Society," pp. 2–3.

99. Zeng Kuoqing, "He Mei xieding," p. 135.

making horizontal links of their own. Such outsiders, Gan argued, ignorantly or malevolently identified the Fuxingshe with the Blue Shirts.

The connection between the mysterious Lixingshe, the Fuxingshe and the Lanyishe was reinforced by other satellite members, many of them younger Whampoa alumni, who knew that at least some of these organizations were formed around 1 March 1932 by the cohort of Chiang loyalists who were prominent in propaganda, military indoctrination and intelligence work. They knew of the existence of a Society for Vigorous Practice, which they believed was based on three principles: Chiang Kai-shek would be the supreme and permanent leader; Whampoa alumni would form the base of the group; and its members would follow the precepts of the Three People's Principles, practise Communist organizational techniques and cultivate the spirit of Japanese samurai.[100] They thought that responsibility for actually forming and organizing the Lixingshe was delegated to five members of the founding group: He Zhonghan, Feng Ti, Teng Jie, Zhou Fu and Kang Ze.[101] They understood that the organization was completely centralized around this "core nucleus" of five men plus some 50 others. And they were told that a number of cells within the Lixingshe held weekly meetings in Chiang Kai-shek's official residence inside the Mingwalang compound, where they were given lectures by their "principal" on the "philosophy of practising with vigour," and where they also studied German and Italian fascist organizations.[102]

The association between this group and the Blue Shirts was reinforced even more when the Japanese became convinced of the group's existence. This came about partly through Liu Jianqun's press conference and partly through the writings of Fu Shenglan, who published a book called *The Inside Story of the Blue Shirts* (*Lanyishe de neimu*) in which he described the Blue Shirts as a secret service organization. Fu was a member of the Communist Party who was persuaded by Kang Ze to join one of the satellite organs of the Lixingshe in 1933. He later transferred his allegiance to the Wang Jingwei puppet government and during the war of resistance served as the collaborationist mayor of Hangzhou. His book on the Blue Shirts was adopted by the Japanese Military Police in Shanghai as teaching material to train Chinese who worked for the Japanese secret service.[103]

Meanwhile, all that the public knew, according to Liu Jianqun, was that membership in the Blue Shirts Society had to be kept a strict secret.

> With a view to attaining the object of immediately overthrowing the feudal influences, exterminating the Red Bandits, and dealing with foreign insult[s], members of the Blue Shirt Society should conduct in secret their activities in various provinces, *xian* and cities, except for the central Kuomintang headquarters and other political organs whose work must be executed in an official manner.[104]

100. These principles are enumerated in Hakano Ken'ichi's studies cited in Hung-mao Tien, *Government and Politics*, pp. 55–56.

101. Zhang Weihan, "Dai Li yu 'Juntong ju', " p. 84; Xiao Zuolin, "Fuxingshe shulüe," p. 12.

102. Huang Yong, "Huangpu xuesheng," p. 12.

103. Deng Yuanzhong, *Sanminzhuyi lixingshe shi*, p. 17. See also Coble, "Super-patriots and secret agents," *passim*.

104. "The Blue Shirt Society," p. 3.

Even though Blue Shirts were supposed to "launch people's movements," they were also told to be prepared to assume "secret service" duties and never to reveal to others that they were from the KMT. Indeed – as the Shanghai Municipal Police Special Branch later remarked – the reason they had so few details about the Blue Shirts during their seven years' existence was precisely because those who had sworn oaths to join the society "were forbidden to admit to outsiders that they were members of the Blue Shirt Society or to disclose its secrets under the penalty of death, which was the only punishment."[105] Needless to say, the existence of the Blue Shirts was never publicly recognized by Chiang Kai-shek.[106]

Liu Jianqun himself, while claiming credit for suggesting the establishment of the society in the first place, had to go on record before the press as not having created the organization. Questioned by a *Beijing chenbao* reporter as to whether or not the Blue Shirts had actually been formed, Liu replied:

> In the winter of 1931, I suggested the reorganization of the Kuomintang with the sole object of promoting universal respect towards the Three Principles of the People. The foundation of the Blue Shirt Society is interlocked with that of the Kuomintang. The Blue Shirt Society will have no new doctrines beyond those of the Kuomintang. We can at once know the object of the organization by understanding the original title, the Blue Shirt Society and not the Blue Shirts Party. This scheme of mine was only a suggestion to the Kuomintang. I have not as a matter of fact participated in any movement of this nature. I am not in a position to give any reply to all kinds of questions relating to the activities of this organization.[107]

The reporter concluded, at the end of the January 1933 press conference, that "from Mr Liu's statement, it was still impossible for us to speak with any certainty of the existence or non-existence of this society."[108] What was certain, however, was that the press, as well as foreign intelligence and police organs, would thereafter equate the activities of the Renaissance Society (and behind it, the Lixingshe) with right-wing Blue Shirts in their midst.[109]

Who, for example, was behind the formation of the new Nationalist version of the Chinese Boy Scouts (Zhongguo tongzi jun) in April 1933? There had been a Boy Scouts movement in China since about 1917, when Jing Hengyi established a national branch that participated in the Boy Scouts world congress after the war. But the Chinese Boy Scouts of the 1930s embodied a much more militaristic effort, closely associated with the Department for National Military Training (Guomin junshi jiaoyu zu) that was formed in July 1932. Zhao Fansheng, a military academy graduate who served as the department's director, and Yang Kejing, head of academic affairs for the Guomin junshi jiaoyu zu, had originally been section and unit heads in the national Boy Scouts headquarters. With the

105. "Memorandum on the Blue Shirt Society," p. 3.
106. Hung-mao Tien, *Government and Politics*, p. 56.
107. "The Blue Shirt Society," pp. 1–2.
108. *Ibid.* p. 2.
109. See, for example, *ibid.* p. 1.

help of Lixingshe founder Gan Guoxun, they drafted a programme, complete with charter and budget, to train Boy Scout officers from around the country. After Chiang Kai-shek approved the proposal, 160 students were recruited for cadre training. One-third were graduates of the military academy, and the rest were Boy Scout officers already serving in schools in the provinces. The purpose of the six-month programme was to train officers and instructors "to reform the Chinese Boy Scouts, to strengthen and enlarge their organization, to stimulate their intellectual and physical capacities, to heighten their consciousness, to firm up their patriotic and revolutionary will, and to give these youths some military knowledge."[110] At the same time, the Lixingshe set up another "satellite" operation in the form of a Society for Vigorous Advancement (Lijinshe), which was specifically charged with penetrating the Boy Scouts. By April 1933 the Lijinshe had 300 members, all of whom were provincial and municipal officers of the newly staffed Zhongguo tongzi jun.[111]

Individual members of these satellite organizations frequently identified themselves as members of the Blue Shirts. They claimed to hold to a common political programme, devoted to strengthening the "dictatorship of General Chiang Kai-shek," if necessary by force.[112] According to them:

> The "Blue Shirt Society" was established in 1931 with a view to achieving an effective "Party Rule" and was sponsored by Chiang Kai-shek with a number of his most ardent supporters. This society was a secret organization and only operated within the Kuomintang, its main object being to create a "strong Kuomintang feeling among the rank-and-file in the army." When this was accomplished, the warlords and their abuse of military power would be defeated.[113]

According to the intelligence reports, three movements were to be launched. First, a "movement to make the army sound" (*jianjun yundong*) was supposed to maintain surveillance over generals throughout the country and carry out a "fascinization" of the Chinese armies by conducting military training classes at the Political Training Institute. This probably corresponded to the "national military training movement" (*guomin junxun yundong*) referred to in accounts of the Society for Vigorous Practice.[114] Secondly, a "movement to make the party sound" (*jiandang yundong*) was intended to drive out competing cliques and restore the full powers of Chiang's presidency, while despatching Blue Shirt elements to local party branches "in order to safeguard the fascist movement of the association." And thirdly, a "movement to make finances sound" (*jiancai yundong*) would equalize land rights, raise loans for state-owned enterprises, and "provide the Fascist movement with material supports."[115]

110. Gan Guoxun, "Guanyu suowei 'Fuxingshe' de zhenqing shikuang," *zhong*, p. 69.
111. *Ibid. shang*, p. 38.
112. "Memorandum on the "The Blue Shirt Society," p. 3; "The Fascist or 'Blue Shirt' Party in China," pp. 1–2.
113. Shanghai Municipal Police Files, D-4685 (C), 3/10/40.
114. Gan Guoxun, "Guanyu suowei 'Fuxingshe' de zhenqing shikuang," *xia*, p. 82; Maria Hsia Chang, *The Chinese Blue Shirt Society*, p. 5.
115. "Blueshirts – Fascisti Movement in China," p. 2; Hung-mao Tien, *Government and Politics*, pp. 58, 64.

This last was probably what the Lixingshe called a "movement for national economic construction" (*guomin jingji jianshe yundong*), which followed Sun's principle of the people's livelihood in seeking to create a nation of owner-cultivators. In an explicit spirit of "self-reliance" (*zili-gengsheng*), the Lixingshe sought to reclaim land, nurture farm labour and productivity, and actively promote agricultural productivity and exports.[116] This programme was to be carried out with funds from the membership dues of the Whampoa Alumni Association. In the summer of 1932, Chiang Kai-shek actually ordered the alumni group to set aside Mex. $350,000 out of its endowment, to which was added $650,000 from the treasury of the Nanchang headquarters command. These moneys were used to set up a Peasants Bank (Nongmin yinhang) for the four provinces of Henan, Hubei, Anhui and Jiangxi. The bank was chartered to provide loans for peasants returned to areas recently reclaimed from "bandits." More funds were added by Chiang Kai-shek in spring 1933, bringing the total to $4,000,000. With this endowment and the approval of the Minister of Finance, a national China Peasants Bank was founded to provide credit unions with low-interest loans. Chen Guofu was named chairman of the board.

As far as the public knew, however, there was no connection at all between the China Peasants Bank and the Blue Shirts, whose ideological principles were evidently being spelled out in speeches and writings by the group's three major "theoreticians," He Zhonghan, Deng Wenyi and Liu Jianqun.[117] The message that their tracts repeatedly put out was that in order to repel foreign invaders the Chinese people had first to unify and strengthen the nation by exterminating the Communist Party. After that eradication was accomplished, there would be a social and economic revival in the countryside, giving the Chinese the resources to build up their armies by concentrating their "racial spirit" (*minzu jingshen*) upon the single leader and party destined to command them against their foreign attackers. There was a vague political programme outlined in these writings, but a former provincial leader of the movement in later years could only remember its general outlines: to support absolutely the leadership of Chiang Kai-shek, carry out the centralization of government, recover lost territory and protect national sovereignty, abolish the unequal treaties, carry out the equalization of land rights, develop agriculture, carry out economic controls, develop national capital, strengthen national defence, carry out a system of conscription, thoroughly train and develop a national people's army, clean out bureaucratic corruption in the government, establish universal education, eradicate the Communist Party completely, and bring peace and social order to the country. Of all these, the two goals he most vividly recalled as being emphatically stressed were to render full support to Chiang Kai-shek's leadership and to exterminate the Communists.[118]

116. Maria Hsia Chang, *The Chinese Blue Shirt Society*, pp. 68–81.
117. "Two Sources of Anti-Japanism," in *The Osaka Mainichi and the Tokyo Nichi Nichi Supplement: The China Emergency*, 20 October 1937, p. 29.
118. Xiao Zuolin, "Fuxingshe shulüe," pp. 30, 43.

*"Fascinization"*

It is difficult to know how seriously to take these calls for "fascinization," or even to estimate how representative they were of the Blue Shirts' ideology as a whole.[119] Certainly, contemporary newspaper reports depicted the Blue Shirts as "fascist" or "semi-fascist" elements with national socialist leanings.[120] Describing a "gang of semi-fascists known as 'Blue Shirts' [who] have established their headquarters in a luxurious flat in Caine Road" in Hong Kong, the *North China Daily News* claimed that they wanted to establish a dictatorship along the grounds of Mussolini's government.[121] "These Chinese Fascists believe that strong-men are needed to hold the reins of government. Hence, 'swastika' methods will be used in dealing with political opponents."[122] Judging from contemporary police reports, however, there does at least seem to have been a segment of the Renaissance Society that was relatively vocal and took its fascist labels to heart. This element among the Whampoa graduates was dominated by former cadets who had studied in Germany, France, Italy and Belgium, and who looked to Feng Ti, first secretary of the Fuxingshe and then later the Chinese military attaché in Berlin, as their leader. Feng in turn allied himself with Tang Zong, who also served as military attaché in Berlin, as well as with Gu Xiping, who had studied in France; with Liu Pan, who had undertaken police training in Belgium; and with Tang Wu, who had studied in Italy.[123] This group, which urged Chiang Kai-shek to model himself after Hitler and Mussolini, was usually identified with the putative and ubiquitous Blue Shirt Society.[124]

Whatever the internal authenticity of the Lanyishe, the Special Branch equated its membership – which the Japanese Foreign Ministry's Bureau of Investigation estimated to be 14,000 by the end of 1935 – with the "fascist wing" of the three-tiered Fuxingshe, and singled out its primary leader as being He Zhonghan.[125] He Zhonghan clearly envisaged himself as becoming the political leader of the so-called "Whampoa clique." The term generally referred to graduates of the first three years of the Academy, but the closest thing that it had to a genuine factional structure was the Renaissance Society.[126] The Blue Shirts were sometimes viewed, therefore, as being purely and simply the Whampoa clique, and as such

119. *China Quarterly*, summer 1937, 2.488, cited in Walter E. Gourlay, " 'Yellow' unionism in Shanghai: a study of Kuomintang technique in labor control, 1927–1937," *Papers on China*, Vol. 7 (Cambridge, MA: Harvard University Committee on International and Regional Studies, 1953), p. 106.

120. "Blue Shirts Organization," p. 4.

121. Maria Hsia Chang, *The Chinese Blue Shirt Society*, p. 22.

122. "The Blue Shirts for China," *The North China Daily News*, 20 June 1933. Clipped in Shanghai Municipal Police (International Settlement) Files, No. D-4685, 8 July 1933.

123. William C. Kirby, *Germany and Republican China* (Stanford: Stanford University Press, 1984), pp. 137, 232

124. Huang Yong, "Huangpu xuesheng," p. 11; Maria Hsia Chang, *The Chinese Blue Shirt Society*, p. 22.

125. "The Blue Shirt Society," p. 7; Xiao Zuolin, "Fuxingshe shulüe," p. 58; "Memorandum on the Blue Shirt Society," p. 4; " 'Blue Shirts' to suspend anti-Japanese activities," *The Shanghai Times*, 21 January 1936, n.p.

126. Hung-mao Tien, *Government and Politics*, p. 53.

members of the Lixingshe and its front groups thought of themselves as being part of Chiang Kai-shek's *dixi* – that is, his direct line of descent or "family."[127]

The term *di*, which was an invidious intrafamilial distinction that referred to the progeny of a wife as opposed to of a concubine, was very revealing. It signalled the creation, below the level of competition between Chiang Kai-shek and rivals Wang Jingwei and Hu Hanmin to control the legitimate institutions of the regime such as the Central Executive Committee and the Political Council, of cliques within the Generalissimo's own power structure. These cliques were competing at the level of policy implementation, where the regime's resources were actually allocated, and their struggles accompanied the rise of Chiang Kai-shek to paramountcy, if not total hegemony, within the governing structure of China.[128] The distinction between direct and indirect "family," therefore, was not even primarily a civil cleavage; it was used by extension to refer to Chiang Kai-shek's "family troops" (*dixi budui*): the half-million men who were commanded by Generals Chen Cheng, Hu Zongnan and Tang Enbo, and who were considered to be the Generalissimo's *cohors praetoria*.[129] From the perspective of these self-styled "wife's sons," other cliques within Chiang's power structure were interlopers. Members of the CC clique, for instance, were viewed as Chiang's "adopted sons" (*minglingzi*), while the Political Study clique leaders Yang Yongtai and Zhang Qun were mere "yamen advisers" (*shiye*) and "household stewards" (*guanjia*).[130] Although the Blue Shirts did not have a particularly hostile attitude toward the Political Study Group, which they regarded as being no more than hired help, they did regard the "adopted sons" of the CC clique as being serious enemies; and from 1933 they began to direct a great deal of activity toward supplanting the Chen brothers' influence, especially in newspaper publishing and educational circles.[131]

Despite the rivalry between the Lixingshe and the CC clique, Chen Lifu was associated in the public's eye with these new "fascist" formations. According to a French intelligence report dated 12 August 1933, Chiang Kai-shek held a summer conference that year at Lushan, which was attended by Chen Lifu, Zeng Kuoqing, Wu Xingya (chief of the Shanghai Social Affairs Bureau) and Pan Gongzhan (chief of the Shanghai Educational Bureau of the KMT), among others.

During the course of the conference, development of the fascist movement in China was discussed. It was decided to establish in the first place fascist cells in the

127. Deng Yuanzhong, *Sanminzhuyi Lixingshe shi*, p. 130.

128. Hung-mao Tien, *Government and Politics*, pp. 46–47.

129. Zhang Xin, "Hu Zongnan qi ren," ("Hu Zongnan the man") in Wenshi ziliao yanjiu weiyuanhui (eds.), *Zhejiang wenshi ziliao xuanji* (*Selected Historical Materials on Zhejiang*, No. 23 (Zhejiang: Renmin chubanshe, 1982), pp. 172–73.

130. Xiao Zuolin, "Fuxingshe shulüe," pp. 54–55.

131. *Ibid.* See also Hung-mao Tien, *Government and Politics*, p. 63. "The Fascist or 'Blue Shirt' Party in China," p. 2; "The Blue Shirt Society and the arrest of Yuan Hsueh Yi," p. 1; Boorman, *Biographical Dictionary of Republican China*, Vol. 1, pp. 48–49, and Vol. 4, p. 18.

Kuomintang headquarters in "loyal military units" and in schools and universities.... We are informed among other things that the influence of the fascist elements begins to be more and more noticeable in the following universities: Sun Yat-sen (Guangzhou), Central (Nanjing), Honan (Kaifeng), and Chinan (Shanghai).[132]

Indeed, earlier that summer the president of Sun Yat-sen University, Zou Lu, accused the Blue Shirts of being a major annoyance at his school. Blaming recent movements of the undergraduates to oust him and to impeach him at the Ministry of Education on them, Zou alleged that "the Blue Shirts were trying to undermine the Kuomintang at the behest of certain militarists who wish to gain absolute powers in government like Benito Mussolini or Adolph Hitler."[133] According to newspaper reports like these, this new body of Chiang loyalists, whose appearance coincided with the advent of the Nazis, was considering adopting various names, including the Chinese Fascist Society and the Black Shirts Party.[134] Finally, they took the name Blue Shirt Society "because they thought that the [other] names ... might cause [the] Kuomintang to think that the new organization would be in violation of the rule of the Kuomintang that there can be no other political party besides the Kuomintang and that there must be no parties in the Kuomintang."[135]

The Lushan conference to which the French intelligence report referred may have been the summer session of the Army Officers Training Brigade (Junguan xunlian tuan), which Chiang Kai-shek addressed on 23 July 1933 during the weekly memorial ceremony for Sun Yat-sen. In that speech, which was entitled "What a modern soldier must know," Chiang described the three "newly developing nations" of Italy, Germany and Turkey as having a "collective slogan": "Labour (*laodong*)! Create (*chuangzao*)! Military force (*wuli*)!" "Labour," he explained, meant that the people of the entire country, from all walks of life and at all levels of society, from rulers to masses (*laobaixing*) and from generals to privates, worked together unstintingly and incessantly. "Create" signified the construction of a new nation, building a fresh society out of the old. "Military force" was the "substantive strength" (*shizhi de liliang*) required to bring forth revolution, sweeping aside all obstacles in order to foster the growth of the nation. All three of these, Chiang insisted, were intertwined and indispensable; they explained why the "newly developing nations" were rising so rapidly.[136]

132. Extract from French Police Daily Intelligence Report, 12 August 1933. In Shanghai Municipal Police (International Settlement) Files, No. D-4685, 26 August 1933.

133. "Blue Shirts for China," *The North China Daily News*, 20 June 1933. Clipped in Shanghai Municipal Police (International Settlement) Files, No. D-4685, 8 July 1933.

134. *Shanghai Times*, 7 January 1935, quoted in Shanghai Municipal Police Files, D-4040, 8/7/35.

135. "The Blue Shirt Society," p. 7. For a characterization of the Blue Shirts as "a party within a party," see "Memorandum on the Blue Shirt Society," p. 3; "Two sources of anti-Japanism," p. 29.

136. "Xiandai junren xu zhi" ("What a modern soldier must know"), in Zhongguo guomindang zhongyang weiyuanhui, Dangshi weiyuanhui, (ed.), *Xian zongtong Jiang gong sixiang yanlun zongji* (*Complete Collection of the Ideas, Speeches, and Writings of the Late President Chiang Kai-shek*) (Taipei, 1984), pp. 321–22. See, for other references by Chiang

### *Confucian Citizenship*

Fascism as a form of modern nationalism was the subject of a speech that Chiang delivered two months later, on 20 September 1933 in Xingzi county, Jiangxi, on "How to be a member of the revolutionary party." Claiming that "solidity" (*shizai*) was the primary essence of being a "revolutionary party member" (*geming dangyuan*), Chiang called for a stoical and even stupid stolidness to counter merely "clever" superficiality of the "city slicker" sort.

> Anytime, anywhere, we must be firm, solid, unadorned, fulfilling. We must have absolutely no fear of difficulty – no opting for temporary ease and comfort, superficiality, luxury, skipping ahead without following the proper order, calculatingly taking advantage. Revolution is an extremely difficult and dangerous enterprise. If we wish to be a member of the revolutionary party we must content ourselves to be slow-witted (*dai*) and dumb (*ben*): what the Ancients referred to as preserving awkwardness (*zhuo*), or what was meant by the phrase, "To counter the clever with clumsiness, to attack the empty with solidity" (*yi zhuo zhi qiao, yi shi ji xu*). Only the slow-witted man (*dai ren*) and the dumb man (*ben ren*) will be engaged in this solid endeavour.[137]

Denouncing modern society for its frivolity and emptiness, Chiang claimed to find this bedrock solidity in the "fundamental essence" (*jiben jingshen*) of a common or "shared" (*gongtong de*) fascism. The essence of that fascist spirit was national self-confidence (*zixin*). A fascist necessarily believes that his own nation is "best of all" (*zui youxiu*), with the most glorious history and superior culture of any country. For Chinese this meant recognizing the fundamental precepts of *The Great Learning* as the "highest culture of our people."

> Loyalty, filial piety, humaneness, charity, righteousness, peace and harmony are one and the same as our nation's traditional virtues of propriety, righteousness, integrity, and frugality. Our traditional national essence (*jingshen*) is the spirit of wisdom, benevolence, and courage. Our nation's one and only revolutionary principle is the Three People's Principles. And all of these spirits and principles come back to the single principle of sincerity (*cheng*). Therefore, as members of the revolutionary party we must dedicate ourselves sincerely to the preservation of the traditional virtues and the traditional spirits. Only by doing so will we be able to revive the highest culture of our nation, to restore our nation's very special standing in this world, to create a glorious and radiant world order for mankind, and in achieving this noble and great enterprise thereby save mankind and save the world.[138]

As an international force, Chiang went on to explain, fascism was characterized by extreme militarization. Although members of the revolutionary party were not always members of an actual military unit, they

---

*footnote continued*

to the success of Turkey, Italy and Germany in nation-building by adhering to social discipline and organizational rules, Maria Hsia Chang, *The Chinese Blue Shirt Society*, p. 26.

137. "Ruhe zuo geming dangyuan" ("How to be a revolutionary party member"), in Zhongguo guomindang zhongyang weiyuanhui, Dangshi weiyuanhui (ed.), *Xian zongtong Jiang gong sixiang yanlun zongji*, p. 564.

138. "Ruhe zuo geming dangyuan" pp. 565–66; Mary Backus Rankin's comments at the "Reappraising Republican China" conference, London, 18–19 December 1995, p. 1.

must consciously adopt a military style of life: "We must all have the soldier's habit and spirit. We must all have the army's organization and discipline. In other words, we must all obey, make sacrifices, be sombre and serious, neat and orderly, tidy and solid, alert and diligent, secretive, unadorned and simple in habit, all of us unanimous in our firmness and courage, sacrificing everything for the collectivity, for the party, for the nation."[139]

Chiang's obsession with neatness and orderliness, coupled with his constant frustration at the slovenliness of the peasant troops he commanded, their leggings unlashed and trousers unbuttoned, lent a fussy air to this imitative fascism, which confounded manners with morals. Clearly impressed by the village neatness and scientific precision that the Germans and Japanese evinced, Chiang Kai-shek somehow seemed to equate tooth-brushing and public sanitation with the collective engine of power and popular will that fascism represented in the mid-1930s. And, of course there was no question but that fascism was associated with premier military qualities which the Chinese attributed to the Germans – a people they may have found less threatening precisely because Germany had lost its privileges of extraterritoriality in China during the preceding World War.[140]

Chiang Kai-shek thus grafted his own view of fascist military discipline onto the classic Neo-Confucian view of community hierarchy and lineage solidarity that no doubt suffused his own "comfortable" upbringing as the member of an affluent village family, dominated by a self-righteous mother who surely believed that sons should sweep the cottage floor with the same care and respect that they showed in bowing to their elders.[141] Fascist militarization, then, was just another way of teaching Confucian citizenship to the people.[142] The Lixingshe's National Military Training Movement (Guomin junxun yundong) was intended to bring together the "sheet of loose sand" (*yi pan san sha*) that constituted Chinese agrarian society by teaching people how to "unite" (*jihui*) and "congregate" (*jieshe*) in order to defend themselves against the Communists and Japanese. A Department of National Military Education (Guomin junxun jiaoyuchu) was established under the auspices of the Ministry of Training and Supervision (Xunlian zongjianbu) to form local training committees in all the provinces and municipalities under the authority of the Executive Yuan. According to one of its initiators, this civilian military training movement was a "social reform movement of a revolutionary nature," designed to move China into "the era of the scientific masses (*kexue de qunzhong shidai*)." Just as the May Fifth Draft

139. "Ruhe zuo geming dangyuan," p. 566.

140. Gan Guoxun, "Guanyu suowei 'Fuxingshe' de zhenqing shikuang," p. 69. For the identification of the Chinese with the misfortunes experienced by the Germans after the First World War, see the articles from *Qiantu* cited in Maria Hsia Chang, *The Chinese Blue Shirt Society*, p. 24.

141. Mary Backus Rankin's comments at the "Reappraising Republican China" conference, London, 18–19 December 1995, p. 3

142. Shanghai tongshe (eds.), *Shanghai yanjiu ziliao* (*Research Materials on Shanghai*) (Shanghai: Zhonghua shuju, 1936), p. 184.

Constitution of 1934 established a General Affairs Office the following year to elect delegates to a national congress, and just as preliminary elections were held in 1935 and 1936, the military training movement was meant to go along with Article 24 of Sun Yat-sen's plan for national reconstruction that called for returning power to the people after 1937. It was all supposedly part, in short, of the political tutelage system that Sun had visualized, and that was called to a halt by the Marco Polo Bridge incident in July 1937.[143]

### *Chinese and European Fascism*

Although Lixingshe insiders may have claimed that the military training activities of the Blue Shirts were actually a form of voter education, the general public thought otherwise. In newspapers and magazines of the period, the Blue Shirts were frequently compared to the Gestapo, and the Blue Shirts themselves took considerable interest in European fascism.[144] This fascination with the Nazis and Fascisti was shared with the general public: in 1933 talk about fascism became a fashion in China, and a large number of publications were advertised in the pages of *Shanghai shenbao* reflecting widespread public interest in the Black and Brown Shirts.[145]

Yet even though a Society for German–Chinese Translation (Zhong–De bianyi xueshe) was established within the Lizhishe headquarters in Nanjing, the editors of the Renaissance Society journal *Qiantu* (*Future*), which was published with funds from the Political Indoctrination Department provided by He Zhonghan, were at first wary about mentioning fascism for fear of offending some of their readers, including Chiang Kai-shek himself.[146] Later, their editors were profoundly distressed by Nazi notions of Aryan racial supremacy.[147] Xiao Zuolin, the editor of another Fuxingshe magazine called *The Chinese Revolution* (*Zhongguo geming*) in 1934, said that although there was great interest in explaining what fascism had to do with the phenomenal rise of Mussolini and Hitler, he and his writers were afraid to write about it initially because Chiang himself did not use the term.

> At the same time we knew what the hows of fascism were but not the whys. When we wanted to say what lay behind it, we couldn't come up with anything. Moreover, even though Chiang Kai-shek was actually carrying out fascism as the Three People's Principles, never was there a moment when the word "fascist" passed through his

143. Gan Guoxun, "Guanyu suowei 'Fuxingshe' de zhenqing shikuang," *xia*, p. 82.

144. "Memorandum on the Blue Shirt Society," p. 2. "The Secret Military Police of China was frankly modeled after the Gestapo," Oliver J. Caldwell, *A Secret War: Americans in China, 1944–1945* (Carbondale: Southern Illinois University Press, 1984), p. 23; Ai Jingwu, "Fuxingshe Henan fenshe de pianduan huiyi," ("Fragments of reminiscences about the Fuxingshe branch in Henan"), in Chinese People's Political Consultative Conference Henan sheng weiyuanhui, Wenshi ziliao yanjiu weiyuanhui (comps.), *Henan wenshi ziliao* (*Historical Materials on Henan*) (Henan: Henan renmin chubanshe, 1981), fascicle 5, p. 108.

145. Deng Yuanzhong, *Sanminzhuyi lixingshe shi*, p. 15.

146. Xiao Zuolin, "Fuxingshe shulüe," p. 35; Deng Yuanzhong, *Sanminzhuyi lixingshe shi*, p. 16.

147. Maria Hsia Chang, *The Chinese Blue Shirt Society*, pp. 22–23.

mouth. Whenever he opened or closed his mouth, it was always *Sanminzhuyi*. Therefore, no one was yet daring enough to openly use the term.[148]

Meanwhile, however, the chief editor of *Future*, Professor Liu Bingli, had decided to devote its sixth issue to a special survey of fascism.[149] The stated purpose of the magazine was vaguely related to doing away with traditional individualism and speedily promoting a new flourishing of corporatism (*jituanzhuyi*) in China.[150] But the articles in this issue on fascist Germany and Italy were quite specific, and many different aspects of fascism – including its economic policies – were examined in some detail.[151]

Furthermore, at least in terms of interest and ideological self-articulation, the Blue Shirts did bear a partial resemblance to fascist movements in Germany and Italy in the 1930s.

I believe that the Blue Shirts may accurately be described as fascist because the methods they employed and ideas they expressed coincided with those of recognizably fascist movements; because they consciously admired, emulated and propagandized European fascist ideas; and because many of them thought of themselves as fascist.[152]

Structurally, however, Chiang's was a military dictatorship; the regime was authoritarian rather than fascist, and the ideology of his Renaissance Society was "a form of reactive, developmental nationalism" that has been identified generically by political scientists as an "ideology of delayed industrialization."[153] Regime and party were based upon an organic conception of state and society that sought to avoid both "the amoral individualism of capitalist society and the class war promised by revolutionary socialism."[154] As Walter Gourlay has pointed out, the relationship of the Nationalist government to the urban working classes was very different from the organizational linkages between European fascist regimes and trade unions.

A conscious effort was made to educate, indoctrinate, and orient labor to play a part in the "new order" of Fascism. Individual workers were constantly encouraged to become the leaders of fascist unions, and a place was made for such leaders in the party hierarchy.... In contrast to this, ... "yellow" unionism was controlled and administered with a minimum of labor participation. The leaders came from outside the ranks of labor .... Chiang was not a fascist; he was uncapable of it. He was a

148. Xiao Zuolin, "Fuxingshe shulüe," p. 35.
149. For Liu Bingli, see also Maria Hsia Chang, *The Chinese Blue Shirt Society*, p. 17.
150. *Ibid.* pp. 33–34.
151. Xiao Zuolin, "Fuxingshe shulüe," pp. 35–36. See also Hung-mao Tien, *Government and Politics*, p. 63.
152. Eastman, "Fascism and Modern China: a rejoinder," p. 841. See also Hung-mao Tien, *Government and Politics*, pp. 64–65.
153. Maria Hsia Chang, *The Chinese Blue Shirt Society*, p. 130; Mary Matossian, "Ideologies of delayed industrialization: some tensions and ambiguities," in John H. Kautsky (ed.), *Political Change in Underdeveloped Countries: Nationalism and Communism* (New York: Wiley and Sons, 1962), pp. 252–264.
154. Joseph Fewsmith, *Party, State, and Local Elites in Republican China: Merchant Organizations and Politics in Shanghai* (Honolulu: University of Hawaii Press, 1985), p. 178.

military bureaucrat. His solution was not to win over the workers but to sit on them.[155]

In short, the most striking contrast with European fascism was the Nationalists' inability or unwillingness to create a true mass movement, which in turn reflected the regime's persistent distrust of social mobilization and political participation.[156]

Consequently, a Blue Shirts training manual written in 1936 repudiated too close an identification with Western fascism. It admitted that "many comrades believe that our organization was founded just at the time that European fascism was rising; that in order to resist the aggression of Japanese imperialism and lay the foundation for order in Chinese society, we opt to move with the world tide and adopt fascism; and that our ideology therefore is fascism." But the manual argued that this view was misguided, if only because the imitation of foreigners would cause the Blue Shirts to ignore China's unique conditions, and fail to realize that the Three People's Principles was an ideology entirely appropriate to the particular conditions of China at the time. Writing many years later, Gan Guoxun, one of the Lixingshe founders, was infuriated by the allegations that the so-called Blue Shirts were fascists. "How can we allow our enemies to calumniate our activities," he asked, "and call us a fascist Blue Shirts secret service?"[157]

According to Gan, a number of journalists and commentators who were never really part of the inner circle of the Lixingshe, being members of the third-tier Renaissance Society, both misunderstood the purpose of the original Whampoa founders of the movement and bandied about all too easily the term "fascist." These figures – including Chen Dunzheng, the author of *Dongluan de huiyi* – were misled by the superficial appearances of some of the Renaissance Society leaders, who appeared to be aping the European fascists. Chen, for instance, who served in the Training Department (Xunlian chu) of the Fuxingshe, described Teng Jie returning from a tour of Germany and Italy garbed in the latest Schutzstaffel style.

Mr Teng was dressed in an olive-green uniform. The jacket was of Sun Yat-sen style. He was wearing a tie. The trousers were riding pants with narrow bottoms. He was wearing riding boots. He was very cocky and arrogant. Mr Teng told me that this was the uniform of Hitler's Germany.[158]

Teng Jie was merely one of several Renaissance Society officers (including Du Xinru, Li Guojun, Feng Ti, Pan Youqiang and Hu Yougui) who went to Germany, Italy, Britain, France and Belgium. Their purpose was not to study fascism as such, but rather – in line with Chiang Kai-shek's policy of *annei rangwai* – to see how Germany and Italy had managed to

155. Gourlay, " 'Yellow' unionism in Shanghai," pp. 128–29.
156. Mary Backus Rankin's comments at the "Reappraising Republican China" conference, London, 18–19 December 1995, p. 1.
157. Gan Guoxun, "Guanyu suowei 'Fuxingshe' de zhenqing shikuang," *xia*, pp. 81, 84.
158. Chen Dunzheng, *Yuanxiage suibi*, quoted in *ibid.* p. 84.

escape the trammels of liberalism that constrained Britain and France from exterminating Communism within their borders.[159]

If the example of European fascists' ruthless attacks on Communists helped strengthen the Lixingshe members' resolve, the German Brown Shirts and Italian Black Shirts also created a new paramilitary style and rally ritual for them to copy.[160] There quickly emerged in the gatherings of some of the front organizations of the Blue Shirts a "proto-fascist" cultural style. This collective quality, which one member later called "the sword and knife culture of the police vanguard" (*jingcha qianwei de daojian wenhua*), did at moments assume a ceremonial manner akin to European fascist ritual.[161]

For example, the Fuxingshe in 1934 founded in Hangzhou a Cultural Vanguard Brigade (Wenhua qianwei dui), which consisted of 300 to 400 students from Zhejiang University, Zhijiang University, and the National Arts School (Guoli yizhuan xuexiao). During the initiation ceremonies, which were held before a sword and dagger to represent the "blood and iron" of the brigade, groups of cadets from the Central Air Force Academy and the Jiangsu Police Training School lined up in military uniform to form a guard of honour under the command of the principal of the police academy, Zhao Longwen, a founding member of the Lixingshe. The thousands of spectators who looked on as the new brigade members swore an oath of allegiance in front of the naked weapons appeared to be deeply moved by the order and solemnity of the occasion.[162]

However, the distances between this relatively small group pledging loyalty to the portrait of Chiang Kai-shek, and the serried ranks at Nürnberg saluting their Führer or the fisted crowds in Piazza di Roma hailing Il Duce, were considerable.[163] A journalist writing at the time spelled out the difference quite perceptively:

> Nor is such an organization as the Blue Shirts unknown in the West. Both Mussolini and Hitler have their personal secret police to watch elements both inside and outside the party. Some commentators, Western and Chinese, have designated the Blue Shirts as Fascist. Such a convenient label, however, is misleading. In the first place, no Fascist party can be or wants to be secret; its strength lies in its ability openly to propagandize and organize on a broad mass base and thus establish a common front

159. *Ibid.*

160. Ai Jingwu. "Fuxingshe Henan fenshe de pianduan huiyi," pp. 107–114.

161. Joshua H. Howard, "Workers at war: industrial relations in the Nationalist arsenals of Chungking, 1932–1949," Ph.D. thesis in progress, University of California, Berkeley, p. 78; Xiong Zhuoyun. "Fandong tongzhi shiqi de Chengdu jingcha" ("The Chengdu police during the period of reactionary rule"), in Chinese People's Political Consultative Conference, Sichuan weiyuanhui, Wenshi ziliao yanjiu weiyuanhui (comps.), *Sichuan wenshi ziliao xuanji* (*Selections of Historical Documents on Sichuan*), No. 17, pp. 108–129 (Chengdu, 1965); Shao Ping, Zhang Yuanyou and Li Ying, "Guomindang 'Zhongtong' zai Chengdu de fandong xinwen huodong" ("The reactionary journalistic activities of the KMT's Central Statistics (Bureau) in Chengdu"), in Chinese People's Political Consultative Conference, Sichuan weiyuanhui, Wenshi ziliao yanjiu weiyuanhui, *Sichuan wenshi ziliao xuanji*, fascicle 24, pp. 64–72. See also, for suggestions along these lines: Mary Backus Rankin's comments at the "Reappraising Republican China" conference, London, 18–19 December 1995, p. 3.

162. Xiao Zuolin, "Fuxingshe shulüe," pp. 40–41.

163. Maria Hsia Chang, *The Chinese Blue Shirt Society*, p. 50.

> of sections of all classes in support of the movement. In the second place, conditions in China are so different from those of any country of Western Europe that political technique was varied too radically to be classified in Western terminology. The Kuomintang itself resembles Western Fascist parties to some extent, but it is far more heterogeneous – and also because it sprang more from Western democratic than from dictatorial traditions, it has not proved very adaptable to the peculiar conditions of modern China.[164]

But even if the European Black and Brown Shirts and the Chinese Blue Shirts were not precisely analogous, the image of fascism throughout the world was powerful and compelling during those years. A large number of Chinese military officers had been sent to Germany and Italy for training, and returned to China full of admiration for fascism "and convinced of its value under present conditions in China."[165] Furthermore, fascism's emotional appeal to Chinese ultra-nationalists must have gained a certain ideological edge if only because the Blue Shirts were so keen to find fresh political ideas with which to challenge the monopoly of the Chen brothers and their partisans over newspaper and magazine publishing.[166]

### *The Symbolic Vagueness of Chinese Culturalism*

It was partly to provide the Blue Shirts with a front organization to expand their activities into cultural circles, that the Chinese Culture Study Society (Zhongguo wenhua xuehui) was founded on 25 December 1933 by a group of Chiang Kai-shek's followers that included Deng Wenyi, his personal secretary. Deng Wenyi had a long-standing commercial interest in cultural affairs, having borrowed money from friends to open the "Give Us a Lift Bookshop" (Tiba shudian), which published and distributed collections of Chiang Kai-shek's speeches and a series of handbooks for the military. As the Blue Shirts sprang into being, Deng's "Give Us a Lift Bookshop" expanded into a chain of stores that distributed the movement's publications in Nanjing, Hankou, Nanchang, Changsha, Guiyang and other cities.[167] The Chinese Culture Study Society was thus grafted on to a simple but extensive propaganda dissemination network that Deng Wenyi had already set in place. Its appearance coincided with the inauguration of the New Life Movement, formally initiated in Jiangxi by Governor Xiong Shihui in February 1934; and it sprang from the same moral revivalism that characterized this "ideological hodgepodge of classical Confucian tenets, a Christian code of ethics, and military ideals."[168]

Within the Lixingshe, the New Life Movement was regarded as one of the Blue Shirts' "four major movements." All society cadres and mem-

164. Burton, "Chiang's secret blood brothers," p. 308–310.
165. Shepherd-Paxton Talk, in *Records of the Department of State, Internal, China, 1930–1939*, No. D130, 00/14127.
166. Xiao Zuolin, "Fuxingshe shulüe," p. 55.
167. *Ibid.* pp. 37, 41, 56.
168. Wei, *Counterrevolution in China*, pp. 76–78.

bers were governed by it, especially insofar as their personal assets and earnings were concerned. By the rules of the Society for Vigorous Practice, all members were supposed to register their personal property. Any increase or decrease in future holdings would have to be justified by their regular salaries, and these assets were supposed to be inspected at random by the secretariat or the inspectorate of the Lixingshe. An embezzlement of 200 *yuan* was supposed to lead to imprisonment; those who stole 500 *yuan* would be punished by death. Local Lixingshe organizations co-ordinating the programme would thereby create "a new atmosphere" which would lead to the eradication of such "evil customs" as extravagance, greed, laziness, deception, treachery, gambling, lust and all that "longing for leisure and abhorrence of labour" (*hao yi wu lao*) characteristic of the "feudal gentry" (*fengjian shidaifu*). Under this new moral order, which would abolish waste and patronage, men and women "would revive (*fuxing*) our ever self-generating and self-renewing national spirit (*minzu jingshen*)" to "recover a confidence lost since the Opium War in the nation's ability to survive."[169]

The primary goal of the Chinese Culture Study Society was, correspondingly, to "renew life" (*gexin shenghuo*) by moving people's minds to common public purpose. The heart of this effort was a programme of "militarization" (*junshihua*) initially restricted to members of the Renaissance Society and later extended to the public at large through the mechanism of the New Life Movement Promotion Association. It was this association that implemented many of the most controversial and intrusive measures of the New Life movement, including restrictions on smoking, dancing and the wearing of certain kinds of Western clothing.[170] The Blue Shirts were consequently blamed by foreigners, and especially the American missionary community, for having subverted the original intent of the New Life experiment by turning it into a fascist-dominated movement.[171]

Were the missionaries right? Was Chiang's regime, after all, a fascist form of government, in intent if not in fact? In truth, "Confucian fascism" remained iconically ambiguous. Its symbols of power quickly merged into hues of traditional social relationships that combined imperial loyalism with the more egalitarian righteousness of medieval knights-errant – "the men of the rivers and lakes" who formed the militant brotherhoods of late imperial China. This profound nativism, which also found expression in the romantic revolutionary nationalism of Communist leaders like Mao Zedong, drew as much upon the vernacular literary tradition of *Water Margin* and *Romance of the Three Kingdoms* as it did upon

169. Gan Guoxun, "Guanyu suowei 'Fuxingshe' de zhenqing shikuang," p. 81.

170. Burton, "Chiang's secret blood brothers," p. 310; Ilona Ralf Sues, *Shark Fins and Millet* (New York: Garden City Publishing Co., 1944.), pp. 47–48; Neale Hunter, "The Chinese League of Left-Wing Writers, Shanghai, 1930–1936," Ph.D. thesis, Australian National University, August 1973, p. 270.

171. "Political implications of 'The New Life Movement' in China." Nanjing dispatch no. 473, 21 May 1937, in *Records of the Department of State, Internal, China, 1930–1939*, No. 00/14127, 19 June 1937. See also Wei, *Counterrevolution in China*, p. 77.

Confucian moralism.[172] Its ambiguousness – its pervasive vagueness – was at once its cultural strength and its ideological weakness. Stripped of structural supports once the "Leader" disappeared from the scene, the Blue Shirts' system of belief subsided into the larger symbolic realm of popular anti-foreignism and ethnic revivalism that characterized many movements in modern China, including the Nationalists' own enemies to the political left. Red Guards and Blue Shirts, as Lloyd Eastman cannily suggested in *The Abortive Revolution*, were not that far apart.

172. See Wen-hsin Yeh, "Dai Li and the Liu Geqing affair: heroism in the Chinese Secret Service during the War of Resistance," *Journal of Asian Studies*, Vol. 48, No. 3 (1989), pp. 545–562.

# The Internationalization of China: Foreign Relations At Home and Abroad in the Republican Era

William C. Kirby

Nothing mattered more. Chinese history during the era of the first Republic was defined and shaped – and must ultimately be interpreted – according to the nature of its foreign relations. While few would dispute the contributions of what Paul Cohen has called a "more interior approach"[1] to modern Chinese historical studies in the past two decades, there is no point searching for some uniquely "China-centred" historical narrative for this period. Everything important had an international dimension. The period is bordered by the inauguration of two "new Chinas," the Republic of 1912 and the People's Republic of 1949, both of which were patterned on international designs. The difference between those governments shows the progression of international influences. Few Chinese were affected in a direct way by the parliamentary experiment of the early Republic. No Chinese would be unaffected by the lethal blend of Leninism and Stalinism that Mao Zedong called Chinese Communism.

Foreign relations in this era became, quite simply, all penetrating, all permeating, all prevailing – *durchdringend*, as the Germans say – ultimately forcing their way into every part of Chinese society. In the realm of high diplomacy, Chinese statecraft delineated and protected the borders of the new nation-state to which all Chinese (and not a few non-Chinese) were now said to belong. "China" – truly a geographic and not a political expression before 1912 – moved from being a ward, if not semi-colony, of the "great powers" to being a great power itself, recovering the sovereignty and autonomy that had been so severely limited in the latter decades of the Qing dynasty.

The transition from pupil to power was even more marked in the military sphere. It is only necessary to compare the duration and outcomes of the first and second Sino-Japanese wars, or contrast the Qing's humiliation by a relative handful of Western soldiers in the Boxer War of 1900 with China's performance at the end of the Republican era. Five years after the Nationalists had outlasted Japan in the war of 1937–45, the People's Republic – whose armies were born of the Republican era – would fight to a draw hundreds of thousands of the best armed troops of the world's most powerful nation. Military strength was made possible in part by industrialization, which was founded in turn on an unprecedented opening to international economic influences. This era witnessed the "golden age" of the Chinese bourgeoisie as well as the birth of modern

1. Paul A. Cohen, *Discovering History in China: American Historical Writing on the Recent Chinese Past* (New York: Columbia University Press, 1984), p. 153.

© The China Quarterly, 1997

state capitalism, neither of which could have existed without foreign partners and investment.

Most striking of all in this period was the self-conscious attempt to overhaul Chinese culture, particularly political culture, according to international categories. Every government would seek legitimacy in the context of one or another internationally authenticated "ism," from constitutionalism to Communism. Most puzzling about the era is the manner in which the Western presence could disappear from China so quickly and completely, if ultimately temporarily, within years of the end of the Republican period.

### *Diplomacy: From Great Muddle to Great Power*

Diplomatic history has not been at the heart of Republican China studies. The examination of foreign policy and of formal, state-to-state relations has never held for scholars of any period of modern Chinese history the cardinal position it enjoyed in European historical writing in the late 19th and early 20th centuries. If Ranke's use of Venetian ambassadorial letters defined a history of *Fürsten und Völker* with more princes than peoples,[2] the book that defined the field of modern China's foreign relations put trade before diplomacy, and treated inter-state relations as but one part of a confused set of economic, cultural and political contests.[3] If in the larger field of international relations the "realist" school of foreign relations long dominated scholarship, treating states as unitary, rational actors pursuing permanent interests, with their actions determined more by external than by internal stimuli (the "primacy of foreign policy"),[4] the most influential work in the history of China's foreign relations has always incorporated the private with the public, the official with the non-official, on a stage where "non-state actors" can steal the show.[5]

Only recently has this broadly conceived and methodologically inclusive approach been graced with a name: "international history." Here foreign policy is but one part of foreign relations, and may in any event be a cultural construct. Hence the importance to this school of "images," "perceptions," "belief system" and "cognitive maps."[6] As important as

2. Leopold von Ranke, *Fürsten und Völker von Süd-Europa im sechzehnten und siebzehnten Jahrhundert, vornehmlich aus ungedrückten Gesandtschafts-Berichten* (Berlin: Duncker und Humblot, 1854).

3. John K. Fairbank, *Trade and Diplomacy on the China Coast. The Opening of the Treaty Ports, 1842–1854* (Cambridge, MA: Harvard University Press, 1954).

4. For a concise overview of realist and "neo-realist" models see Ore R. Holsti, "International relations models," in Michael J. Hogan and Thomas G. Paterson (eds.), *Explaining the History of American Foreign Relations* (Cambridge: Cambridge University Press, 1991), pp. 57–88.

5. A splendid example is Michael H. Hunt, *The Making of a Special Relationship: The United States and China to 1914* (New York: Columbia University Press, 1983).

6. This has been a particularly big theme in Chinese–American relations. Most recently see R. David Arkush and Leo O. Lee (eds.), *Land Without Ghosts: Chinese Impressions of American from the Mid-Nineteenth Century to the Present* (Berkeley: University of California Press, 1989); and Jonathan Goldstein, Jerry Israel and Hilary Conroy (eds.), *America Views China: American Images of China Then and Now* (Bethlehem: Lehigh University Press, 1991).

the interests and actions of other nation-states is the "set of lenses" through which information about them is viewed.[7] Among theoreticians of international relations, the work of Pierre Renouvin and Jean-Baptiste Duroselle comes closest to the work of international historians in incorporating a long list of factors, among them cognitive issues, interest group politics and processes of demographic and cultural change, while not ignoring the traditional concerns of power politics and geopolitics.[8] Yet as practised by such master historians as Akira Iriye and Michael Hunt, international history still lacks anything like a theory.[9]

But while the study of China's foreign relations has generally been theory-poor,[10] it has not lacked poor theories. The Marxist-Stalinist-Maoist tradition stressed the economic and class dimensions of foreign relations, subject to frequent reinterpretation according to the dictates of contemporary politics. In the People's Republic of China (PRC), Lenin's linkage of imperialism with finance capital during capitalism's "highest stage" remained a standard interpretation well into the PRC's own capitalist phase, even though it explained nothing about the imperialist West's activities in China.[11] More recently the narrative of modern Chinese history has been shorn of complexity and contingency in order to fit it into a "world systems" approach.[12] And – with the notable exception of the work of Prasenjit Duara[13] – postmodernist approaches to

7. See Ore Holsti, "The belief system and national images," in James N. Rosenau (ed.), *International Politics and Foreign Policy* (New York: The Free Press, 1969). More recently see Richard Little (ed.), *Belief Systems and International Relations* (Oxford: Oxford University Press, 1990). For an excellent review of the literature see David Shambaugh, *Beautiful Imperialist: China Perceives America, 1972–1990* (Princeton: Princeton University Press, 1991), pp. 17–20.

8. See Pierre Renouvin and Jean-Baptiste Duroselle, *Introduction à l'histoire des relations internationales*, 4th ed. (Paris: Armand Colin, 1991).

9. Akira Iriye, "Culture and international history," in Hogan and Patterson, *Explaining*, pp. 214–15; and Michael H. Hunt, "Normalizing the field," in Michael H. Hunt and Niu Jun (eds.), *Toward a History of Chinese Communist Foreign Relations, 1920s–1960s* (Washington, DC: Asia Program of the Woodrow Wilson Center, 1994), pp. 163–191. Hunt (p. 167) urges the "theoretically enthralled" to "enter the fray, usually monopolized by historians, over what the evidence may actually mean." As Emily S. Rosenberg writes, "International history is not a methodological prescription but, to switch the metaphor, a vast empty plain with undetermined borders and topography that must be sketched by the historian-guide." Emily S. Rosenberg, "Walking the borders," in Hogan and Patterson, *Explaining*, pp. 24–25.

10. On the limitations of theory in a specific context see Michael H. Hunt, "Beijing and the Korean Crisis," *Political Science Quarterly*, No. 107 (Fall 1992).

11. The classic, simple account is that of Hu Sheng, *Imperialism and Chinese Politics* (Beijing: Foreign Languages Press, 1955). More recently see Xiang Rong, "Lun menhu kaifang zhengce" ("On the open door policy"), *Shijie lishi* (*World History*), No. 5 (1980); *Lun dangdai diguozhuyi* (*On Contemporary Imperialism*) (Shanghai: Renmin, 1984). On the continued uses of "imperialism" as an analytical category in policy see Shambaugh, *Beautiful Imperialist*, pp. 53ff. For a superb discussion of the historical literature see Jürgen Osterhammel, "Semi-colonialism and informal empire in twentieth-century China: towards a framework of analysis," in Wolfgang J. Mommsen and Jürgen Osterhammel (eds.), *Imperialism and After: Continuities and Discontinuities* (London: Allen & Unwin, 1986), pp. 290–314.

12. Frances K. Moulder, *China, Japan, and the Modern World Economy: Toward a Reinterpretation of East Asian Development, ca. 1600 to ca. 1918* (Cambridge: Cambridge University Press, 1977).

13. Prasenjit Duara, *Rescuing History from the Nation: Questioning Narratives of Modern China* (Chicago: University of Chicago Press, 1996).

the study of the historiography of China's foreign relations seem unable to escape ancient political debates.[14]

In all this excitement comparatively few have given serious scholarly attention to China's diplomatic history. John Garver, Andrew Forbes, Donald Jordan, Odd Arne Westad, Youli Sun, Nicholas Clifford and others whose work is cited below have made vital contributions, but few among these would consider themselves diplomatic historians. It may be that international history has chased diplomatic history, that is, the study of the practice of diplomacy, almost entirely from that small patch of the China field that has continued to study foreign relations. As a result there is no standard text in the West on the diplomatic history of 20th-century China. (Even for the 19th century, the work of H. B. Morse has not been surpassed in English.)[15] For detailed, general narratives of diplomatic affairs in the Western literature one must retreat to contemporary accounts, such as those of Robert T. Pollard, Claude A. Buss and Werner Levi.[16] While Chinese authors have more readily written general diplomatic histories, and indeed published several outstanding volumes during the Republican era, scholarship has been limited until recently by the political restrictions of several Chinese governments.[17] Only in the 1990s and only in the PRC, where archival restrictions on Foreign Ministry archives have been fewer than in Taiwan, have there appeared comprehensive, largely unpoliticized, archive-based surveys of the diplomatic history of the Chinese Republic.[18]

The paucity of energy in the study of diplomatic history, compared to other fields, is all the more regrettable because the story of Chinese diplomacy in the Republican era is one of stunning accomplishments from a position of unenviable weakness. The Republican government of

14. See Tani E. Barlow's attempt to strike out the baleful influence of the "Cold War founders" of American China studies, who allegedly displaced colonialism from the history of China's foreign relations. Tani E. Barlow, "~~Colonialism's~~ career in postwar China studies," *positions* 1, No. 1 (1993), p. 225. See also James Der Derian and Michael J. Shapiro, *International/Intertextual Relations: Postmodern Readings of World Politics* (Lexington, MA.: Lexington Books, 1989).

15. H. B. Morse, *The International Relations of the Chinese Empire* (London: Longmans Green, [1910] 1918).

16. Robert T. Pollard, *China's Foreign Relations, 1917–1931* (New York: Macmillan, 1933); Claude A. Buss, *War and Diplomacy in Eastern Asia* (New York: Macmillan, 1941); Werner Levi, *Modern China's Foreign Policy* (Minneapolis: University of Minnesota Press, 1953).

17. Among the most distinguished works are older ones that deal primarily with the early (pre-Nationalist government) period of the Republic: Zhang Zhongfu, *Zhonghua minguo waijiaoshi* (*Diplomatic History of the Republic of China*) (Beijing: Beijing daxue chubanshe, 1936; Chongqing, 1943); Hong Junpei, *Guomin zhengfu waijiaoshi* (*Diplomatic History of the Nationalist Government*) (1930; reprint Taipei: Wenhai chubanshe, 1968). Two works that represent well the ideological divide of the Taiwan Strait are Ding Minnan, *Diguozhuyi qin Hua shi* (*History of Imperialism's Aggression against China*) (Beijing, 1958, 1985); and Fu Qixie, *Zhongguo waijiaoshi* (*Diplomatic History of China*), Vol. 2 (Taipei: Sanmin, 1957).

18. Wu Dongzhi (ed.), *Zhongguo waijiaoshi: Zhonghua minguo shiqi, 1911–1949* (*History of China's Foreign Relations: The Period of the Republic of China, 1911–1949*) (Zhengzhou: Henan renmin, 1990); and especially Shi Yuanhua, *Zhonghua minguo waijiaoshi* (*Diplomatic History of the Republic of China*) (Shanghai: Shanghai renmin, 1994).

1912 inherited not what one might call "historical China" but the *Da Qing Guo*, the vast Qing empire, the multinational and multicultural expanse that included Manchuria, Mongolia, Eastern Turkestan and Tibet, among other areas. No Chinese empire had ever been so big for so long as the Qing realm of the Manchus. The first decade of the 20th century was full of portends of its dissolution. But the amazing fact of the Republican era is that this space was not only redefined, as "Chinese" and as the sacred soil of China, but also *defended* diplomatically to such a degree that the borders of the PRC today are essentially those of the Qing, minus only Outer Mongolia. The Qing fell but the empire remained. More accurately, the empire became the basis of the Chinese national state. This was perhaps the greatest accomplishment of Republican diplomacy.

*Defending the boundaries.* The task of defending the Republic's far-flung and militarily indefensible borders fell mainly to a diplomacy that was hard-pressed, often creative and always obstinate. For example President Yuan Shikai announced in 1912 that he was "restoring" the titles of the Dalai Lama of Tibet – who had fled to India in 1910 – even as the Dalai Lama was declaring himself in full control of Tibetan territory. Two years later China refused to sign a convention with British and Tibetan authorities that would underscore China's "suzerainty," but not full sovereignty, over Tibet. In the 1920s and 1930s China played up the authority of the Panchen Lama, who had fled to China proper, in contrast to the stubbornly autonomous Dalai Lama. But when in 1940 a new Dalai Lama was named, the Nationalist regime once again acknowledged his claim to spiritual, if not temporal, authority, on the premise that the title was its to bless. When in 1942 Tibet opened its own Foreign Ministry, China, unlike Britain, refused to deal with it.[19] As British influence – the main external support of Tibetan autonomy – disappeared in the post-war years, Tibet's formal reassociation with the Chinese state was but a matter of time. In short, a series of Republican governments refused to resolve the Tibetan question until it could be settled in China's favour, as it was in 1950.

A determined policy of non-recognition and an even greater degree of diplomatic patience was required to maintain the several regions of Xinjiang within China's potential pull if not its orbit. Here the cause was helped by the political dominance of the essentially self-appointed Han Chinese governors Yang Zengxin and Sheng Shicai, whose self-interest in suppressing ethnic separatism and, to the degree possible, setting limits to Soviet influence, served the long-term purpose of retaining the concept of Chinese suzerainty in a realm in which the Chinese state had almost no real power. Even when, in the late 1930s, Xinjiang became "a virtual territorial extension of the Soviet Union"[20] at a time when China was

19. A brief survey may be found in Marc Mancall, *China at the Center: 300 Years of Foreign Policy* (New York: Free Press, 1984), pp. 251–54.

20. Andrew D. W. Forbes, *Warlords and Muslims in Chinese Central Asia: A Political History of Republican Sinkiang* (Cambridge: Cambridge University Press, 1986), p. 157.

dependent upon Soviet military aid in the war against Japan, the Nationalist regime refused to abandon its claim. Instead, it bided its time until Soviet power was diverted and it could perform a "delicate surgical procedure"[21] to install Nationalist Chinese leadership of the province in what John Garver has called a "brilliant" and well timed diplomacy that possibly "saved Xinjiang for the Chinese nation."[22] It then dealt with the contemporaneous rebellion known as the "Eastern Turkestan Republic," which sought less separation from China than local autonomy, and ultimately would be granted neither.[23] Xinjiang, too, was saved for the Chinese Communists, who inherited it intact on 12 October 1949.

The non-recognition of unpleasant realities in China's border areas was carried to an art form in the case of Manchuria. But here diplomacy was accompanied by a willingness to fight. Surely it speaks volumes about the obsessive and unitary conception of Chinese nationalism that the Chinese Republic would mobilize for war in defence of the *Manchu* homeland. (Although Chinese had begun to settle in southern Manchuria in the 18th century, Han migration was legalized only in 1907.) When the Republic was established, northern Manchuria was *de facto* a Russian colony and southern Manchuria a sphere of Japanese influence. The Republic negotiated and fought over this territory almost continuously throughout its existence, including outright hostilities with the Soviet Union in 1929 and full-scale war with Japan from 1937 to 1945. The greatest success came in Chinese diplomacy toward "Manzhouguo," the Japanese-administered state that aimed to give political legitimacy to the conquest of the region by Japanese forces in 1931. By itself China could not alter the fact of Japanese control. But through a globally orchestrated diplomacy that made the "non-recognition doctrine" part of a standard political lexicon, it could and did deny Manzhouguo any semblance of legality: in its early years, apart from Japan only El Salvador saw fit to recognize the new Manchu paradise. And China's uncompromising posture would make it a suitable ally for other, later, enemies of Japan, including the two powers that would ultimately return Manchuria to Chinese rule, the United States and the Soviet Union.

If the case of Outer Mongolia turned out differently, this was perhaps because there China confronted a combination of circumstances present nowhere else: coherent, internal resistance to Chinese rule, which had grown significantly after the Qing opened Mongolia to Han settlement in 1902; and a determined effort by a powerful neighbour to support a separatist movement. After both Chinese warlordism and the Russian civil war spilled into Mongolia in 1918–19, Mongolian partisans found allies in the new Soviet state and declared a republic in 1924. This was the one case in which Chinese non-recognition would have no effect. On maps printed in Taipei, Outer Mongolia still forms the northern border of

21. Mancall, *China at the Center*, p. 250.
22. John W. Garver, *Chinese-Soviet Relations, 1935–1945* (New York: Oxford University Press, 1988), p. 178.
23. See Linda Benson, *The Ili Rebellion: The Moslem Challenge to Chinese Authority in Xinjiang, 1944–1949* (Armonk: M. E. Sharpe, 1990).

the Republic of China. But the Nationalist regime itself legitimized Mongolian independence in the Sino-Soviet treaty of 1945, although this was done only *in extremis*. To Chiang Kai-shek, who went against the majority opinion of the Kuomintang leadership, this was the "maximum sacrifice," bearable only – and perhaps not forever – if alliance with the Soviet Union could avert the "national calamity" of Communist rebellion.[24] It didn't, but Mongolians ratified their independence in the Stalinesque plebiscite of October 1945 (the vote was some 487,000 to *nothing*), an outcome that Mao Zedong's People's Republic would be forced to live with in the following decades.

By 1945 all border regions of the Qing empire, save for Outer Mongolia, had been recovered. In all border areas except Mongolia, the level of external influence was much less than in 1911, and the residual rights of the Soviet Union in Xinjiang and Manchuria would disappear within a decade. Indeed, the Republic went beyond the borders of 1911 in regaining Chinese sovereignty over Taiwan, which the Qing had lost to Japan in 1895.[25] The tenacity, obduracy and overall *success* of Chinese diplomacy regarding the most distant regions of the Manchu realm may help to explain the PRC's unyielding determination to "recover" once again for China the territory of Taiwan, even though it has never governed it for a single moment.

*Internal frontiers.* An even more consistent purpose of Chinese diplomacy during the Republic was the recovery of sovereignty *within* China proper. When Mao Zedong declared that the Chinese people had finally "stood up" in 1949, he overlooked the fact that the People's Republic, unlike the Republic, inherited a state unburdened by foreign "concessions" and settlements outside government control, not to mention the institution of extraterritoriality, which had immunized foreigners against Chinese law. This did not happen by itself. It was the result of a stubborn resolve to do away with the residue of the "politics of imperialism." While once at the centre of Western writings on China's foreign relations,[26] with the signal exception of Akira Iriye's *After Imperialism*,

24. See the marvellous account of the Moscow negotiations of 1945 in Xiaoyuan Liu, *A Partnership for Disorder: China, the United States, and their Policies for Postwar Disposition of the Japanese Empire, 1941–1945* (Cambridge: Cambridge University Press, 1996). The citations are from a manuscript version, pp. 304, 306. See also Odd Arne Westad, *Cold War and Revolution: Soviet-American Rivalry and the Origins of the Chinese Civil War* (New York: Columbia University Press, 1993), pp. 40–41.

25. Taiwan's loss, interestingly enough, had been taken for granted. Until Japan's defeat in the war of 1937–45 seemed likely, no Republican government had challenged the legality of the Treaty of Shimonoseki by which the Qing had ceded the island to Japan; and for no major political movement, including the Communists, had it been *terra irredenta*.

26. Zhang Zhongfu, *Diplomatic History of the Republic of China*; Hong Junpei, *Diplomatic History of the Nationalist Government*; Robert T. Pollard, *China's Foreign Relations, 1917–1931* (New York: Macmillan, 1933); *Syllabus on Extraterritoriality in China* (Nanjing: Citizen's League, 1929); G. W. Keaton, *The Development of Extraterritoriality in China* (2 vols.) (London: Longmans, 1928); Liu Shih-Shun, *Extraterritoriality: Its Rise and Its Decline* (New York: Columbia, 1925); G. Soulié Morant, *Extraterritorialité et intérêts étrangers en Chine* (Paris: Paul Geuthner, 1925); Li Tz-hyung (ed.), *Abolition of Extraterritoriality in China* (Nanjing: International Relations Committee, 1929); Thomas F.

published nearly 30 years ago, this diplomacy has received scant attention in the West, although it has been recounted in loving detail by Chinese historians.[27]

The Nationalist regime in particular had what one foreign diplomat called an "extraterritoriality complex."[28] Its rise followed the failure (from China's viewpoint) of the Washington Conference of 1921–22 and was accompanied, in the Northern March of 1926, by a wave of popular anti-foreignism unmatched since the Boxer years. Unlike Boxer xenophobia, this was orchestrated anti-foreignism, linked to a "revolutionary diplomacy" that included the economic boycott as a weapon.[29] If there was a single turning point in the century-long struggle to undo Western privilege, it was the January 1927 overrunning of the British concession at Hankou, which was returned to Chinese governance without a shot being fired. This came after 18 months of anti-British agitation and boycotts in Kuomintang-held China, and after Britain had already made, in the Christmas Memorandum of the previous month, the extraordinary (and for some foreign powers, traitorous) offer of the "sympathetic adjustment of treaty rights" – including unconditional tariff autonomy – to meet the "legitimate aspirations of the Chinese people."[30] But when the concession was taken the prospect of a military response on the part of the powers, as in 1900, seemed very real.

---

*footnote continued*

Millard, *The End of Extraterritoriality in China* (Shanghai: A.B.C. Press, 1931); Wu K'ai-sheng, *La politique étrangère du gouvernement national de Chine et la révision des traités inégaux* (Paris: M. Giard, 1931). Contemporary documentation of diplomatic activity included: Carnegie Endowment for International Peace, Division of International Law, *Treaties and Agreements with and concerning China, 1919–1929* (Washington, DC: Carnegie Endowment for International Peace, 1929); China, Ministry of Foreign Affairs, *Treaties of 1928 and Related Papers* (Shanghai: Kelly and Walsh, 1929); Permanent Court of International Justice, *Affaire relative à la denonciation du traité sino-belge du 2 novembre 1865* (Leyde: Société d'éditions A. W. Sijthoff, 1929); Adolphe Dubois, "Les accords franco-cinois," thèse, Univ. de Paris, 1928; *Sino-Foreign Treaties of 1928: Texts of the Documents Which Lay the New Foundations for Sino-Foreign Relations* (Beijing: Peking Leader Press, 1929); Great Britain, Foreign Office, *Exchange of Notes between His Majesty's Government of the United Kingdom and the Chinese Government Regarding the Rendition of the British Concession of Chinkiang, Nanking October 31, 1929* (London: H.M. Statioinery Office, 1930).

27. This is true also for the latest histories from the PRC: see Shi Yuanhua, *Zhonghua minguo waijiaoshi*, chs. 4 and 6. This diplomatic history has, of course, long been written from the perspective of foreign powers (e.g. Dorothy Borg, *American Policy and the Chinese Revolution, 1925–1928* (New York: Macmillan, 1947)). Although recent work on British policy and on the international community in China has employed Chinese materials in an imaginative way, the focus has not been on *Chinese* diplomacy. See Edmund S. K. Fung's excellent work, *The Diplomacy of Imperial Retreat: Britain's South China Policy, 1924–1931* (Hong Kong: Oxford University Press, 1991); and Nicholas Clifford's marvellous *Spoilt Children of Empire: Westerners in Shanghai and the Chinese Revolution of the 1920's* (Hanover, N.H.: Middlebury College Press, 1991).

28. British Minister to China Miles Lampson, quoted in Iriye, *After Imperialism*, p. 286.

29. For an enlightening discussion of boycotts as a diplomatic weapon in a later context see Donald A. Jordan, *Chinese Boycotts versus Japanese Bombs: The Failure of China's "Revolutionary Diplomacy," 1931–32* (Ann Arbor: University of Michigan Press, 1991).

30. United States State Department, *Papers Relating to the Foreign Relations of the United States* (Washington, DC: U.S. Government Printing Office, 1926), Vol. I, pp. 923–27. On the American Minister's sense of betrayal see *ibid.* pp. 930–34.

Instead the British negotiated the rendition of the Hankou concession in less than two months. Chinese diplomats then pursued four years of talks that "succeeded in adding a diplomatic to their nationalist revolution"[31] and which almost certainly would have culminated in the general end of extraterritoriality in 1931, were it not for the intervening Manchurian crisis. By the early 1930s, negotiations had restored Chinese control over maritime customs, tariffs, postal communications, salt monopoly revenues and almost two-thirds of the foreign concessions in China. In all these Chinese negotiators employed a diplomacy of what Arthur Waldron has called (in a different context) an "inexorable legalistic gradualism," which was perhaps more effective than the unilateral denunciation of old treaties.[32] For such painstaking and expert work the Foreign Ministry recruited, as Julia Strauss has shown, "the most cosmopolitan and well educated group of young men in all of China."[33] Even before the formal return of all concessions in 1943, the regime had regained judiciary control over Chinese residents in foreign concessions, and (as I have discussed elsewhere) strove to tame the wildest part of China's inner frontiers: the international society of the treaty ports.[34] The end of the old treaty system set the stage for the post-war negotiation of new legal, commercial and cultural treaties with the West that fulfilled the most basic element of China's diplomatic agenda since the first Opium War. Only Hong Kong and Macau remained under colonial authority and not, it seemed, for long.[35] Elsewhere, with extraterritoriality gone, Chinese laws began to govern and increasingly restrict the activities of foreigners in China. They still do.

*International environment.* The preservation of the nation's borders – even when China was in no position to fight for them – and the recovery of internal authority depended in no small measure on the international setting. Frontier policy was aided by the common determination of Chinese *and* foreign governments to view the Chinese Republic as a nation-state. As in the 19th century, when the imperialist powers gave rhetorical support to the empire's territorial integrity (in part to avoid

31. Levi, *Modern China's Foreign Policy*, p. 192.

32. Waldron refers to Beiyang-era negotiations in his review of Yongjin Zhang, *China in the International System*, in *The China Quarterly*, No. 131 (September 1992), p. 797.

33. Julia C. Strauss, *Strong Institutions in Weak Polities: Personnel Policies and State Building in China, 1927–1940* (Oxford: Oxford University Press, 1998). (Citation is from manuscript, p. 246.)

34. William C. Kirby, "Traditions of centrality, authority, and management in modern China's foreign relations," in David Shambaugh and Thomas W. Robinson (eds.), *Chinese Foreign Policy: Theory and Practice* (Oxford: Clarendon Press, 1994), pp. 13–29.

35. On wartime negotiations over Hong Kong see Liu Xinli, "Chongqing guomin zhengfu yu Yingguo zhengfu guanyu Xianggang wenti de jiaobu" ("Diplomatic initiatives of the Chongqing National Government and the British Government regarding Hong Kong"), *Jindaishi yanjiu* (*Modern Historical Research* No. 4 (1994), pp. 191–200. Chan Lau Kit-ching, *China, Britain and Hong Kong, 1895–1945* (Hong Kong, Chinese University Press, 1990), p. 327, shows how the Pacific War delayed the issue of Hong Kong and that during the war even Churchill had come to believe that Hong Kong would go the way of Wei-hai-wei. See also Kevin P. Lane, *Sovereignty and the Status Quo: The Historical Roots of China's Hong Kong Policy* (Boulder: Westview, 1990).

fighting over it themselves), foreign powers remained convinced that the new Chinese Republic would be even more trouble divided than united. Tibet had announced its independence in 1913. At various times, in various ways, so did a lot of Chinese provinces. None would have their independence sanctioned by the Republic, and none, save the north-eastern provinces reorganized as Manzhouguo, would receive formal recognition by a single foreign power. For better or (as in the case of the Qing's international debts) for worse, the Republic's status as the successor to the Qing was unchallenged internationally.

As the Chinese nation-state established itself, its assertion of internal control benefited from a broader international trend: the beginning of the end of European pre-eminence in global power politics. Take again the example of 1927: the British surrender of Hankou reveals as much about the decline of Western power in China as it does about the Nationalist revolutionaries. Britain's "one real weapon," thought John Pratt of the Foreign Office's Far Eastern Department, was "the vague threat of force." The actual dispatch of troops was certainly considered, but deemed worthless, for against economic boycotts, the Nationalists' most potent weapon, "troops [were] no protection."[36] A bluff was tried at Shanghai, where a small force was gathered to defend the International Settlement, but the British Chiefs of Staff knew that no conceivable British force could defend it against a determined attack by the Nationalist military.[37] In any event any significant British military action was politically impossible at a time when British public opinion had become anti-interventionist and anti-imperialist. "Far away from England, and with the constant provocations of the Chinese ever before your eyes and ears," wrote Foreign Minister Austin Chamberlain to his Minister in China, Miles Lampson, "you can have no conception of how profoundly pacific our people now are."[38]

The West not only began its retreat from China, but broke apart as a distinct entity after the First World War. The unity of the Western powers in dealings with the Qing had come to include Japan after the turn of the century, and had severely restricted the empire's diplomatic freedom. This was one reason why the Qing state could take no part, even when it wanted to, in the international alliance system of the late 19th and early 20th centuries. The European catastrophe of 1914–18 changed that, and made China a player in a reorganizing, multi-polar, international system.

One could read widely on the history of the First World War and never know that China took part in it. But however painful the experience of what Guoqi Xu calls Republican China's "age of innocence," China's entry into the war was a major turning point in its foreign rela-

36. Great Britain, Foreign Office, F979/156/10, minute by Pratt, 31 January 1927, cited in Clifford, *Spoilt Children of Empire*, p. 189.

37. Great Britain, Foreign Office, FO 405/252/16, Chamberlain to Tilley, 13 January 1927; *Survey of International Affairs* (London: Royal Institute of International Affairs), 1927, p. 377.

38. Great Britain, Foreign Office, FO 800/260/421, Chamberlain to Lampson, 4 April 1927. Quoted also in Fung, *Diplomacy*, pp. 131–32.

tions.[39] As Zhang Yongjin has shown, the Republic self-consciously entered "international society" for the first time in its diplomacy of 1918–20, agreeing to abide by the rules and norms that in theory governed international behaviour.[40] China became an active participant in the "universal partnership" (to use Robert Keohane's term)[41] of the League of Nations. But the League's inability to enforce its principles, as China would discover to its anguish in the Manchurian Crisis of 1931, only strengthened the Republic's desire to pursue its interests through an independent diplomacy.[42] It was, then, less the ideal than the practice of foreign relations in the inter-war period that permitted China for the first time to deal with foreign powers individually, not as a unit. This bilateralism was a leading factor in the success enjoyed in treaty revision in 1928–31, and it would lead to modern China's first international alignments or alliances of any significance.

*Allies and enemies.* These alignments became matters of national life or death as tensions with Japan increased through the Republican era, culminating in the War of Resistance from 1937 to 1945. China's survival and ultimate victory depended on a search for foreign patrons and allies in a fast-changing international environment. The Nationalist government after 1927 moved rapidly from an era when China was an object of great power co-operation at China's expense, to one in which it formed important economic or strategic associations with three of the world's most powerful nations – Germany, the Soviet Union and the United States – in order to defend itself against the fourth. In 1927 China remained a "muddle," in the assessment of the British Foreign Office.[43] By 1945 it had become an important factor in the global balance of power and in the victory of the Allied coalition that it had joined, this time – unlike its role in the First World War – as a partner more than a supplicant. Indeed China was formally now a "great power," a status attained by performance in war and diplomacy,[44] and confirmed by a permanent seat on the Security Council of the new United Nations.

With Germany, the Nanjing government entered into modern China's first co-operative relationship based upon both the principle and practice

39. See Guoqi Xu, "Age of innocence: the First World War and China's quest for national identity," Ph.D. dissertation, Harvard University, in progress.

40. Zhang Yongjin, *China in the International System, 1918–20* (London: Macmillan, 1991). Zhang's conception of international society as the expansion of "the international society of European states" is drawn from Hedley Bull and A. Watson (eds.), *The Expansion of International Society* (Oxford: Clarendon 1984).

41. Robert Keohane, "Partnerships and alignments: neorealist and institutionalist analyses," p. 6. Paper presented to the conference on Patterns of Cooperation in the Foreign Relations of Modern China, Wintergreen, August 1987.

42. On Chinese reactions to the failure of League internationalism see Ian Nish, *Japan's Struggle with Internationalism: Japan, China and the League of Nations, 1931–33* (London: Kegal Paul International, 1993).

43. W. R. Louis, *British Strategy*, p. 135.

44. Garver, *Chinese-Soviet Relations*, pp. 192–96, shows that this status was not simply a gift to China, based on future expectations of it by the Americans, British and Soviets, but a hard-won diplomatic achievement.

of equality and mutual benefit. That relationship – in many ways the most successful of the Republican period – was grounded in economic, military and ideological ties, and arguably gave China the military-industrial capacity to survive the first years of the Sino-Japanese war.[45] It was *Realpolitik* and little more – the common fear of Japan – that led to the alignments with the Soviet Union (1938–40), studied so well by John Garver and He Jun,[46] and the United States (1941–45), studied by so many, though until recently almost entirely from the American perspective.[47] These partnerships assured China's survival, trained Chinese armies and brought the Republic into the very centre of global power politics. None of these relationships proved permanent, but each was crucial in its time. How each was pursued, managed, institutionalized and ultimately concluded is one of the more interesting stories of modern China's diplomacy.[48] Together they demonstrate the versatility of Chinese diplomacy in pursuing broadly consistent goals through an extraordinarily diverse set of relationships within a short span of years.

Of course the most influential, complicated, dangerous and ultimately disastrous of China's foreign relationships was that with Japan. War is the ultimate category of foreign relations, and the eight-year struggle with Japan inflicted staggering losses on the Chinese people, the Chinese economy and the Chinese government, which never really recovered

45. William C. Kirby, *Germany and Republican China* (Stanford: Stanford University Press, 1984); Françoise Kreissler, *L'Action culturelle allemande en Chine. De la fin du XIXe siècle à la Seconde Guerre mondiale* (Paris: Editions de la Maison des sciences de l'homme, 1989); Kuo Heng-yü (ed.), *Von der Kolonialpolitik zur Kooperation. Studien zur Geschichte der deutsch-chinesischen Beziehungen* (München: Minerva, 1986).

46. See Garver, *Chinese-Soviet Relations*; He Jun, "Lun 1929–1939 nian de Zhong Su guanxi" ("Sino-Soviet relations, 1929–39"), dissertation, Nanjing University, 1986.

47. A small sample of work includes: Dorothy Borg, *The United States and the Far Eastern Crisis of 1933–1938* (Cambridge, MA, 1964); Warren I. Cohen, *America's Response to China* (New York, 1980); Ta-jen Liu, *History of Sino-American Relations, 1840–1974* (Taipei, 1978); Michael Schaller, *The U.S. Crusade in China, 1938–1945* (New York, 1979); Wilma Fairbank, *America's Cultural Experiment in China, 1912–1949* (Washington, DC, 1976). Contemporary Chinese perspectives include Zhang Zhongfu, *Sinian laide Meiguo yuandong waijiao* (*U.S. Far Eastern Policy in the Past Four Years*) (Chongqing, 1941), and *Meiguo zhanqiande yuandong waijiao* (*U.S. Far Eastern Policy Before the War*) (Chongqing, 1944). More recently see Li Changjiu (ed.), *Zhong Mei guanxi erbainian* (*200 Years of Sino-American Relations*) (Beijing, 1984). All the above work had to be based on little or no Chinese archival evidence. Exceptions were works that sought to make a point in an international scholarly/political dispute, as in the never-ending Stilwell controversy (see for example Ching-chun Liang, *General Stilwell in China, 1942–1944: The Full Story* (New York: St John's University Press, 1972). However, since the early 1980s there has been an explosion of publication on Sino-American relations in the PRC, much of which takes account of newly available Chinese materials. For a bibliography, see Yang Yunheng and Hu Yukun (eds.), *Zhongguo Meiguoxue lunwen zhongmu* (*Guide to Chinese Essays on American Studies*) (Shenyang: Liaoning daxue chubanshe, 1991). For a survey of such scholarship see Chen Jian, "Sino-American relations studies in China," in Warren I. Cohen (ed.), *Pacific Passage: The Study of American–East Asian Relations on the Eve of the 21st Century* (New York: Columbia University Press, 1996), pp. 3–35. The field of Chinese–American relations in the 20th century in the same volume by William C. Kirby, Charles W. Hayford and Nancy Bernkopf Tucker.

48. See William Kirby, "Nationalist China's search for a partner: relations with Germany, the Soviet Union, and the United States, 1928–1945," in Harry Harding (ed.), *Patterns of Cooperation in Modern China's Foreign Relations*, forthcoming.

from it.[49] With Japan too, China had pursued broadly consistent goals and policies. But the same measures that had proven so successful with respect to Western imperialism – obduracy, legalism and econ-omic boycotts – proved unsuccessful at best and counter productive at worst in Sino-Japanese relations, which moved from diplomatic dispute to open military conflict and finally into the realm of barbarism.

The "Asian Holocaust"[50] of the Second Sino-Japanese War is still understudied, particularly in Western scholarship, but pre-war Sino-Japanese relations have been the subject of much recent work. Although there is still no comprehensive diplomatic history of Sino-Japanese relations,[51] here the multi-dimensional approach of "international history" has made important contributions. The domestic aspects of China's Japan policy in the 1930s and the evolving role of "public opinion" in policy debate and formulation are at the heart of Parks Coble's fine study.[52] Donald Jordan emphasizes the unpredictable results of a new version of Nationalist "revolutionary diplomacy," particularly anti-Japanese boycotts, in the early 1930s, which he suggests not only failed to deter Japanese aggression but in fact helped to bring it about in the first place.[53] Youli Sun's stimulating, revisionist account of China's "appeasement" diplomacy during the 1930s stresses the cultural construction of Chinese foreign policy, which, he argues, was defined and implemented according to conceptions of "imperialism" that assumed an inevitable conflict between Japan and the Western powers. This *idée fixe* emerges in Chiang Kai-shek's great gamble for war in July 1937 and his determination over the next four years to make world politics fit his preconception.[54] To this Akira Iriye has added the challenge that Sino-Japanese relations in this period are looked at primarily in cultural terms, first as partners in cultural internationalism, then as enemies whose struggle became all the more deadly once it was defined as a battle of cultures.[55]

Japan's defeat ended the wartime alliance structure and China's

49. Chi Jingde, *Zhongguo dui Ri kangzhan sunshi diaocha shishu* (*Historical Account of China's Losses During the War with Japan*) (Taipei: Guoshiguan, 1987); Han Chi-tong, *Zhongguo dui Ri zhanshi sunshi wenguji* (*Estimated Chinese Losses During Hostilities with Japan*) (Shanghai: Zhonghua, 1946); William C. Kirby, "The Chinese war economy," in James Hsiung and Steven I. Levine (eds.), *China's Bitter Victory: The War with Japan, 1937–1945* (Armonk: M. E. Sharpe, 1992, pp. 185–213).

50. Hsiung and Levine, *China's Bitter Victory*, p. v.

51. Compilations of documentation from either side of the Taiwan Strait include: *Zhongguo waijiaoshi ziliao xuanbian* (*Selections of Materials on China's Diplomatic History*), Vol. 3, 1937–1945 (Beijing: Waijiao xueyuan, 1958); *Zhonghua minguo zhongyao shiliao chubian: dui Ri kangzhan shiqi, ti san bian, zhanshi waijiao* (*Preliminary Compilation of Important Historical Materials for the Republic of China, the Period of the War of Resistance Against Japan, Vol. 3, Wartime Diplomacy*) (Taipei: Kuomintang dangshi weiyuanhui, 1981).

52. Parks M. Coble, *Facing Japan: Chinese Politics and Japanese Imperialism, 1931–1937* (Cambridge, MA.: Council on East Asian Studies, 1991).

53. Jordan, *Chinese Boycotts versus Japanese Bombs.*

54. Youli Sun, *China and the Origins of the Pacific War* (New York: St Martin's Press, 1993).

55. Akira Iriye, *China and Japan in the Global Setting* (Cambridge, MA: Harvard University Press, 1992.) See also, on the more positive side of cultural relations, Joshua A. Fogel, *The Cultural Dimension of Sino-Japanese Relations: Essays on the Nineteenth and Twentieth Centuries* (Armonk: M. E. Sharpe, 1995).

position in it. If China was recognized as a great power, it now had to navigate in a bipolar world dominated by two "superpowers," the United States and the Soviet Union, and complicated by a Chinese Communist insurgency that neither power could control. Nationalist China would win the war – not only the war with Japan but the struggle for China's sovereignty and self-assertion in the world – only to lose the country. This outcome, unexpected then and still astounding in retrospect, is one reason why the post-war era has long been the most contested field of Republican China's diplomatic history. Steven I. Levine's pathbreaking study, *Anvil of Victory*, demonstrated the interlocking nature of international and domestic settings in explaining, better than anyone else, how the Communists won in Manchuria and set the stage for their conquest of China.[56] Most recently Odd Arne Westad has explored the origins of the Civil War in the context of the Cold War politics and in the light of new Soviet and Chinese materials.[57] He stresses the nearly universal ineptitude (at best, limited vision and gross miscalculation) that marked leading policy-makers in all four corners (that is, in Chongqing, Yan'an, Moscow and Washington) but shows clearly how the *civil* war was fundamentally shaped and its outcome partly determined by *Cold* war diplomacy, in which the Chinese Communist Party (CCP) was now a player.[58] Michael Hunt goes further to suggest the emergence of a distinctively Chinese Communist approach to foreign relations, autonomous from those of other post-imperial Chinese regimes and eventually even from its Comintern and Soviet mentors. In the foreign policy of the Communist "state in embryo" one finds themes that would endure past 1949, not the least of which (and this is my reading more than Hunt's) was the dominance of an opinionated leader with dangerous limitations in foreign affairs.[59] But Mao Zedong would inherit a state and a history of diplomatic achievement that would allow the People's Republic to play a major role in world affairs from the start.

### *The Internalization of Foreign Relations*

The definition and defence of the Chinese *zuguo* took place in an environment of inescapable internationalization at home. The physical dimensions of this were most obvious in the cities, particularly the treaty ports, with their paved streets, electric lights, public parks and big cinemas showing mostly Hollywood films, not to mention the thousands of foreigners who lived there. But internationalization would be evident across the land, wherever railway lines were laid with foreign financing;[60]

56. Steven I. Levine, *Anvil of Victory: The Communist Revolution in Manchuria, 1945–1948* (New York: Columbia University Press, 1987).

57. Westad, *Cold War and Revolution*.

58. In this regard see also Brian Murray, "Stalin, the Cold War, and the division of China: a multi-archival mystery," Woodrow Wilson Center Cold War International History Project No. 12, June 1995.

59. Michael H. Hunt, *The Genesis of Chinese Communist Foreign Policy* (New York: Columbia University Press, 1996).

60. Ralph Heunemann, *The Dragon and the Iron Horse* (Cambridge, MA: Harvard University Press, 1984).

or in the skies, where Pan American and Lufthansa introduced civil aviation to China in partnership with the Chinese government;[61] or wherever soldiers marched, in Western-style uniforms, carrying imported guns and ammunition, ordered about by generals weighted down by the medals and epaulets of current fashion, and trained by successive missions of foreign military advisers. And even remote areas could be changed overnight by the force of the international economy.

An example is Dayu *xian*, in south-western Jiangxi province, which in the 20th century enjoyed its second or third, and certainly its most dramatic, incorporation into global markets. This former prefectural seat had for centuries been a major trading depot, being the first city to the north of the Meiling pass from Guangdong, on one of the most frequented trading routes linking Guangzhou to east-central China. As the Frenchman du Halde described the city in 1736, it was "as large as Orléans [ca. 100,000], populous and handsome, has a great trade, and is a place of much resort."[62] Dayu prospered during the heyday of the Guangzhou system of Sino-Western trade, trafficking in tea, silk and opium. But by the time Shi Dakai's expedition passed through the city during the Taiping Rebellion in 1858, Dayu's decline had begun. With the expansion of the treaty-port system and the growth of Shanghai, the route over the Meiling became limited to regional traffic. Dayu became a backwater, worthy of only the lowest form of substation to collect the *lijin* transit tax. Its cultivable land was capable of feeding only half its population, and increased production of local tea, bamboo paper and the once-famous *Dayu banya*, or Dayu pressed duck, did not prevent its downward slide.[63]

Then tungsten was found at Dayu. The presence of the ore was discovered in the late 19th century by a foreign missionary who owned property at nearby Xihua Mountain, which, it turned out, held the largest concentration of wolframite, the ore from which tungsten is mined, in the world. He was soon bought out by local gentry who made the mountain "public property," but such civic-mindedness lasted only until 1916 – the height of the First World War and of a frenzied demand for tungsten, essential for the making of modern armaments and special steels. A frenetic land rush ensued, with the mountain subdivided into hundreds of small holdings and with 20,000 miners extracting the world's most

61. Bodo Wiethoff, *Luftverkehr in China, 1928–1949* (Wiesbaden: Otto Harrassowitz, 1975).

62. Père du Halde, *The General History of China* (trans. R. Brookes) (London, 1936), p. 161. See also Stanley Wright, *Kiangsi Native Trade and its Taxation* (Shanghai, 1920), pp. 12, 116; Tan Xichuan, Wang Baojun (comps.), *Dayu xian xu zhi* (1851).

63. Jen Yu-sen, *The Taiping Revolutionary Movement* (New Haven: Yale University Press, 1973), p. 307; John K. Fairbank, "The creation of the treaty system," in J. K. Fairbank (ed.), *The Cambridge History of China*, Vol. 11, Part 1 (Cambridge: Cambridge University Press, 1978), p. 245; Wright, *Kiangsi Native Trade*, p. 12, and Appendix A; Liu Daqian, "Dayu shehui jingji zhi xiankuang tan" ("On the current situation of Dayu's society and economy"), in Jiangxi sheng zhengfu (ed.), *Jingji xunkan* (*Economic Periodical*), Vol. 2, No. 14 (11 May 1934), pp. 15–17; *Jiangxi zhi techan* (*Local Products* of *Jiangxi*) (Nanchang, 1935), p. 106.

valuable strategic ore.[64] Dayu became a boom town. It developed a thriving market for delicate silks, imported Western woollens and even Western cosmetics. Tea and wine houses thrived. While the provincial governments of Jiangxi and Guangdong fought with each other and with Nanjing on how to modernize and monopolize China's most precious export commodity, Dayu enjoyed two decades as the centre of the world's tungsten trade.[65]

Incorporation into world markets was wildly uneven between industries and regions. One famous example was the silk industry, where inferior Chinese quality and marketing had endangered one of the nation's most important export industries. In 1932 the national and provincial governments worked with the Silk Reform Association (*Canci gailiang hui*) of private industrialists to set national quality standards for silk manufacture that were designed above all to meet international standards.[66]At the suggestion of experts from the League of Nations, the government began to regulate both the industry and individual producers. Chinese farmers were forced to have their homes or other buildings used in silk production sprayed with disinfectant, and required to buy eggs only from the government. These reforms – largely successful – were not the first steps toward the nationalization of the industry but toward its internationalization.[67] The Chinese state had internalized international standards, and made them its own.

*Political prototypes.* The same can be said, in a general sense, of political standards.[68] No government of the Republican era, except possibly that planned by Zhang Xun in 1916, believed that China's 20th-century crises could be solved by a return to the Qing state. There were certainly no clear precedents in Chinese political history for the task of integrating a new set of social groups – among them a bourgeoisie, a proletariat, an intelligentsia and a permanent, professional military – into the altogether new structure of a nation-state. This was an era, and indeed has been a century, of continual experimentation with political forms, not

64. Zhou Daolong, (ed.), *Gannan wukuang zhi* (*Tungsten Mines of Southern Jiangxi*) (Nanchang, 1936), pp. 121–22; *Jiangxi jingji wenti* (*Jiangxi Economic Issues*) (Nanchang: Jiangxi sheng zhengfu, 1934), pp. 255ff; L. Fabel, "Le Tungstène: minerai le plus important de la Chine," *Bulletin de l'Université l'Aurore*, Vol. 4 (1943), p. 128.

65. "Shishi wusha tongzhi zhi buzhu" ("Steps toward the control of tungsten ore"), *Economic Periodical*, Vol. 4, No. 5 (15 February 1935), p. 5; Liu Daqian, "Dayu," pp. 16–17.

66. Terry M. Weidner, "Local political work under the Nationalists: the 1930's silk reform campaign," *Illinois Papers in Asian Studies*, No. 2 (1983), p. 67; See also Lillian Li, *China's Silk Trade: Traditional Industry in the Modern World* (Cambridge, MA: Harvard University Press, 1981), p. 200.

67. Second Historical Archives, Nanjing 44 (1719), "Quanguo jingji weiyuanhui gongzuo baogao" ("Report of the work of the National Economic Council"), 1937, pp. 33–40; *ibid.*, Chin Fen, "The National Economic Council" (March 1935), pp. 67–70; Lau-King Quan, *China's Relations with the League of Nations, 1919–1936* (Hong Kong: Asiatic Litho Press, 1939); Tao Siu, "L'Oeuvre du Conseil National Economique Chinois," dissertation, L'Université de Nancy, 1936.

68. On the linkage between "national identity" and the national question as addressed by Marxism see the stimulating work by Germaine Hoston, *The State, Identity, and the National Question in China and Japan* (Princeton: Princeton University Press, 1994).

one of which was indigenous in origin: the parliamentary republic of 1912–13, the military dictatorship of 1913–16, the attempt at constitutional monarchy in 1916 and, most enduringly, the Leninist party-state.

The party-state became the central arena of Chinese politics from 1924 to the present. While the large majority of scholarly literature has dealt with the Communist variant – what Su Shaozhi has called "party-cracy with Chinese characteristics"[69] – the intellectual lineage of the party-state may be traced from Lenin to Stalin to alternative sets of Chinese leaders in both the Nationalist and Communist camps. It was under Russian tutelage that Sun Yat-sen coined the concept *yi dang zhi guo* (government by the party). It was surely no accident that, when the Nationalists drew up their blueprints for the new capital at Nanjing – now to be an international city patterned on Paris and Washington – the structure housing the national government was literally in the shadows of a massive Kuomintang headquarters (*Zhongyang dangbu*), an architectural marvel combining the most distinct features of Beijing's Temple of Heaven and the U.S. Capitol building.[70] By the 1930s the attempt to "partify" (*danghua*) political and even cultural life was second nature to the Nationalist regime. Until very recently, and then largely on Taiwan, the dominance of *zhengdang* (ruling party) political culture has overwhelmed consideration of alternatives to the party-state both in political practice and in scholarship.[71]

Of course the working and practice of Chinese politics sometimes remoulded political models nearly beyond recognition. If all governments planned, or claimed they were working toward, a "constitution," this did not always mean a willingness to adhere to constitutional rule.[72] A cynical New York friend told the American political scientist Frank Goodnow, who was counselling Yuan Shikai as Yuan was setting up his dictatorship, that even the most reactionary government could not do without a constitutional adviser, "any more than the large corporations here who intend to disregard the law start out without the best lawyer of the land in their cabinet."[73] China's self-styled fascists of the 1930s had their advisers and models too, and certainly placed their stamp on the historical image of the Nanjing regime. But what passed for Chinese "fascism" would bear little resemblance to the European phenomenon. At most there was an attempt to import the superstructure of an existing fascist state – the rhetoric, marching, music and propaganda – never the essence

69. Paper delivered to the Conference on the Formation of the Communist Party State, Colorado Springs, 1993.

70. Guodu sheji jishu zhuanyuan banshichu (Office of Technical Experts for Planning the National Capital) (comp.), *Shoudu jihua* (*Plan for the Capital*) (Nanjing, 1929).

71. For the first extensive scholarly treatment of minor parties in 20th-century China see Roger Jeans (ed.), *Roads Not Taken* (Boulder: Westview Press, 1992).

72. See Andrew J. Nathan, *Peking Politics, 1918–1923: Factionalism and the Failure of Constitutionalism* (Berkeley: University of California Press, 1976). On constitutional politics in the Beiyang and Nationalist periods, respectively, see the forthcoming Harvard dissertations of Allen Fung and Paulo Frank.

73. Letter, Charles E. Bigelow to Frank Goodow, New York, 8 February 1914, cited in Ernest P. Young, *The Presidency of Yuan Shikai* (Ann Arbor: University of Michigan Press, 1977), p. 174.

of a fascist social *movement*, which was at the core of the political strength of contemporary German National Socialism and Italian Fascism, and for which the Kuomintang leadership had no taste. In the vast literature on the nature of fascism, there is no definition that can accommodate its various, often disputatious, admirers in China. Indeed fascism never even found an adequate Chinese translation, but remained in abstract transliteration: *faxisi zhuyi*.[74]

Such, however, was not the case with Chinese Communism, whose determination to "share production" (*gongchan zhuyi*) would translate into an unprecedented redistribution of wealth and status in the territories under its control. It is easy to see features that distinguished Chinese Communism, particularly in its Maoist form, from Communism as practised in Stalin's Soviet Union or as understood by Western Communist leaders from Ernst Thälmann to Gus Hall. Much of the literature on Chinese Communism, from the seminal work of Benjamin Schwartz to Mark Selden's powerful study of the "Yan'an Way," to the newest accounts of the CCP's origins,[75] has taken such pains to emphasize the Party's indigenous dimensions that it is easy to forget how strongly this movement was connected to international forces in its youth and how deeply it came to internalize the discipline of international Communism.[76] Certainly the political history of the Party makes no sense without constant reference to the Comintern, the leaders of the USSR and that country's massive intervention in Chinese political life in the Republican era.[77] In foreign policy, recent work demonstrates anew that even when united front policies led CCP leaders to flirt with Washington in 1944–46, they knew they were married to Moscow.[78] Both

74. William C. Kirby, "Images and realities of Chinese 'fascism', " in S. Larsen (ed.), *Fascism Outside Europe* (New York: Columbia University Press, forthcoming), and *Germany and Republican China*, pp. 152–185, 264–65. One critic put it: fascism in China was "a stalk without roots, a river without a source." See Xu Daquan, "Suowei Zhongguo faxisiti de pipan" ("Critique of so-called Chinese fascism"), *Sanmin zhuyi yuekan* (*Three People's Principles Monthly*), Vol. 4, No. 5 (15 November 1934).

75. Benjamin I. Schwartz, *Chinese Communism and the Rise of Mao* (Cambridge, MA: Harvard University Press, 1951); Mark Selden, *The Yenan Way in Revolutionary China* (Cambridge, MA: Harvard University Press, 1971); Dirlik, *The Origins of Chinese Communism*.

76. This was not an overnight process, as Hans J. van de Ven has shown in his *From Friend to Comrade: The Founding of the Chinese Communist Party, 1920–1927* (Berkeley: University of California Press, 1991). On the international if not particularly cosmopolitan experiences of Chinese Communists in Europe see Marilyn A. Levine, *The Found Generation: Chinese Communists in Europe During the Twenties* (Seattle: University of Washington Press, 1993).

77. See C. Martin Wilbur and Julie Lien-Ying How, *Missionaries of Revolution: Soviet Advisers and Nationalist China, 1920–1927* (Cambridge, MA: Harvard University Press, 1988); *Die Komintern und die national-revolutionäre Bewegung in China. Dokumente, Band I, 1920-1925* (Paderborn: Schöningh, 1996).

78. Niu Jun, *Cong Yan'an zouxiang shijie* (*From Yanan to the World*) (Fuzhou: Fujian renmin chubanshe, 1992). Most persuasively see Michael M. Sheng, *Ideology and Foreign Policy: Mao, Stalin, and the United States* (Princeton: Princeton University Press, 1997); and John Garver, "Little chance," *Diplomatic History*, Vol. 21, No. 1 (Winter 1997), pp. 87–94. On the fundamental conflicts between the CCP and the United States see also Zi Zhongyun, *Meiguo dui Hua zhengce de yuanqi he fazhan* (*Origins and Development of U.S. Policy Towards China*) (Chongqing: Chongqing chubanshe, 1987).

out and in power, in the arts as in industry, in internal as in foreign policy, the CCP followed the Soviet road much more than it diverged from it. One must always recall the elementary fact: without the Soviet Union there would be no Chinese Communist Party. There would be no People's Republic of China.

*The military persuasion.* Finally, it may be noted that the political success of the Chinese party-state is related to an even more enduring foreign influence that became a permanent part of modern Chinese politics, that of modern militarism. Both the Nationalists and the Communists fought their way to power in the first half of the 20th century, when China was the world's largest market for Western arms and munitions. It had more men under arms for longer periods than any other part of the world. More to the point, Western militarism (in its Soviet, German and American national forms) was undoubtedly the single most successful cultural export from the West to China.

Foreigners were not needed to teach Chinese to make war or be violent. China's capacity for warfare was already "awesome."[79] What changed, beginning with the new, national army under Yuan Shikai in the late Qing, was the institutionalization of a standing, professional military that measured success in relation to concrete models of military organization abroad. The politicized forces trained by Soviet advisers in Guangdong in 1924–26, the Central Army of Chiang Kai-shek under Prussian-German tutelage from 1927 to 1938, and the several armies advised by first Russians and then Americans during the War of Resistance were all variations on this theme.

To this one may add the militarization of political authority, beginning under and immediately after Yuan Shikai, made manifest as a regional phenomenon in the so-called "warlord" era, and institutionalized at the political center in the dominance of the Military Affairs Commissions of both the Kuomintang and Communist party-states. Beyond that one may turn to the attempted militarization (*junshihua*) of citizenry in Chiang Kai-shek's New Life Movement and ultimately to the mobilization of the entire country in unending "campaigns" and the reconstitution of social units as "brigades" on the forced march to Communism in Mao's People's Republic. And to maintain order on the streets of the major cities, first under the Nationalists and then under the Communists, China would be the beneficiary, if that is the correct term, of the latest in police training from both West and East.[80]

David Shambaugh's recent effort to revise the history of Chinese politics by "bringing the soldier back in" demonstrates how internal and external security issues were nearly always at the top of the CCP political agenda; how soldier-politicians played central roles in CCP and PRC

79. Hans van de Ven, "War in the making of modern China", paper presented to the Fairbank Center for East Asian Research, Harvard University, September 1995, p. 1.

80. On the use of Western and Japanese models in Republican-era policing see Frederic Wakeman, Jr., *Policing Shanghai, 1927–1937* (Berkeley: University of California Press, 1995), p. 58.

governance in an "interlocking directorate"; how military values crowded out others and became the source of political campaigns; and how economic priorities were made on the basis of defence strategy.[81] All this was at least equally true of the Nationalist regime, which bequeathed to the Communists what I would call the Chinese "national security state" with a large state industrial sector geared above all to national defence and the creation of military-economic strength.[82]

*Cultural and Economic Internationalism*

However important the role of foreign policy for the Republican state and foreign prototypes for Republican politics, particularly distinguishing features of the Republican era were the scope and depth of cultural and economic connections with foreigners. It was in those realms that China would be most deeply integrated into global patterns. First, and not least, was the greater possibility of having living foreign relations, that is, relatives who lived, worked or studied abroad, who communicated, remitted funds and occasionally returned home from South-East Asia, North America, Western and Central Europe, the Soviet Union and Japan.

*Missionaries.* Beyond the experiences of Chinese sojourning abroad were those of Westerners in China. At no other time in its modern history was China so open and accessible, even to the greatest scoundrels. Where else could the picaresque J. T. Trebitsch-Lincoln, in his own words "the greatest adventurer of the twentieth century," make his fortune? This Hungarian Jew, who became an Anglican priest and a member of the British parliament, was already wanted for espionage and sedition in three countries when he emerged in China in 1921 with plans "to develop the country into a first class military and naval power." He became chief military adviser to three major militarists of the "warlord" era, including Wu Peifu, and pursued mammoth armaments and industrial negotiations on their behalf. Only with the Nationalist reunification of China did he return to the contemplative life, now as a Buddhist monk, residing in a monastery near Nanjing. But his itinerant urge would send him abroad again as a "Buddhist missionary" to Europe, where he would be arrested for swindling.[83]

Missionaries of a more familiar sort have been the subject of study and controversy ever since Mark Twain's warning that "every convert runs a

81. David Shambaugh, paper delivered to the Conference on the Construction of the Party-State and State Socialism in China, 1936–1965, Colorado Springs, May 1993.

82. William C. Kirby, "Technocratic organization and technological development in China: the nationalist experience and legacy," in Merle Goldman and Denis Simon (eds.), *Science and Technology in Post-Mao China* (Cambridge, MA: Harvard University Press, 1989), pp. 23–43.

83. J. T. Trebitsch-Lincoln, *Der größte Abenteuerer des XX. Jahrhunderts!? Die Wahrheit über mein Leben* (Leipzig, 1931), pp. 226–258; Kirby, *Germany and Republican China*, pp. 26–28; Bernard Wasserstein, *The Secret Lives of Trebitsch-Lincoln* (New Haven: Yale University Press, 1988).

risk of catching our civilization" inaugurated a sceptical literature that competed with missionary-friendly accounts of "God's work in China."[84] Only recently, however, has scholarship begun to address the relationship between mission work and international political interests in this period.[85] At the same time, the subject of religion, which curiously has seldom been at the heart of missionary studies, is being taken seriously. The work of Daniel Bays in particular is demonstrating how Christianity, too, could be "internalized" in 20th-century China and could find a place among "indigenous" Chinese religions.[86]

Missionary work of a more secular kind is highlighted by recent works, including novels, revolving around the history of the YMCA in China.[87] Even doctors, according to Wolfgang Eckart, may be viewed as "cultural missionaries."[88] Technical missionaries, if one may use that term, are the subject of Randall Stross's critical account of the work of American agriculturalists in China, while Chen Yixin has shown how international models for agricultural collectives were domesticated in the Republican era.[89]

Military advisers and mercenaries (can one consider the euphemism "military missionaries"?) have been cultural go-betweens of another kind. In the case of Sino-American relations, attention has been focused almost exclusively on the high politics of the Stilwell and Wedemeyer missions of the 1940s, usually with a strongly partisan perspective.[90] Ultimately more interesting are the institutional history of these missions,[91] particularly in contrast to those of the Soviet mission to the early Nationalist movement[92] or with the German military advisership to the Nationalist

84. See Charles W. Hayford, "Sino-American cultural relations, 1900–1945, cultural criticism, and post-semi-colonial historiography," paper presented for a Workshop on the Historiography of American-East Asian Relations, Wilson Center, Washington DC, 1994.

85. On relationships between missionary "mentalities" and activities on the one hand, and official attitudes on the other, see Patricia Neils (ed.), *United States Attitudes and Policies Toward China: The Impact of American Missionaries* (Armonk: M. E. Sharpe, 1990); James Reid, *The Missionary Mind and American East Asian Policy, 1911–1915* (Cambridge, MA: Council on East Asian Studies, 1983); and Jessie G. Lutz, *Chinese Politics and Christian Missions: The Anti-Christian Movement of 1920–28* (Indiana: Cross Roads Books, 1988). See also Jean-Paul Wiest, *Maryknoll in China: A History, 1918–1955* (Armonk: M. E. Sharpe, 1988).

86. This is the working assumption of the Luce Foundation project on the History of Christianity in China Project, headed by Daniel Bays at the University of Kansas.

87. See John Epsey, *Minor Heresies, Major Departures: A China Mission Boyhood* (Berkeley: University of California Press, 1994); John Hersey, *The Call* (New York: Knopf, 1985).

88. Wolfgang Uwe Eckart, *Deutsche Ärzte in China 1897–1914: Medizin als Kulturmission im Zweiten Deutschen Kaiserreich* (Stuttgart: G. Fischer, 1989).

89. R. E. Stross, *The Stubborn Earth: American Agriculturalists on Chinese Soil, 1898–1937* (Berkeley: University of California Press, 1986).

90. Of which the best examples are Barbara Tuchman, *Stilwell and the American Experience in China* (New York: Macmillan, 1971); and Ching-chun Liang, *General Stilwell in China, 1942–1944: The Full Story* (New York: St John's University Press, 1972).

91. Charles F. Romanus and Riley Sunderland, *Stilwell's Mission to China* (Washington, DC: Office of the Chief of Military History, Department of the Army, 1953), *Time Runs Out in CBI* (Washington, DC: Office of the Chief of Military History, Department of the Army, 1959), and *Stilwell's Command Problems* (Washington, DC: Office of the Chief of Military History, Department of the Army, 1956).

92. Wilbur and How, *Missionaries of Revolution.*

government during 1928–38. The latter has been lately the subject of detailed research not only on its leadership but also on its organization, institutional culture and influence on a range of military, economic, ideological and political matters. This also provides material from which to gauge the personal, almost teacher–student relationship between adviser and master, as with Chiang Kai-shek's interaction with his first and most trusted German adviser, Max Bauer. The curriculum imparted to a generation of Chinese officers, which was *au courant* enough to include a required course on "The Influence of Race on Politics," is known too.[93]

*Education.* The broadest influence of international education would be felt outside the official sphere, sometimes by political design, in the case of cultural activities broadly sponsored by a foreign power,[94] but more commonly by the coming together of young Chinese in international institutions in China, in an era of vibrant, initially uncoordinated, educational exchange, when China housed a cosmopolitan and diverse collection of institutions of higher learning. This has become one of the most fertile fields in the study of China's foreign relations, as scholars trace the beginning of modern academic disciplines and the training of Chinese students, in China, on a high international standard.[95]

93. See for example, Bernd Martin (ed.), *Die deutsche Beraterschaft in China, 1927–1938* (Düsseldorf: Droste, 1981); Hsi-Huey Liang, *The Sino-German Connection: Alexander von Falkenhausen between China and Germany, 1900–1941* (Assen: Van Gorcum, 1978). On Bauer see Kirby, *Germany and Republican China*, ch. 3; on racism see *ibid.* pp. 167–69, and more completely, in terms of China's relationship to international racial discourse, the bold study of Frank Dikötter, *The Discourse of Race in Modern China* (Stanford: Stanford University Press, 1992).

94. Françoise Kreissler, *L'Action culturelle*; Rotraut Bieg-Brentzel, *Die Tongji-Universität. Zur Geschichte deutscher Kulturarbeit in Shanghai* (Frankfurt: Haag und Herchen, 1984).

95. On the diversity of the higher educational enterprise in China see above all, Yeh Wen-hsin, *The Alienated Academy: Culture and Politics in Republican China* (Cambridge MA: Council on East Asian Studies, 1990). For a broad set of essays on cultural and education interactions see Priscilla Roberts (ed.), *Sino-American Relations Since 1900* (Hong Kong: University of Hong Kong Centre of Asian Studies, 1991). Further see Mary Bullock, *An American Transplant: The Rockefeller Foundation and Peking Union Medical College* (Berkeley: University of California Press, 1980), and "The legacy of the Rockefeller Foundation in China," paper presented to the American Historical Association annual meeting, 1990; Peter Buck, *American Science and Modern China, 1876–1936* (Cambridge: Cambridge University Press, 1980); William J. Haas, *China Voyager: Gist Gee's Life in Science* (Armonk: M.E. Sharpe, 1996); James Reardon-Anderson, *The Study of Change: Chemistry in China* (New York: Cambridge University Press, 1991); Laurence A. Schneider, "The Rockefeller Foundation, the China Foundation, and the development of modern science in China," *Social Science in Medicine*, No. 16 (1982); Yang Tsui-hua, "Geological sciences in Republican China, 1912–1937," Ph.D. dissertation, State University of New York at Buffalo, 1985; Bettina Gransow, *Geschichte der chinesischen Soziologie* (Frankfurt: Campus Verlag, 1992); Chiang Yung-chen, "Social engineering and the social sciences in China, 1898–1949," Ph.D. dissertation, Harvard University, 1986; and Joyce K. Kallgren and Denis Fred Simon (eds.), *Educational Exchanges: Essays on the Sino-American Experience* (Berkeley: Institute of East Asian Studies, 1987).

Paradoxically, when higher education was gradually brought back under the control of the Chinese state in the 1930s, this too was on the basis of – or was at least legitimized by – international advice in the form of a commission from the League of Nations' programme on International Intellectual Co-operation. This "Becker Commission," named for its leader, the former Prussian minister of education C. H. Becker, decried the disorganization of Chinese education (which for some reason it blamed on the Americans). It aimed to strengthen the state's hand in setting educational agendas; to rationalize geographically and fiscally the system of national (*guoli*) universities; and to establish a nation-wide system of entrance examinations that would permit authorities to channel admissions to specific disciplines. The result was to reorganize, centralize and ultimately to nationalize Chinese higher education[96] on the basis of an "authoritarian view of knowledge"[97] shared and, in time, implemented vigorously by the Nationalist regime. In terms of disciplines, the reforms that took place in the early 1930s marked a fundamental, and so far permanent, shift of priorities in Chinese higher education away from the humanities and social sciences, in which enrolment began to be limited, in favour of science, mathematics and engineering.

The greatest international schools of all were simply the treaty ports, the multi-cultural arenas of learning, meeting and nationalist conflict. These were the hubs of modern economic growth and the central meeting places between Chinese and foreigners (not to mention between Chinese of different regions) in the first part of the 20th century. They were the most conspicuous breeding grounds of new social classes with international connections. Their heyday co- incided with Chinese capitalism's first "golden age"; of China's first – and last – independent workers' movement; and of an internationally-oriented intelligentsia poorly connected to the state. Here are the best examples of the world of Republican China's "private" foreign relations.[98]

In the field of Republican Chinese history Shanghai, at once an international and a Chinese city, has been a natural focus of new work. In the study of that metropolis alone Emily Honig and Elizabeth Perry have reopened the field of labour history, which had lay dormant in the West since the work of Jean Chesneaux; Frederic Wakeman has brought to light the dark, underworld struggles of the police and their adversaries;

96. C. H. Becker *et al.*, *The Reorganization of Education in China* (Paris: League of Nations' Institute of Intellectual Co-operation, 1932); Zhu Jiahua, *Jiuge yue lai jiaoyubu zhengli quanguo jiaoyu zhi shuoming* (*Explanation of the Ministry of Education's Reform of National Education in the Past Nine Months*) (Nanjing, 1932).

97. Ruth E. S. Hayhoe, "China's higher curricular reform in historical perspective," *The China Quarterly*, No. 110 (June 1987), p. 203. See also Ernst Neugebauer, *Anfange pädagogische Entwicklungshilfe under dem Völkerbund in China, 1931 bis 1935* (Hamburg: Institut für Asienkunde, 1971).

98. See David Strand, *Rickshaw Beijing: City People and Politics in 1920's China* (Berkeley: University of California Press, 1989); Christian Henriot, *Shanghai, 1927–1937* (Berkeley: University of California Press, 1993); Marie-Claire Bergère, *The Golden Age of the Chinese Bourgeoisie, 1911–1937* (Cambridge: Cambridge University Press, 1990).

Emily Honig has investigated migrant culture, Jeffrey Wasserstrom student culture, Wen-hsin Yeh banking culture – all assisted by archival sources that were not open to research just a few years ago.[99]

Yet the international social history of these cities remains to be written. The "sojourners" studied by Wakeman, Yeh and others consist of the Chinese bankers, industrialists, workers, students, journalists, gangsters and prostitutes who gradually came to think of themselves as "Shanghai people." It is not the Shanghai of international sojourners – businessmen, adventurers and refugees from around the globe – who are the protagonists in Nicholas Clifford's recent study. Nor is it the Shanghai of young John Hay Thornburn, the British permanent resident who murdered, and was murdered, in defence of the place that once was known as the Ulster of the East.[100] These cities were sites not just to visit – the scope of international tourism being what it was in the days before transcontinental air travel – but places to live, work, and to be a home abroad for foreign nationals who made China their primary domicile. Above all it is the history of the interaction between Chinese and foreign sojourners in China that is the missing story of modern Sino-foreign relations. The opening of Chinese and international archives now permit this history now to be written, and, simply put, to "bring the West back in" by treating the foreign presence in China as an integral part of modern Chinese history.[101]

*Business.* Certainly a history that includes the foreigner-in-China is fundamental to any new work on the history of Chinese business enterprise, on patterns of Sino-foreign economic co-operation and competition, and on the long-term development of modern Chinese capitalism in an international context.[102] There is no point, as Marie-Claire Bergère argues persuasively, in distinguishing between a "national" versus a "compradore" bourgeoisie: all important businesses had vital international connections, even as almost all had nationalistic ownership.[103]

99. Emily Honig, *Sisters and Strangers: Workers in the Shanghai Cotton Mills, 1919–1929* (Stanford: Stanford University Press, 1986); Elizabeth J. Perry, *Shanghai on Strike* (Stanford: Stanford University Press, 1993); Jean Chesneaux, *The Chinese Labor Movement, 1919–1927* (Stanford: Stanford University Press, 1968); Frederic Wakeman, Jr., *Shanghai Police* (Berkeley: University of California Press, 1994); Emily Honig, "Migrant culture in Shanghai: in search of a Subei identity," and Jeffrey Wasserstrom, "The evolution of Shanghai student protest repertoire," both in Frederic Wakeman, Jr., and Wen-hsin Yeh (eds.), *Shanghai Sojourners* (Berkeley: Institute of East Asian Studies of the University of California, Berkeley, 1992); Wen-hsin Yeh, "Corporate space, communal time: everyday life in Shanghai's Bank of China," *American Historical Review*, No. 9 (February 1995), pp. 97–123. On the Chinese municipal government of Shanghai see Henriot, *Shanghai.*

100. Wakeman and Yeh, *Shanghai Sojourners*; Clifford, *Spoilt Children of Empire*; Robert A. Bickers, "Death of a young Shanghailander: the Thorburn Case and the defence of the British Treaty Ports in China in 1931," *Modern Asian Studies*, Vol. 29, No. 3 (1995).

101. See in particular the forthcoming work of Robert A. Bickers, *Colonial Attitudes and Informal Empire: The British in the Chinese Treaty Ports, 1843–1943* (Manchester: Manchester University Press.)

102. See Rajeswary Ampalavanar Brown (ed.), *Chinese Business Enterprise in Asia* (London: Routledge, 1995). On patterns of both emulation and competition with Western enterprise see Sherman Cochran, *Big Business in China* (Cambridge, MA: Harvard University Press, 1980); and Bergère, *Golden Age.*

103. Bergère, *Golden Age.*

Nor is there any point in limiting discussion of economic internationalization just to the treaty ports. The dynamics of Republican-era economic growth, if one applies the findings of Thomas J. Rawski, began with but extended well beyond the treaty port and urban sectors. Rawski traces a pattern of sustained economic expansion of the national economy during the period 1912–37 that was "rooted in the expansion of foreign trade."[104]

The same could be said for the dramatic expansion of the state sector of the economy in the second half of the Republican period. Chinese state capitalism developed, and could only have developed, in partnership with foreign firms and governments and with foreign technical assistance. This was as true of the joint ventures that funded civil aviation as it was of foreign participation in the expansion of the national rail network, as of the establishment of China's first automotive manufacturing company, and, most strikingly, of the creation of the state heavy industrial sector that would be the economic heart of the late Nationalist and early Communist regimes. The engineers and planners in charge of Chinese state capitalism were mostly trained abroad, or were sent abroad to work with partner firms or governments. They would prove ingenious in adapting to difficult, indigenous circumstances, as when the National government relocated to Sichuan during the war. But their plans and their training were based on state-of-the-art technology and permanent connections to the most advanced industrial economies. When more than two-thirds of China's total industrial capital was in the hands of the state by the end of the Republican era, this was the result not just of nationalization, but of internationalization.[105] It was the result, indeed, of what Sun Yat-sen had once called, in his industrial blueprint for the Chinese Republic, "the international development of China."[106]

*Epilogue*

If the Republican era was indeed such a high tide of internationalism, how can one account for what followed it? In the first years of the People's Republic, China cut off formal relations with all but one Western power and then was diplomatically derecognized by the rest. It was excluded from the central forum of global diplomacy, the United Nations. At home almost all Westerners were thrown out of China, their missions, businesses and homes confiscated, their Chinese partners and friends placed under a political cloud. By 1952 even the receipt of mail from a Western country could be viewed as a seditious act. The Chinese

104. Thomas J. Rawski, *Economic Growth in Prewar China* (Berkeley: University of California Press, 1989), p. 344.

105. See Kirby, "Technocratic Organization," and "Continuity and change in Modern China: economic planning on the Mainland and on Taiwan, 1943–58," *Australian Journal of Chinese Affairs* (July 1990).

106. Sun Yat-sen, *The International Development of China* (New York and London, 1922). See Michael R. Godley, "Socialism with Chinese Characteristics: Sun Yat-sen and the international development of China," *Australian Journal of Chinese Affairs*, No. 18 (July 1987), pp. 109–125.

people "stood up," in Mao's words, only to give the boot to the most intense set of foreign relations in China's modern history.

One explanation is that the PRC was reacting, if not overreacting, to a period of unprecedented interpenetration on the part of Chinese and foreigners. But it also followed a regime that had successfully defended China's status internationally while regaining its full sovereignty internally. Could it not have simply built on those accomplishments? One thing should be clear from the above account: the Republican state had given China what it had not had under the late Qing: the capacity to take the lead in its external relations, and to regulate, or redirect, foreign relations within China to the service of the state. The PRC had this capacity from the start and would use it to the extreme.

A more compelling general explanation is that the early PRC did not diminish China's foreign relations so much as point them all in one direction: East.[107] China was never so deeply incorporated into an international system as it was in the hottest years of the Cold War. Certainly it had never entered into a foreign relationship of the intensity and scope of the Sino-Soviet alliance in all its dimensions. This was an alliance of (initially) shared ideology, and built on decades of Soviet mentoring of the CCP. Beyond that it was the most fully articulated military alliance in China's history. It was a cultural and educational alliance, confirmed by the thousands of Chinese who studied in the USSR and the thousands of Russians who taught in China. And it was an economic alliance of greater depth and complexity than any of modern China's foreign economic relationships. Through long-term plans and annual negotiation, China's economy would become linked to those of its Eastern European and Soviet brothers. At times China would even be a donor nation to its allies, as in its sending of emergency food aid to the tottering East German regime in 1953. On the whole China was the beneficiary of the largest planned transfer of technology in world history, which gave the People's Republic a new core of state industries. For the People's Republic, as for the Nationalist regime before it, industrialization meant internationalization.

Only the total mismanagement of both China's foreign relationships and its domestic politics – and these were interconnected phenomena under Mao Zedong's leadership after the end of the First Five-Year Plan – could have left China in the diplomatic quarantine and economic isolation of the 1960s, when it faced, as it had not since the Boxer War, a world of enemies. But this has proven to be the great exception to the rule of onrushing internationalization that has marked China's modern history from the beginning of the Republican era.

107. "East," that is, in the convoluted geospeak of the Cold War, for China's new allies were of course north by north-west.

# Index